THE INVI
IRON MAN

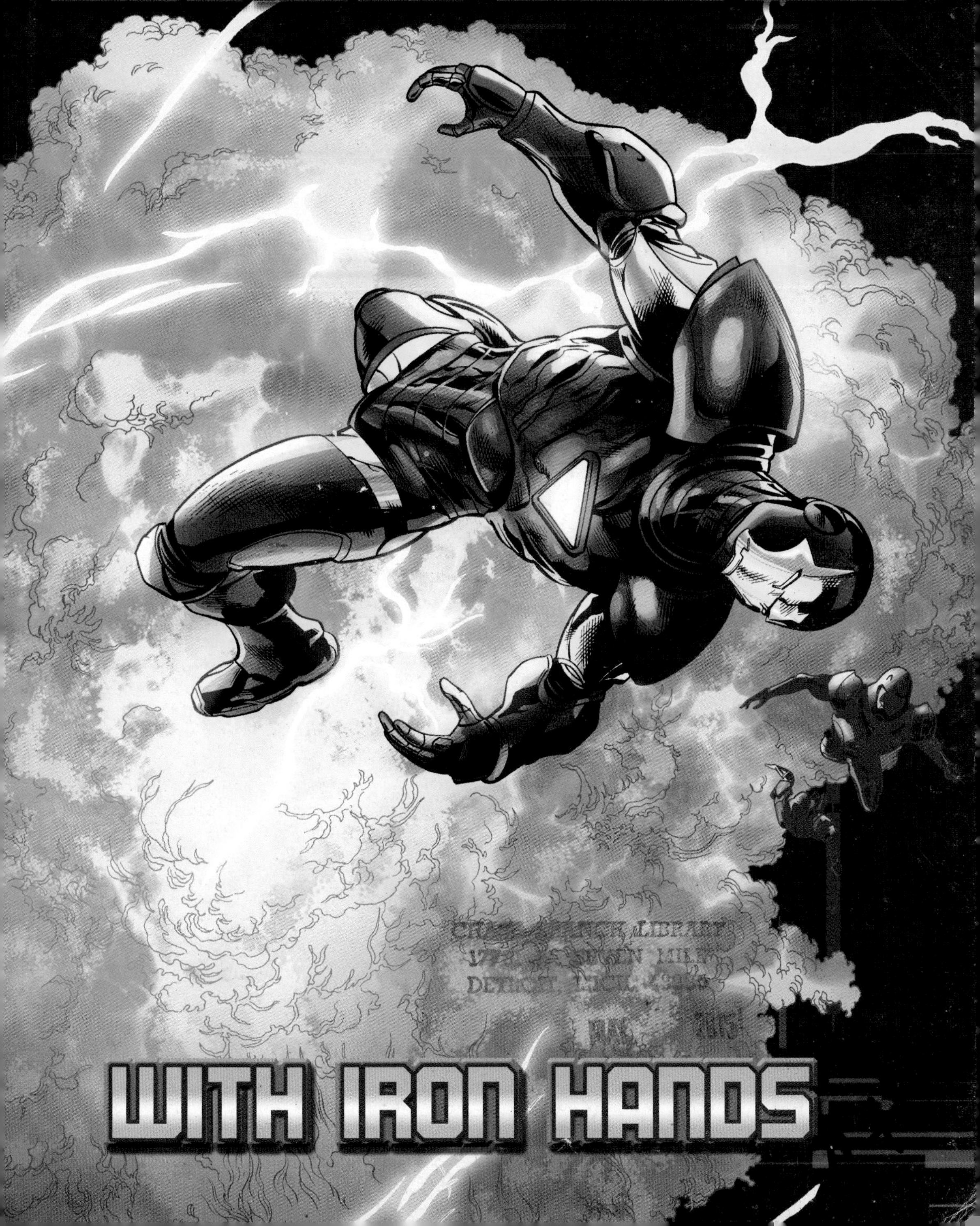

WITH IRON HANDS

THE INVINCIBLE IRON MAN

WITH IRON HANDS

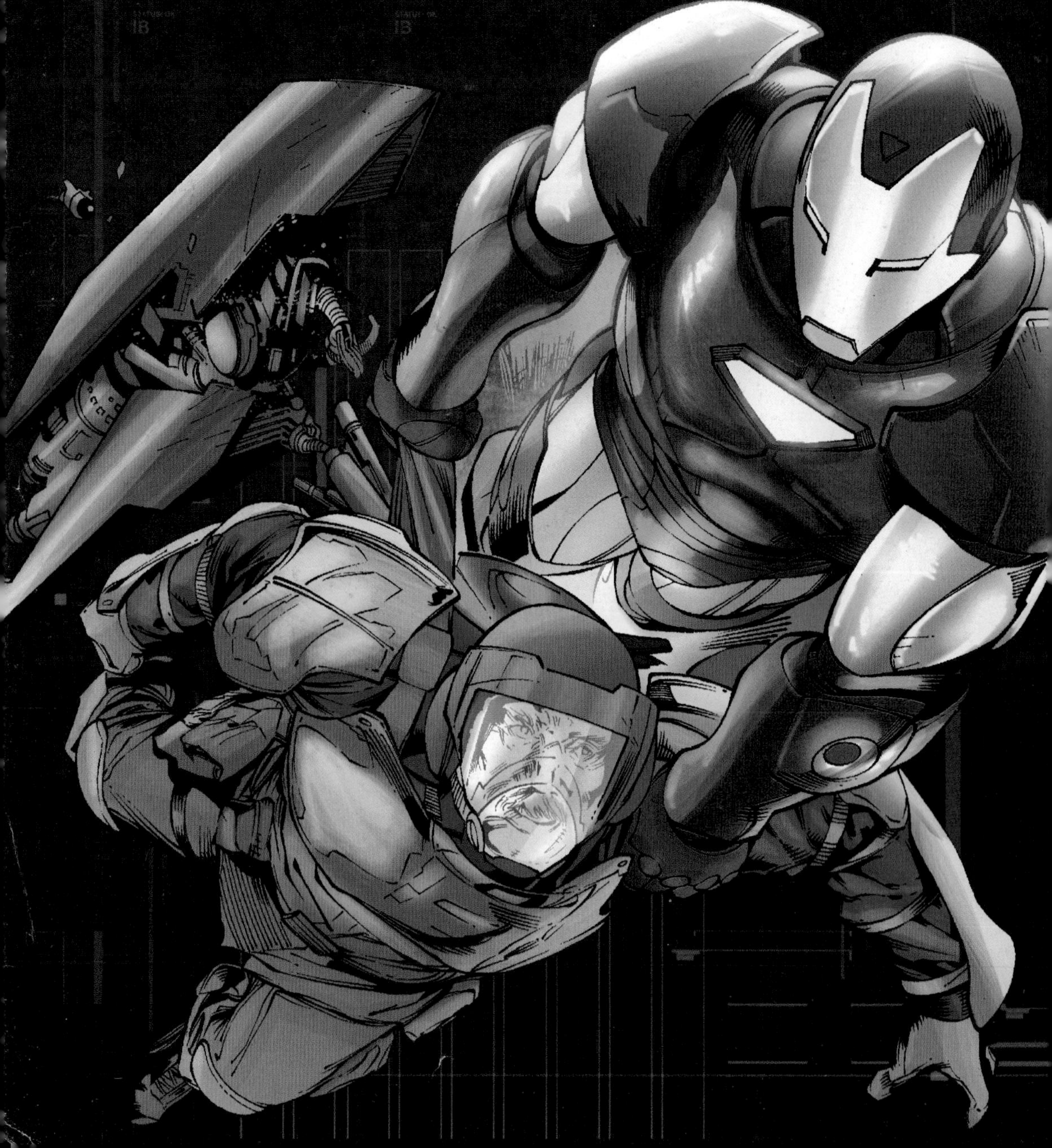

WRITER: Stuart Moore
PENCILERS: Roberto de la Torre, Carlo Pagulayan
& Steve Kurth
INKERS: Roberto de la Torre, Jeffrey Huet
& Andrew Hennessy
COLOR ART: Dean White & Joel Séguin
LETTERER: Virtual Calligraphy's Joe Caramagna
COVER ART: Adi Granov

ASSISTANT EDITORS: Lauren Sankovitch & Lauren Henry
ASSOCIATE EDITOR: Molly Lazer
EDITOR: Nicole Boose with Bill Rosemann
EXECUTIVE EDITOR: Tom Brevoort

"DANGER DEEP"
from *Iron Man (1998) #36*
WRITER: Chuck Dixon
PENCILER: Paul Ryan
INKER: Mark Pennington
COLOR ART: Steve Oliff
LETTERER: Richard Starking & Comicraft's Troy Peteri
COVER ART: Keron Grant

ASSISTANT EDITOR: Brian Smith
EDITOR: Bobbie Chase

COLLECTION EDITOR: Cory Levine
EDITORIAL ASSISTANT: Alex Starbuck
ASSISTANT EDITOR: John Denning
EDITORS, SPECIAL PROJECTS: Jennifer Grünwald & Mark D. Beazley
SENIOR EDITOR, SPECIAL PROJECTS: Jeff Youngquist
SENIOR VICE PRESIDENT OF SALES: David Gabriel
PRODUCTION: Jerron Quality Color

EDITOR IN CHIEF: Joe Quesada
PUBLISHER: Dan Buckley

WHEN BILLIONAIRE INDUSTRIALIST TONY STARK DONS SOPHISTICATED STEEL-MESH ARMOR OF HIS OWN DESIGN, HE BECOMES A LIVING HIGH-TECH WEAPON-- THE WORLD'S GREATEST HUMAN FIGHTING MACHINE.

THE INVINCIBLE IRON MAN

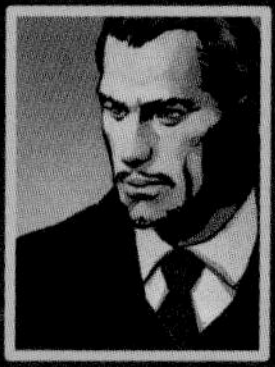

Tony Stark

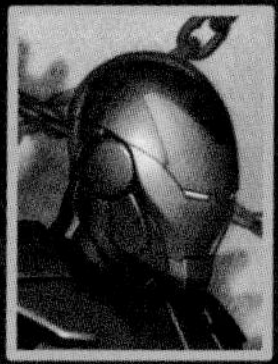

Iron Man

Tony Stark is the Director of S.H.I.E.L.D. (Strategic Hazard Intervention Espionage Logistics Directorate), a worldwide intelligence agency specializing in anti-terrorism operations. International in its membership, scope, and jurisdiction, many of S.H.I.E.L.D.'s top agents have been recruited from the world's foremost national intelligence agencies.

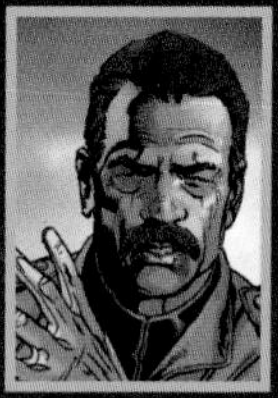

Timothy "Dum Dum" Dugan
Deputy Director of S.H.I.E.L.D.

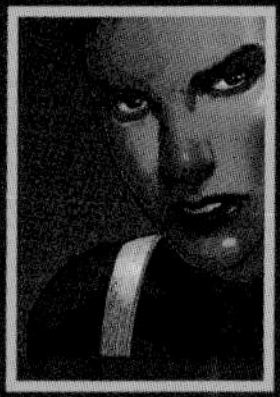

Maria Hill
Deputy Director of S.H.I.E.L.D.

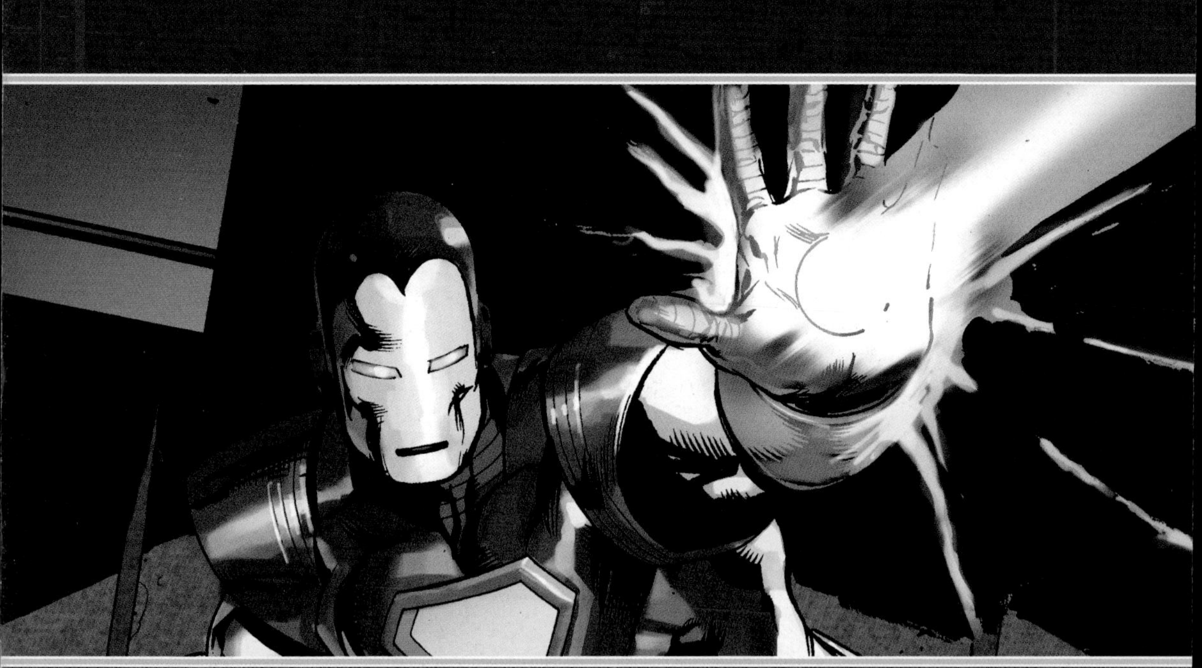

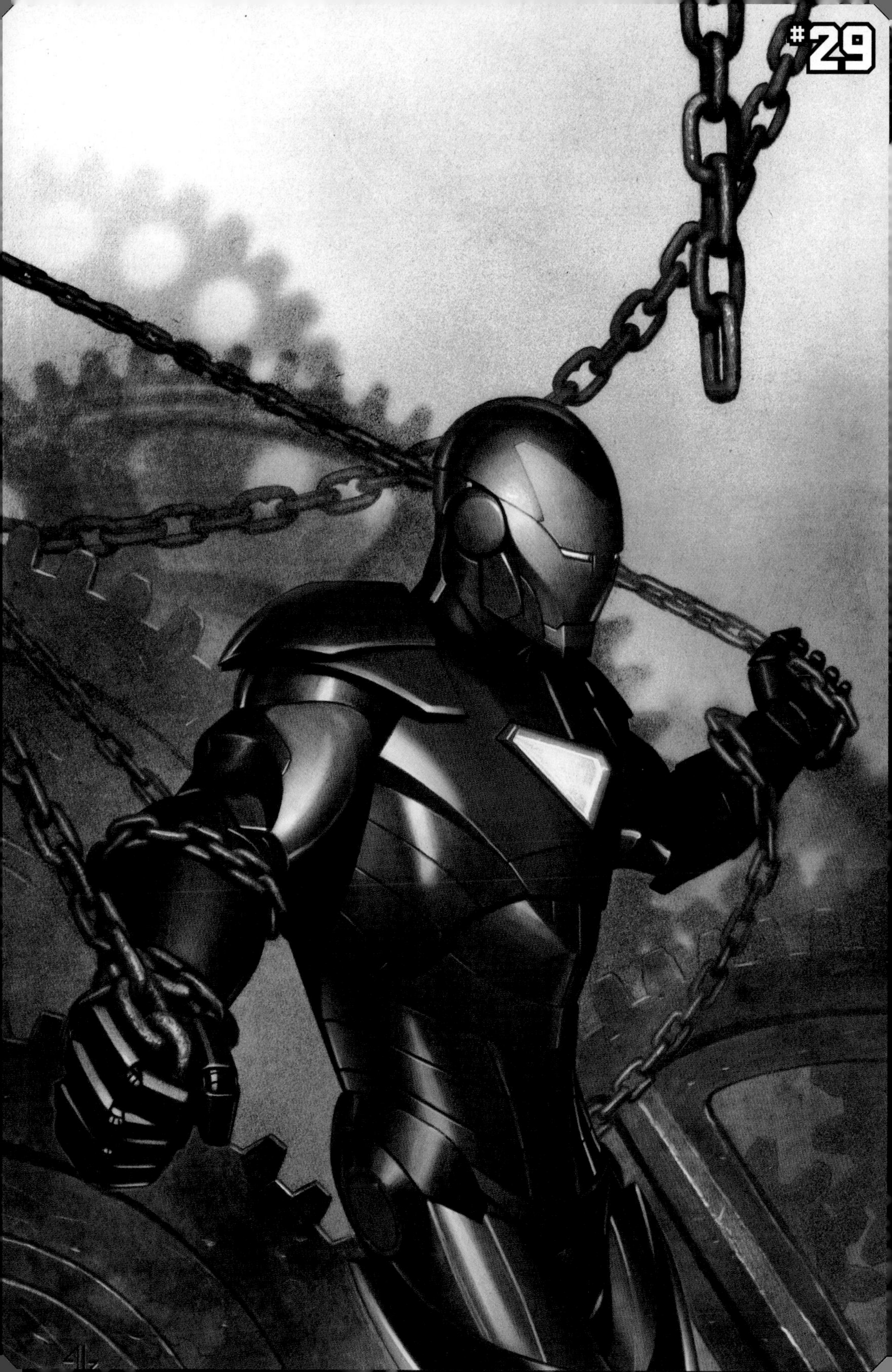
#29

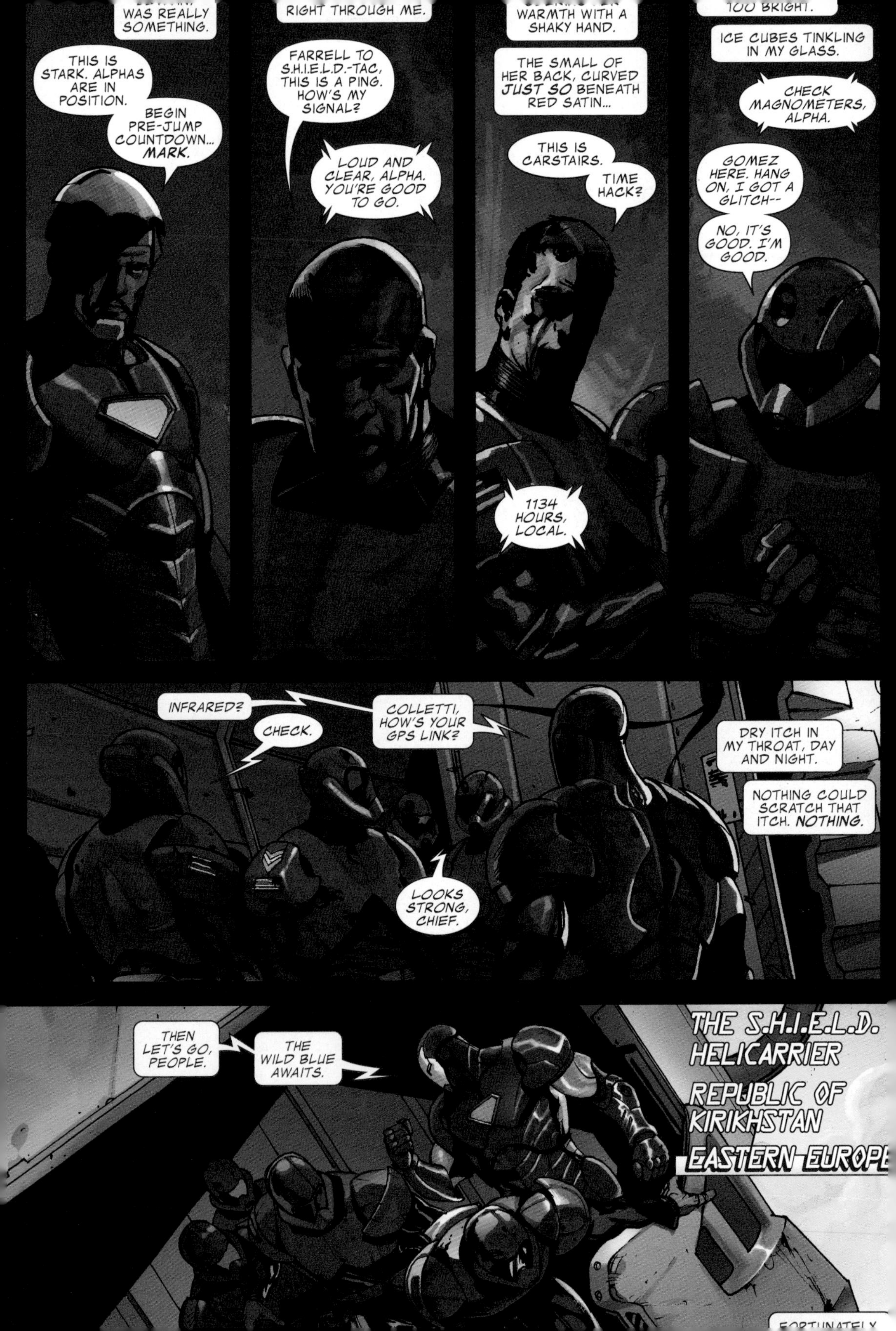
WAS REALLY SOMETHING.
THIS IS STARK. ALPHAS ARE IN POSITION.
BEGIN PRE-JUMP COUNTDOWN... MARK.
RIGHT THROUGH ME.
FARRELL TO S.H.I.E.L.D.-TAC, THIS IS A PING. HOW'S MY SIGNAL?
LOUD AND CLEAR, ALPHA. YOU'RE GOOD TO GO.
WARMTH WITH A SHAKY HAND.
THE SMALL OF HER BACK, CURVED JUST SO BENEATH RED SATIN...
THIS IS CARSTAIRS.
TIME HACK?
1134 HOURS, LOCAL.
TOO BRIGHT.
ICE CUBES TINKLING IN MY GLASS.
CHECK MAGNOMETERS, ALPHA.
GOMEZ HERE. HANG ON, I GOT A GLITCH--
NO, IT'S GOOD. I'M GOOD.
INFRARED?
CHECK.
COLLETTI, HOW'S YOUR GPS LINK?
LOOKS STRONG, CHIEF.
DRY ITCH IN MY THROAT, DAY AND NIGHT.
NOTHING COULD SCRATCH THAT ITCH. NOTHING.
THEN LET'S GO, PEOPLE.
THE WILD BLUE AWAITS.
THE S.H.I.E.L.D. HELICARRIER
REPUBLIC OF KIRIKHSTAN
EASTERN EUROPE

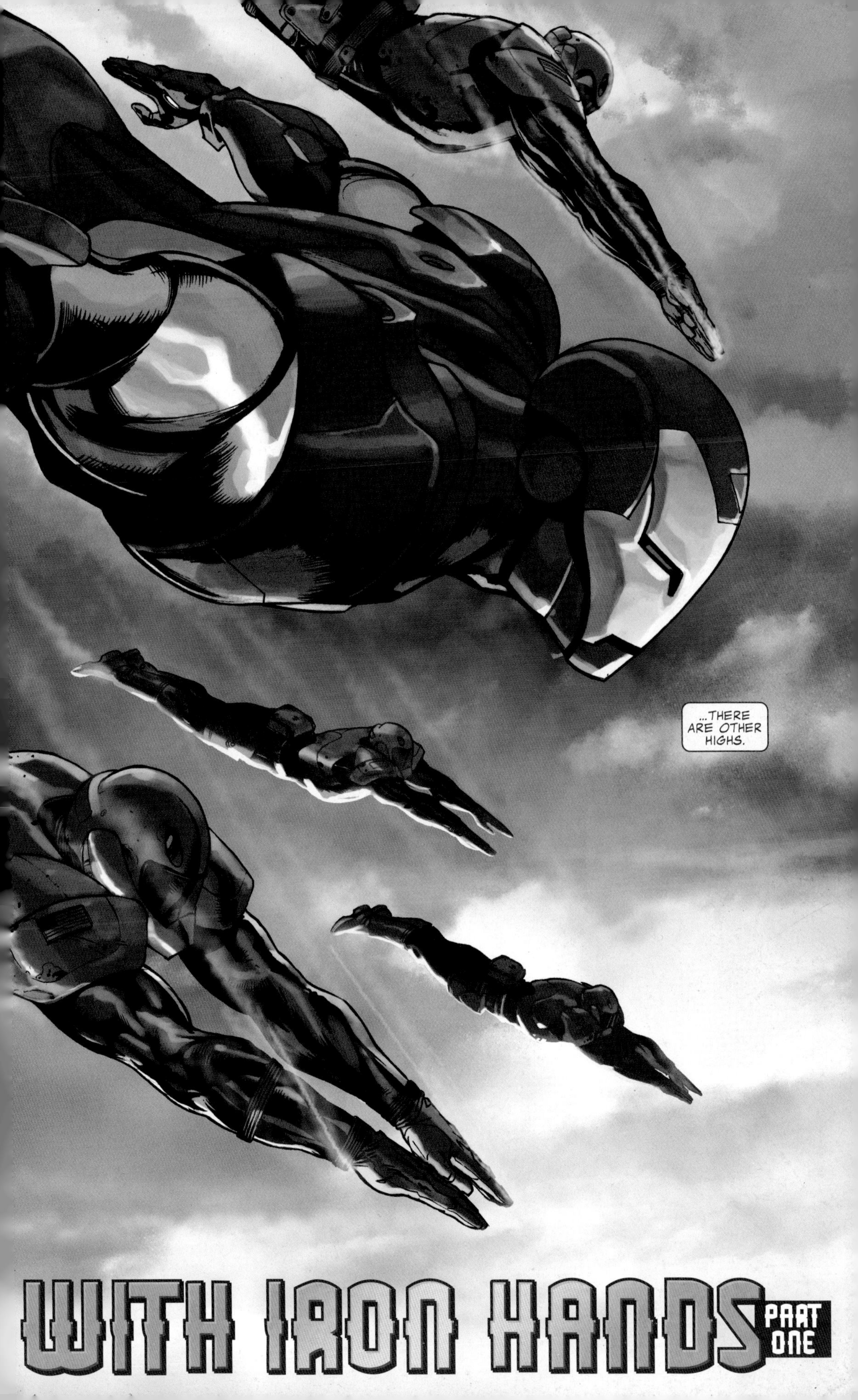
...THERE ARE OTHER HIGHS.
WITH IRON HANDS PART ONE

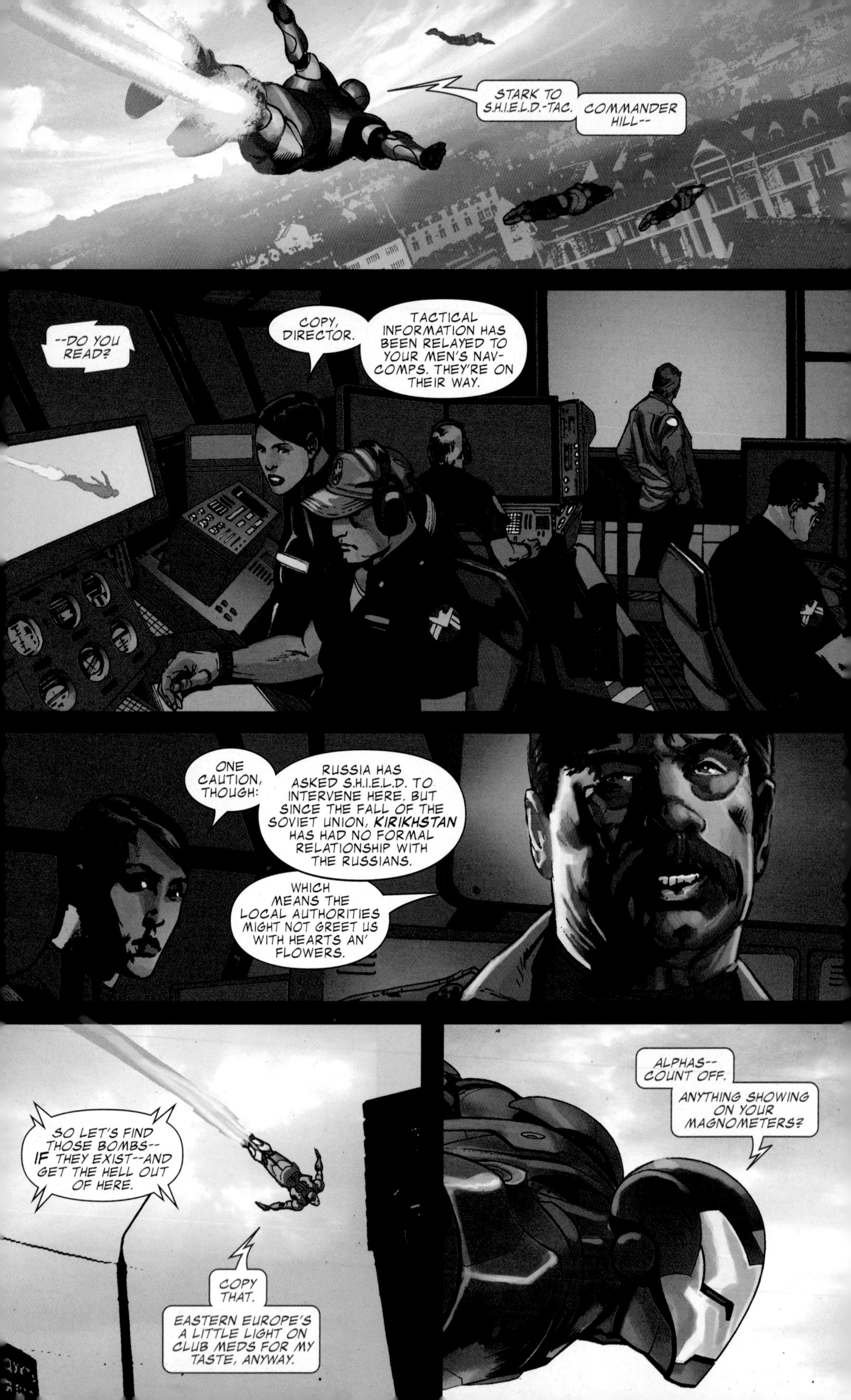
STARK TO S.H.I.E.L.D.-TAC.
COMMANDER HILL--
--DO YOU READ?
COPY, DIRECTOR.
TACTICAL INFORMATION HAS BEEN RELAYED TO YOUR MEN'S NAV-COMPS. THEY'RE ON THEIR WAY.
ONE CAUTION, THOUGH:
RUSSIA HAS ASKED S.H.I.E.L.D. TO INTERVENE HERE. BUT SINCE THE FALL OF THE SOVIET UNION, KIRIKHSTAN HAS HAD NO FORMAL RELATIONSHIP WITH THE RUSSIANS.
WHICH MEANS THE LOCAL AUTHORITIES MIGHT NOT GREET US WITH HEARTS AN' FLOWERS.
SO LET'S FIND THOSE BOMBS--IF THEY EXIST--AND GET THE HELL OUT OF HERE.
ALPHAS--COUNT OFF.
ANYTHING SHOWING ON YOUR MAGNOMETERS?
COPY THAT.
EASTERN EUROPE'S A LITTLE LIGHT ON CLUB MEDS FOR MY TASTE, ANYWAY.

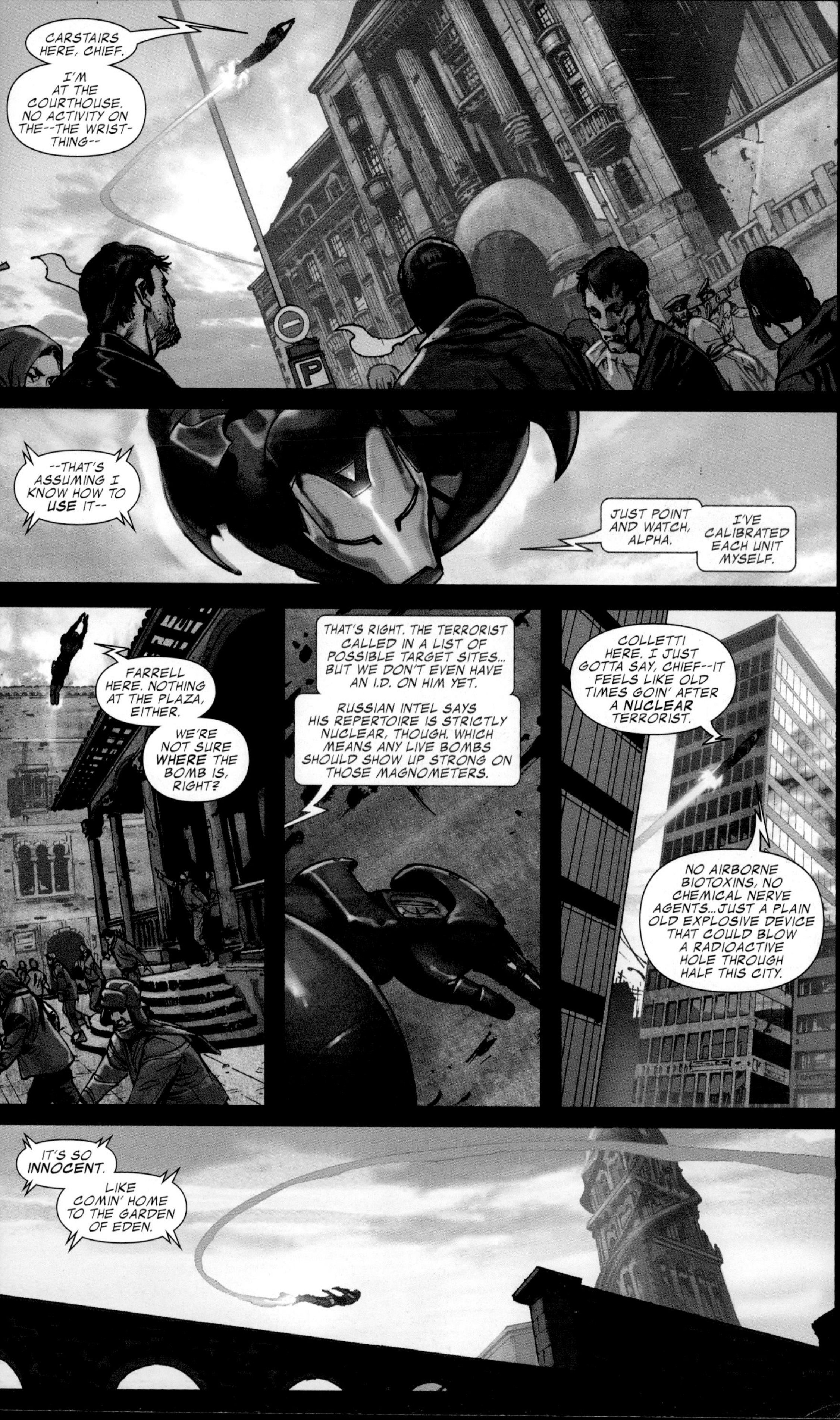
CARSTAIRS HERE, CHIEF.
I'M AT THE COURTHOUSE. NO ACTIVITY ON THE--THE WRIST-THING--
--THAT'S ASSUMING I KNOW HOW TO USE IT--
JUST POINT AND WATCH, ALPHA.
I'VE CALIBRATED EACH UNIT MYSELF.
FARRELL HERE. NOTHING AT THE PLAZA, EITHER.
WE'RE NOT SURE WHERE THE BOMB IS, RIGHT?
THAT'S RIGHT. THE TERRORIST CALLED IN A LIST OF POSSIBLE TARGET SITES... BUT WE DON'T EVEN HAVE AN I.D. ON HIM YET.
RUSSIAN INTEL SAYS HIS REPERTOIRE IS STRICTLY NUCLEAR, THOUGH. WHICH MEANS ANY LIVE BOMBS SHOULD SHOW UP STRONG ON THOSE MAGNOMETERS.
COLLETTI HERE. I JUST GOTTA SAY, CHIEF--IT FEELS LIKE OLD TIMES GOIN' AFTER A NUCLEAR TERRORIST.
NO AIRBORNE BIOTOXINS, NO CHEMICAL NERVE AGENTS...JUST A PLAIN OLD EXPLOSIVE DEVICE THAT COULD BLOW A RADIOACTIVE HOLE THROUGH HALF THIS CITY.
IT'S SO INNOCENT.
LIKE COMIN' HOME TO THE GARDEN OF EDEN.

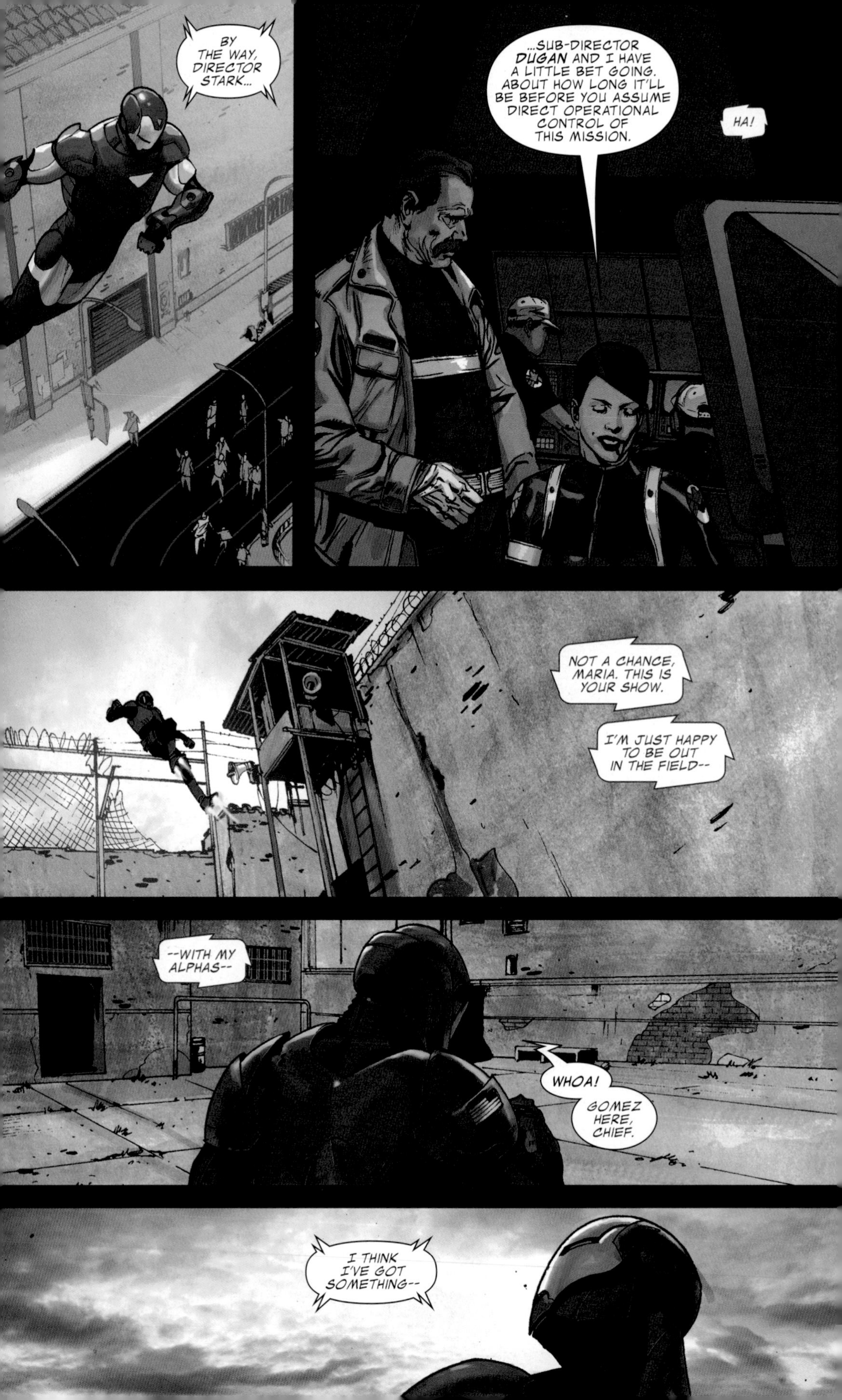
BY THE WAY, DIRECTOR STARK...
...SUB-DIRECTOR DUGAN AND I HAVE A LITTLE BET GOING. ABOUT HOW LONG IT'LL BE BEFORE YOU ASSUME DIRECT OPERATIONAL CONTROL OF THIS MISSION.
HA!
NOT A CHANCE, MARIA. THIS IS YOUR SHOW.
I'M JUST HAPPY TO BE OUT IN THE FIELD--
--WITH MY ALPHAS--
WHOA!
GOMEZ HERE, CHIEF.
I THINK I'VE GOT SOMETHING--

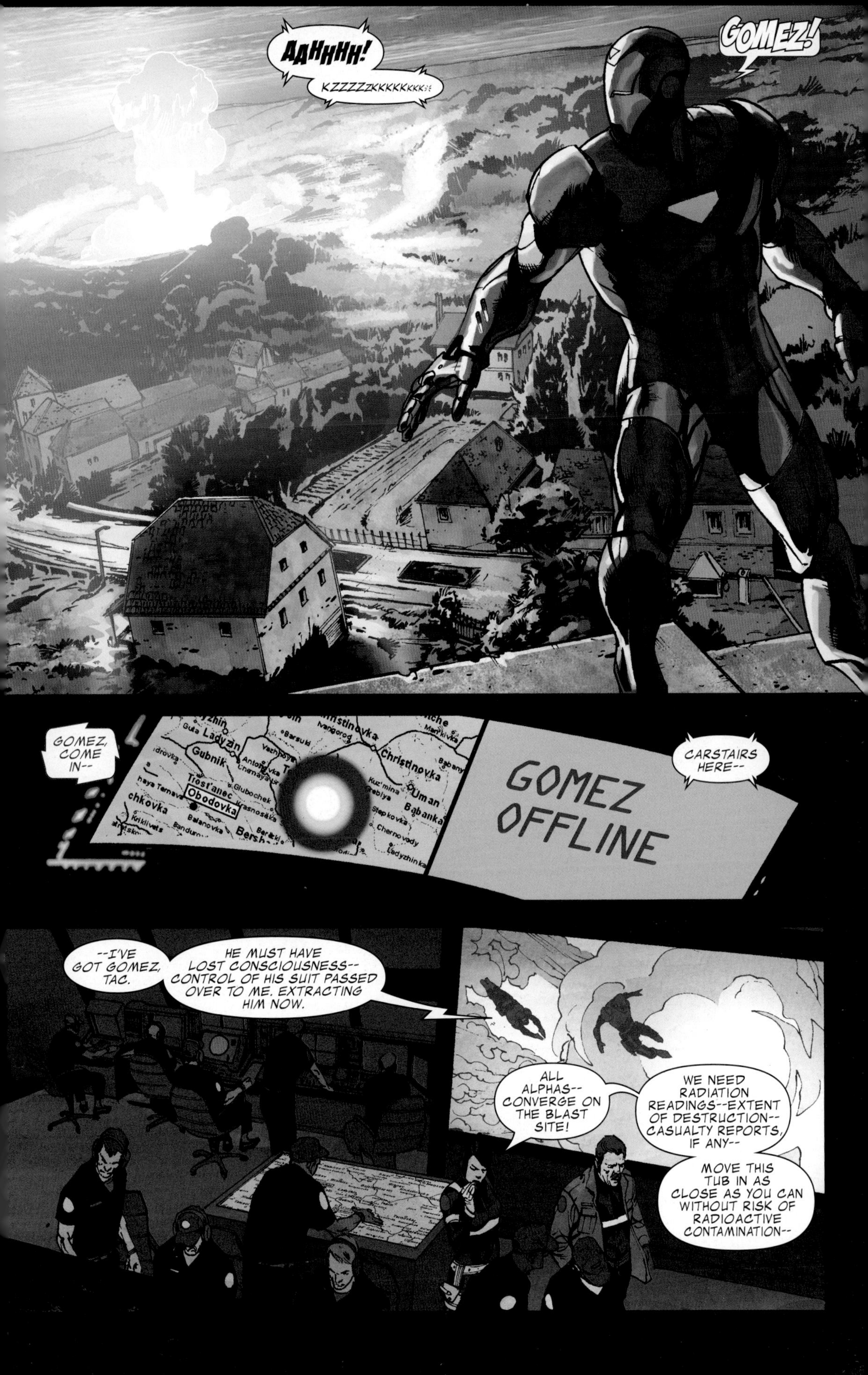
AAHHHH!
KZZZZZKKKKKKKK
GOMEZ!
GOMEZ, COME IN--
Ladyzin
Gubnik
Obodovka
Christinovka
Uman
CARSTAIRS HERE--
GOMEZ OFFLINE
--I'VE GOT GOMEZ, TAC.
HE MUST HAVE LOST CONSCIOUSNESS--CONTROL OF HIS SUIT PASSED OVER TO ME. EXTRACTING HIM NOW.
ALL ALPHAS--CONVERGE ON THE BLAST SITE!
WE NEED RADIATION READINGS--EXTENT OF DESTRUCTION--CASUALTY REPORTS, IF ANY--
MOVE THIS TUB IN AS CLOSE AS YOU CAN WITHOUT RISK OF RADIOACTIVE CONTAMINATION--

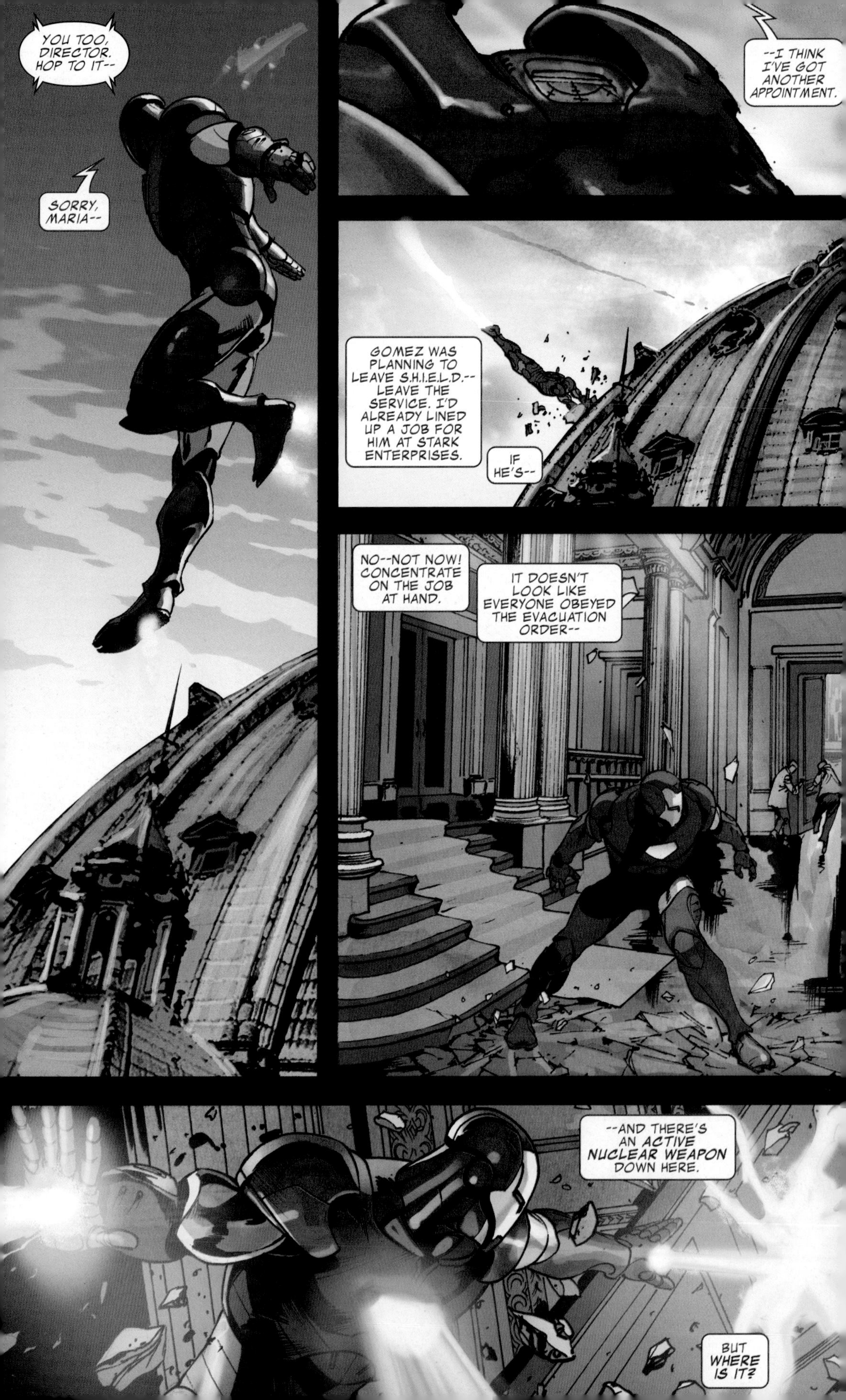
YOU TOO, DIRECTOR. HOP TO IT--
SORRY, MARIA--
--I THINK I'VE GOT ANOTHER APPOINTMENT.
GOMEZ WAS PLANNING TO LEAVE S.H.I.E.L.D.-- LEAVE THE SERVICE. I'D ALREADY LINED UP A JOB FOR HIM AT STARK ENTERPRISES.
IF HE'S--
NO--NOT NOW! CONCENTRATE ON THE JOB AT HAND.
IT DOESN'T LOOK LIKE EVERYONE OBEYED THE EVACUATION ORDER--
--AND THERE'S AN ACTIVE NUCLEAR WEAPON DOWN HERE.
BUT WHERE IS IT?

AH!

THAT'S *IT*. NO BIGGER THAN A HOLLOWPOINT...BUT THE FISSIONABLE MATERIAL'S BEEN COMPRESSED DOWN TO FIT.

DOESN'T ANYBODY BUILD WEAPONS YOU CAN *SEE* ANYMORE?

NOT THAT I SHOULD TALK.

THESE BABIES CAN AFFECT ANYTHING DOWN TO THE *NANO* SCALE--

--WHICH SEEMS TO BE WHAT WE'RE DEALING WITH HERE.

CAREFUL... CAREFUL. DON'T KNOW HOW THE TRIGGER MECHANISM WORKS YET...

OKAY, NORMAL DEFUSING METHODS ARE OUT OF THE QUESTION. FORTUNATELY, I ANTICIPATED THAT...AND INSTALLED *ATOMIC FORCE MICROSCOPES* IN BOTH GAUNTLETS.

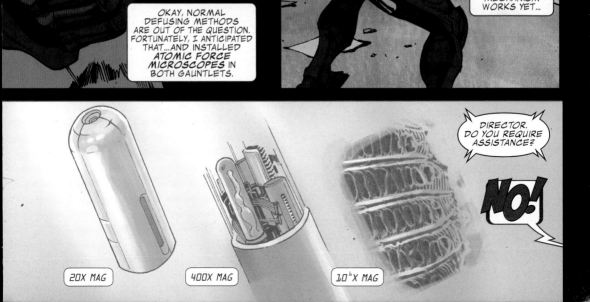

DIRECTOR. DO YOU REQUIRE ASSISTANCE?

NO!

20X MAG

400X MAG

10^6X MAG

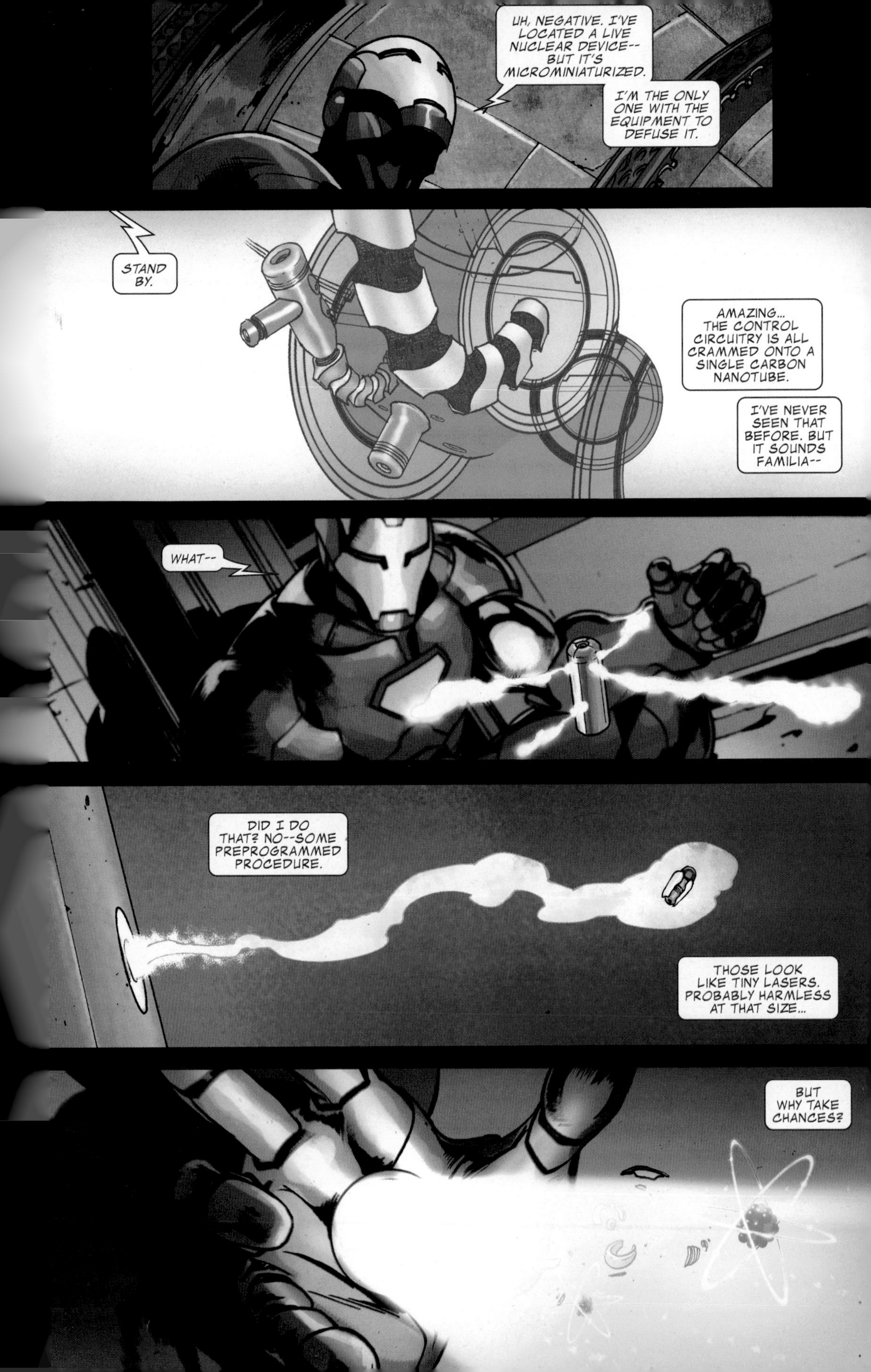
UH, NEGATIVE. I'VE LOCATED A LIVE NUCLEAR DEVICE-- BUT IT'S MICROMINIATURIZED.
I'M THE ONLY ONE WITH THE EQUIPMENT TO DEFUSE IT.
STAND BY.
AMAZING... THE CONTROL CIRCUITRY IS ALL CRAMMED ONTO A SINGLE CARBON NANOTUBE.
I'VE NEVER SEEN THAT BEFORE. BUT IT SOUNDS FAMILIA--
WHAT--
DID I DO THAT? NO--SOME PREPROGRAMMED PROCEDURE.
THOSE LOOK LIKE TINY LASERS. PROBABLY HARMLESS AT THAT SIZE...
BUT WHY TAKE CHANCES?

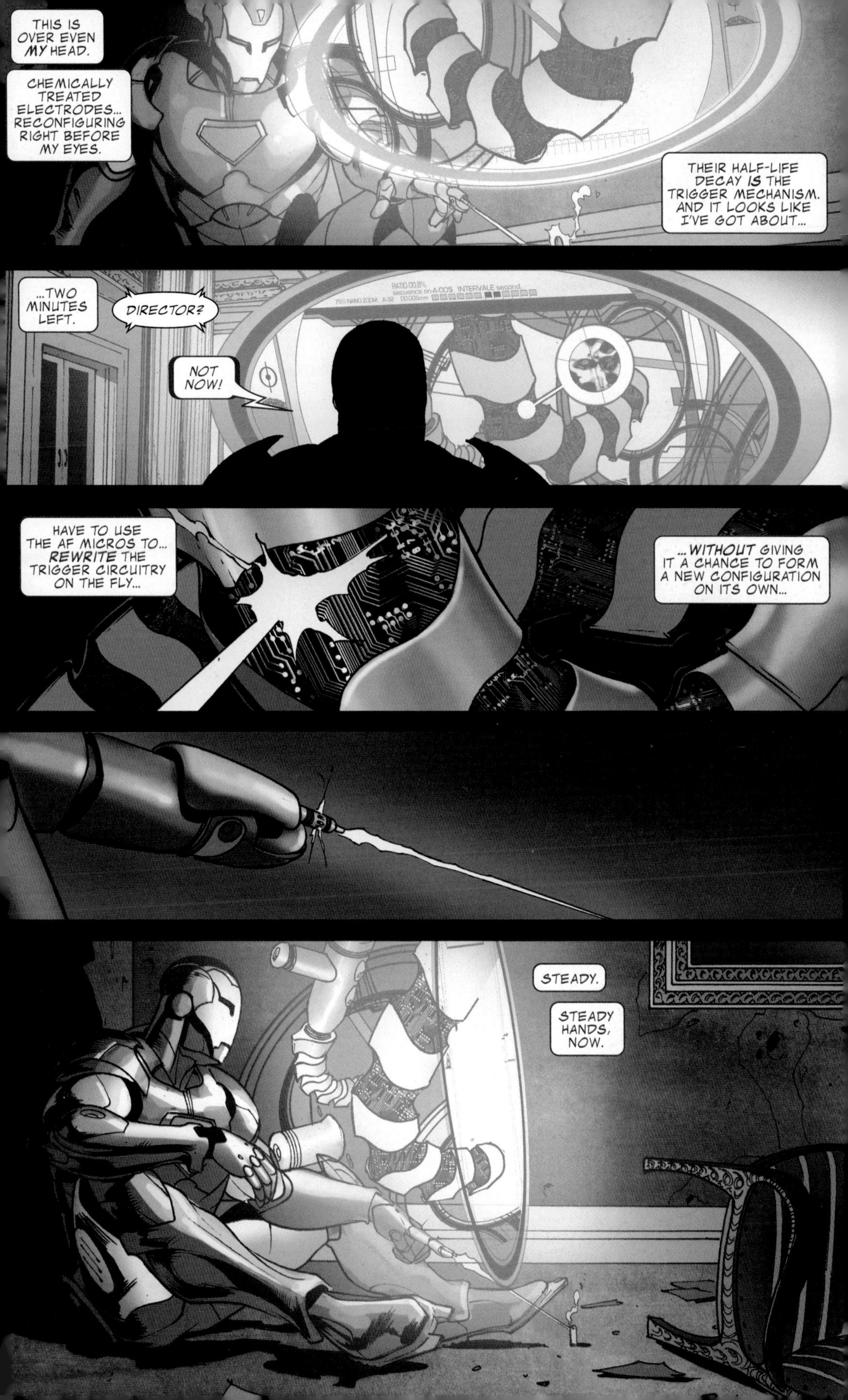
THIS IS OVER EVEN *MY* HEAD.
CHEMICALLY TREATED ELECTRODES... RECONFIGURING RIGHT BEFORE MY EYES.
THEIR HALF-LIFE DECAY **IS** THE TRIGGER MECHANISM. AND IT LOOKS LIKE I'VE GOT ABOUT...
...TWO MINUTES LEFT.
DIRECTOR?
NOT NOW!
HAVE TO USE THE AF MICROS TO... ***REWRITE*** THE TRIGGER CIRCUITRY ON THE FLY...
...***WITHOUT*** GIVING IT A CHANCE TO FORM A NEW CONFIGURATION ON ITS OWN...
STEADY.
STEADY HANDS, NOW.

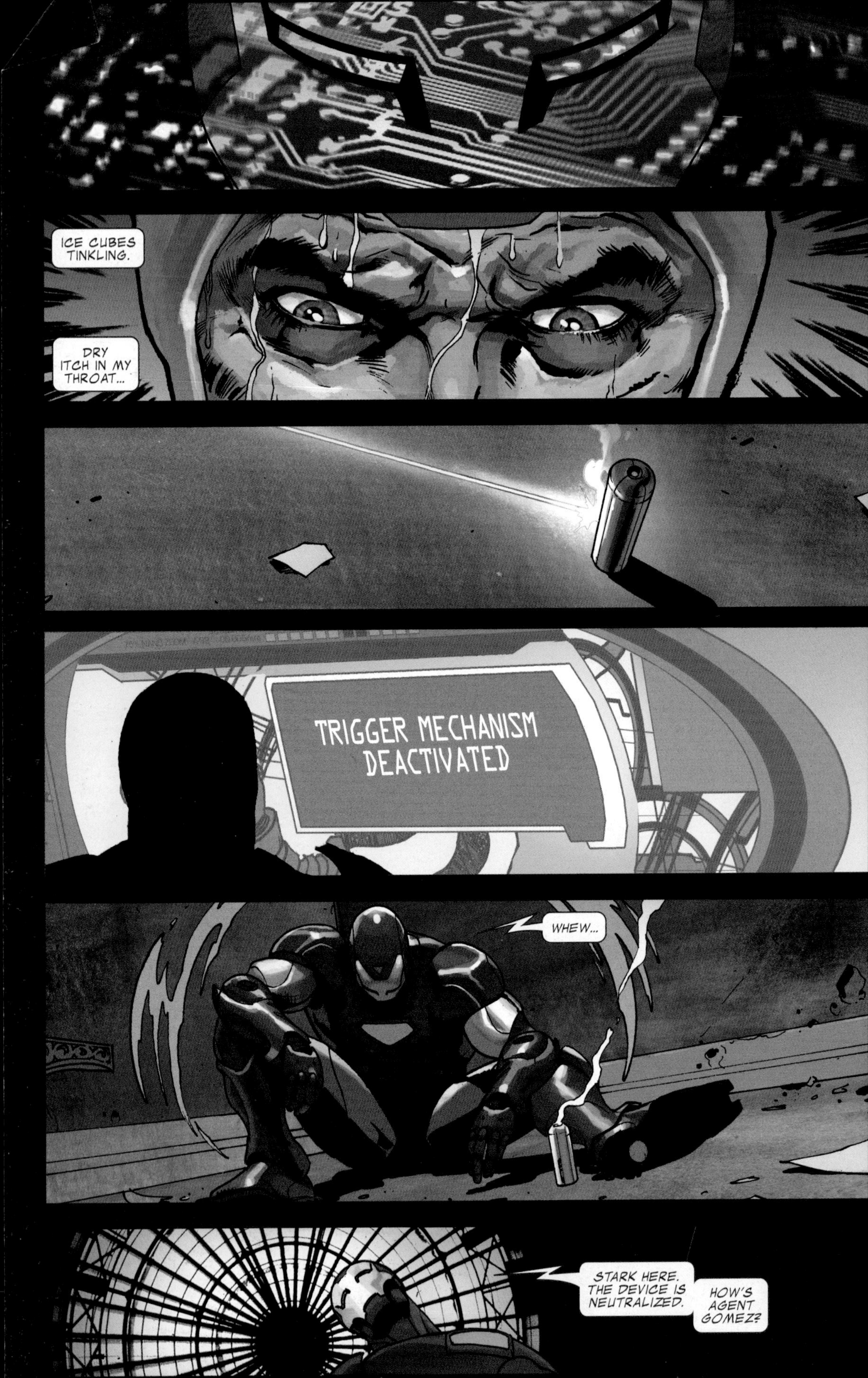
ICE CUBES TINKLING.
DRY ITCH IN MY THROAT...
TRIGGER MECHANISM DEACTIVATED
WHEW...
STARK HERE. THE DEVICE IS NEUTRALIZED.
HOW'S AGENT GOMEZ?

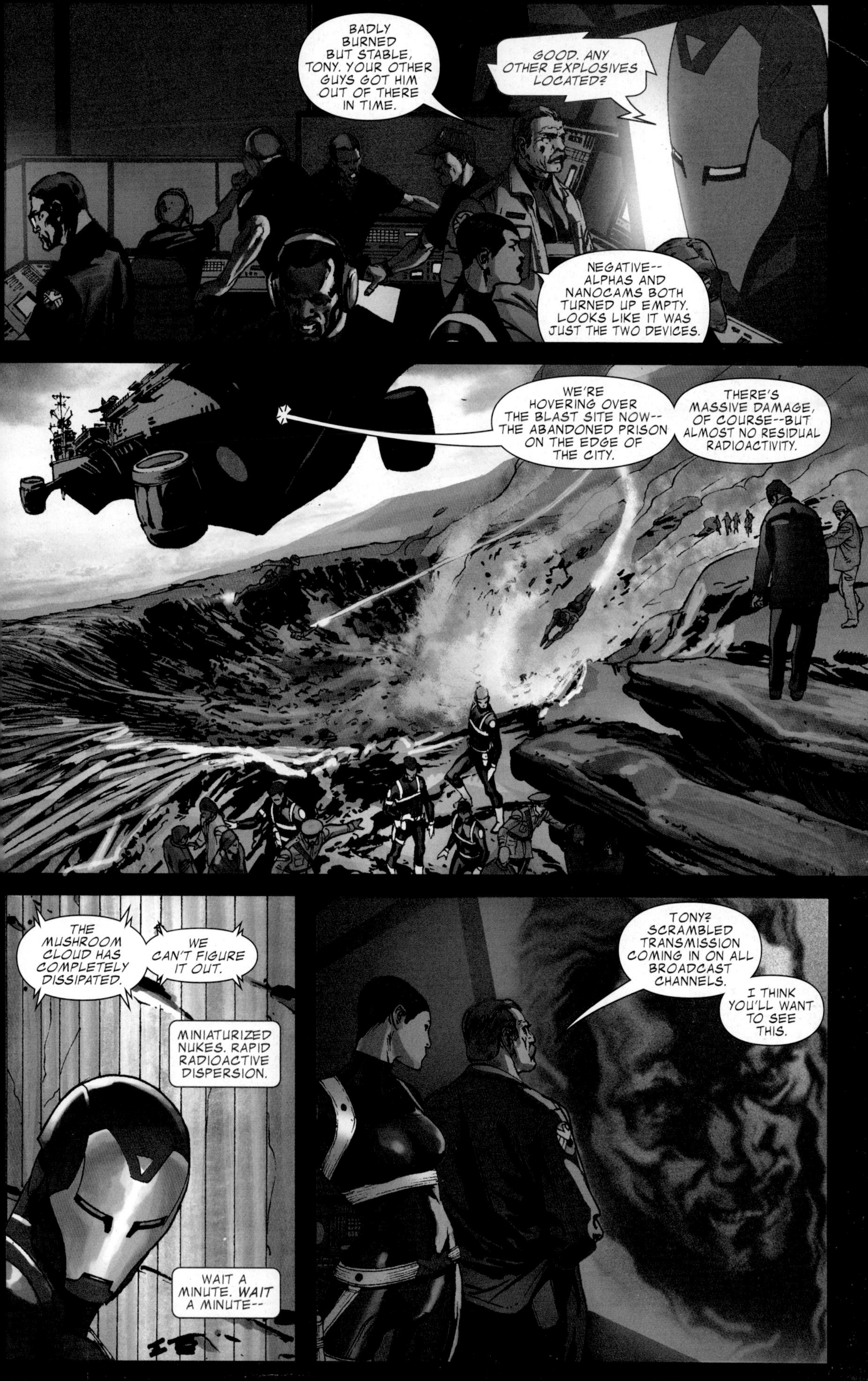
BADLY BURNED BUT STABLE, TONY. YOUR OTHER GUYS GOT HIM OUT OF THERE IN TIME.
GOOD. ANY OTHER EXPLOSIVES LOCATED?
NEGATIVE-- ALPHAS AND NANOCAMS BOTH TURNED UP EMPTY. LOOKS LIKE IT WAS JUST THE TWO DEVICES.
WE'RE HOVERING OVER THE BLAST SITE NOW-- THE ABANDONED PRISON ON THE EDGE OF THE CITY.
THERE'S MASSIVE DAMAGE, OF COURSE--BUT ALMOST NO RESIDUAL RADIOACTIVITY.
THE MUSHROOM CLOUD HAS COMPLETELY DISSIPATED.
WE CAN'T FIGURE IT OUT.
MINIATURIZED NUKES. RAPID RADIOACTIVE DISPERSION.
WAIT A MINUTE. WAIT A MINUTE--
TONY? SCRAMBLED TRANSMISSION COMING IN ON ALL BROADCAST CHANNELS.
I THINK YOU'LL WANT TO SEE THIS.

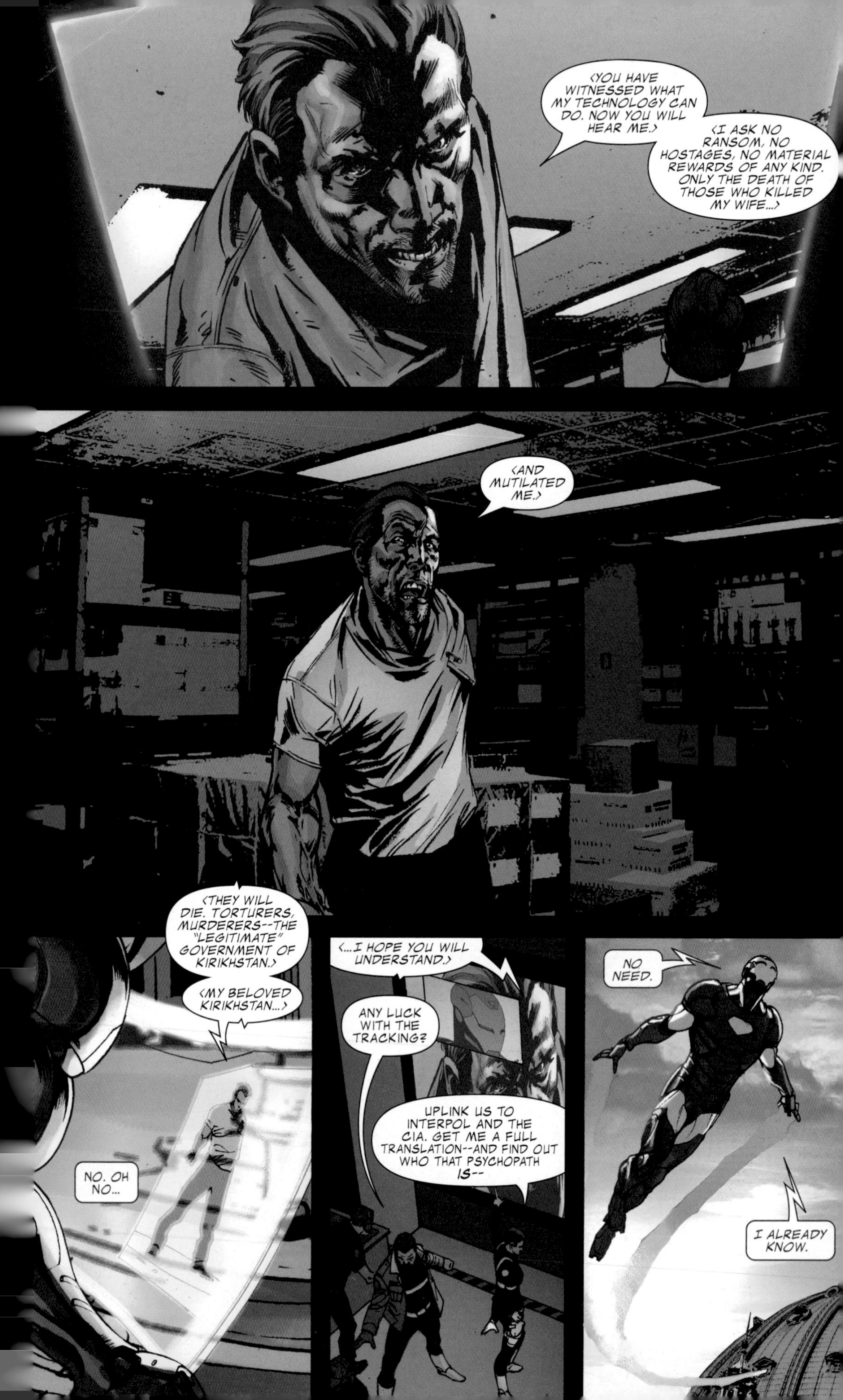

<YOU HAVE WITNESSED WHAT MY TECHNOLOGY CAN DO. NOW YOU WILL HEAR ME.>
<I ASK NO RANSOM, NO HOSTAGES, NO MATERIAL REWARDS OF ANY KIND. ONLY THE DEATH OF THOSE WHO KILLED MY WIFE...>
<AND MUTILATED ME.>
<THEY WILL DIE. TORTURERS, MURDERERS--THE "LEGITIMATE" GOVERNMENT OF KIRIKHSTAN.>
<MY BELOVED KIRIKHSTAN...>
NO. OH NO...
<...I HOPE YOU WILL UNDERSTAND.>
ANY LUCK WITH THE TRACKING?
UPLINK US TO INTERPOL AND THE CIA. GET ME A FULL TRANSLATION--AND FIND OUT WHO THAT PSYCHOPATH IS--
NO NEED.
I ALREADY KNOW.

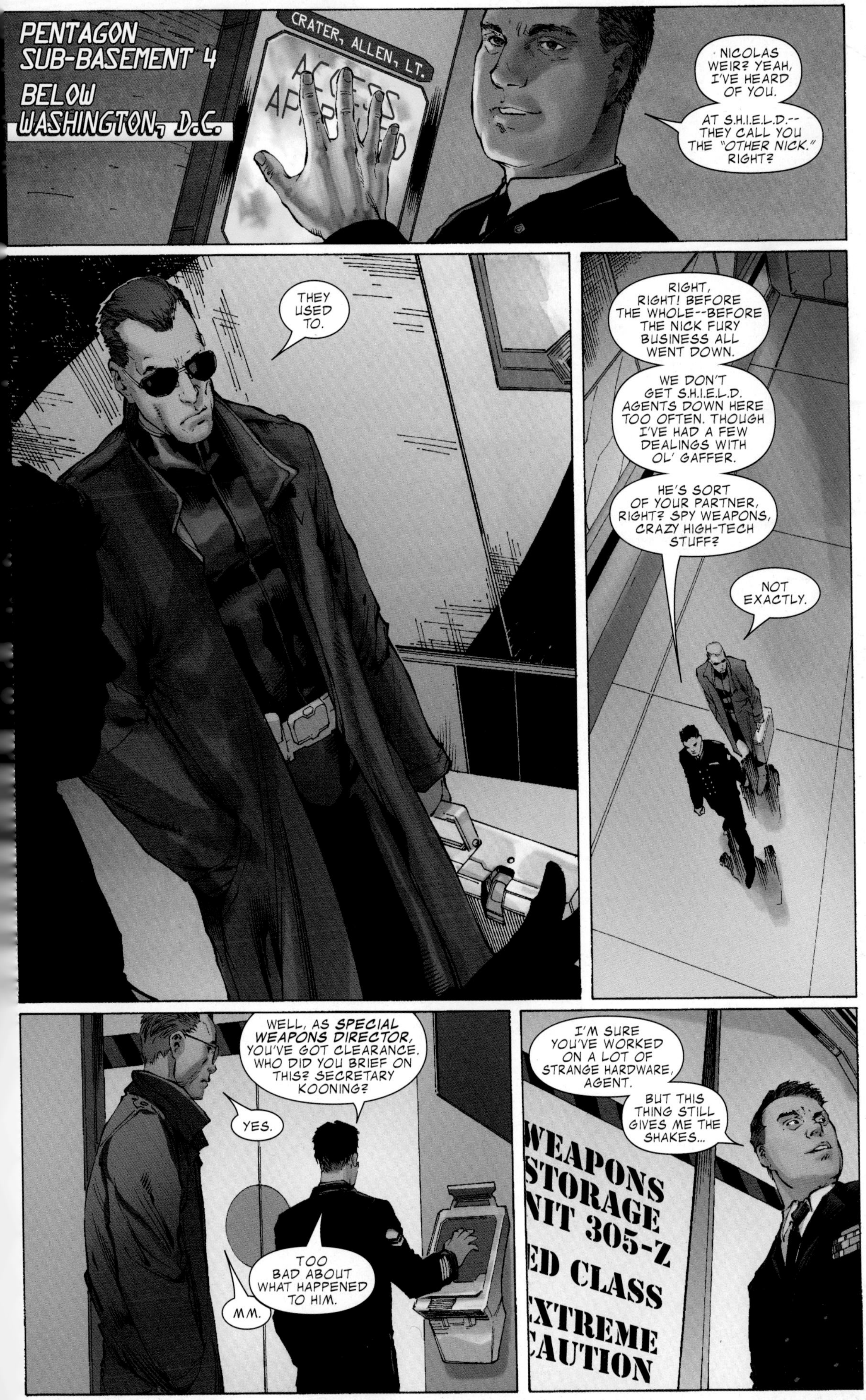
PENTAGON SUB-BASEMENT 4
BELOW WASHINGTON, D.C.
CRATER, ALLEN, LT.
ACCESS APPROVED
NICOLAS WEIR? YEAH, I'VE HEARD OF YOU.
AT S.H.I.E.L.D.-- THEY CALL YOU THE "OTHER NICK." RIGHT?
THEY USED TO.
RIGHT, RIGHT! BEFORE THE WHOLE--BEFORE THE NICK FURY BUSINESS ALL WENT DOWN.
WE DON'T GET S.H.I.E.L.D. AGENTS DOWN HERE TOO OFTEN. THOUGH I'VE HAD A FEW DEALINGS WITH OL' GAFFER.
HE'S SORT OF YOUR PARTNER, RIGHT? SPY WEAPONS, CRAZY HIGH-TECH STUFF?
NOT EXACTLY.
WELL, AS SPECIAL WEAPONS DIRECTOR, YOU'VE GOT CLEARANCE. WHO DID YOU BRIEF ON THIS? SECRETARY KOONING?
YES.
TOO BAD ABOUT WHAT HAPPENED TO HIM.
MM.
I'M SURE YOU'VE WORKED ON A LOT OF STRANGE HARDWARE, AGENT.
BUT THIS THING STILL GIVES ME THE SHAKES...
WEAPONS STORAGE NIT 305-Z
ED CLASS
XTREME AUTION

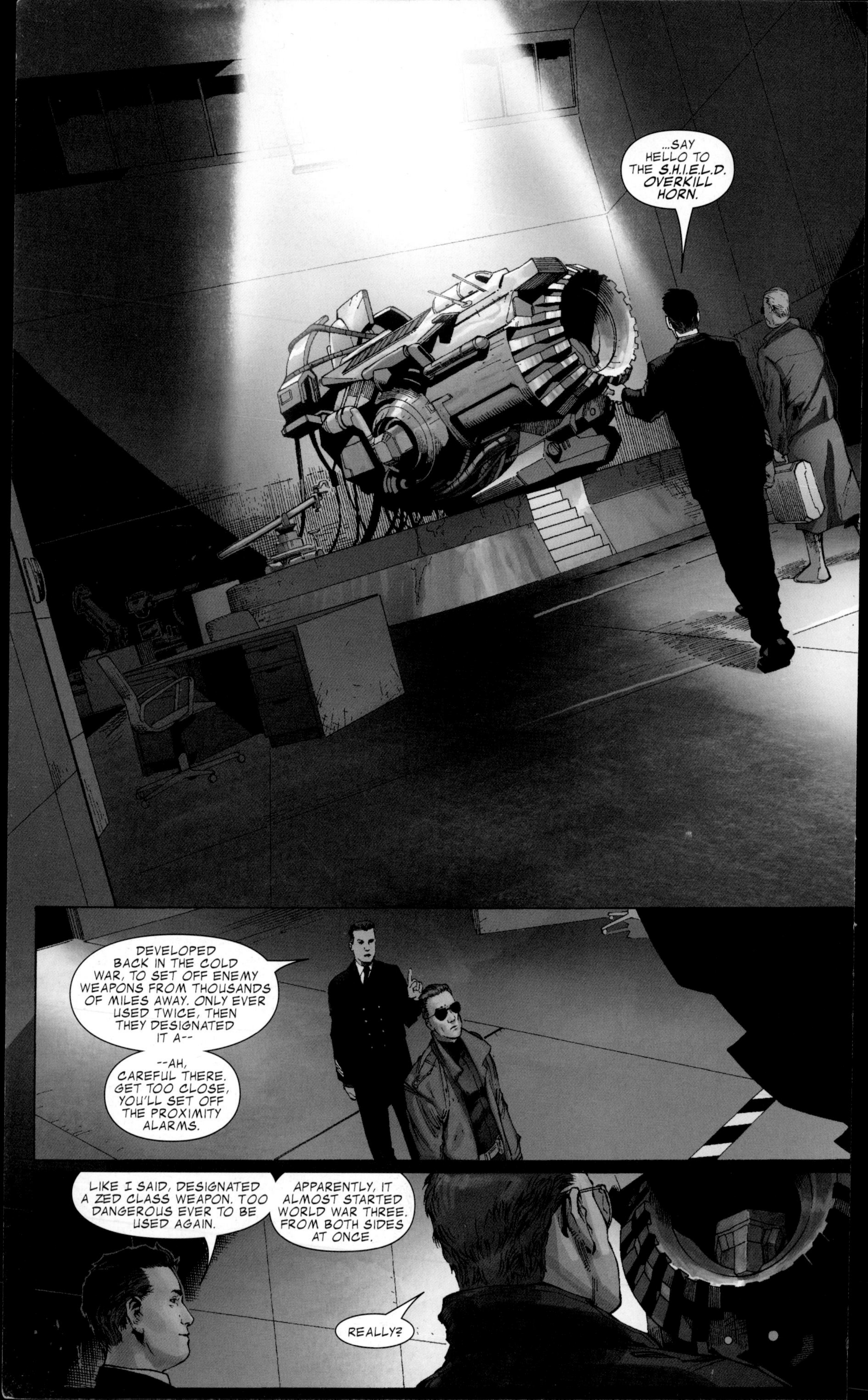
...SAY HELLO TO THE S.H.I.E.L.D. OVERKILL HORN.
DEVELOPED BACK IN THE COLD WAR, TO SET OFF ENEMY WEAPONS FROM THOUSANDS OF MILES AWAY. ONLY EVER USED TWICE, THEN THEY DESIGNATED IT A--
--AH, CAREFUL THERE. GET TOO CLOSE, YOU'LL SET OFF THE PROXIMITY ALARMS.
LIKE I SAID, DESIGNATED A ZED CLASS WEAPON. TOO DANGEROUS EVER TO BE USED AGAIN.
APPARENTLY, IT ALMOST STARTED WORLD WAR THREE. FROM BOTH SIDES AT ONCE.
REALLY?

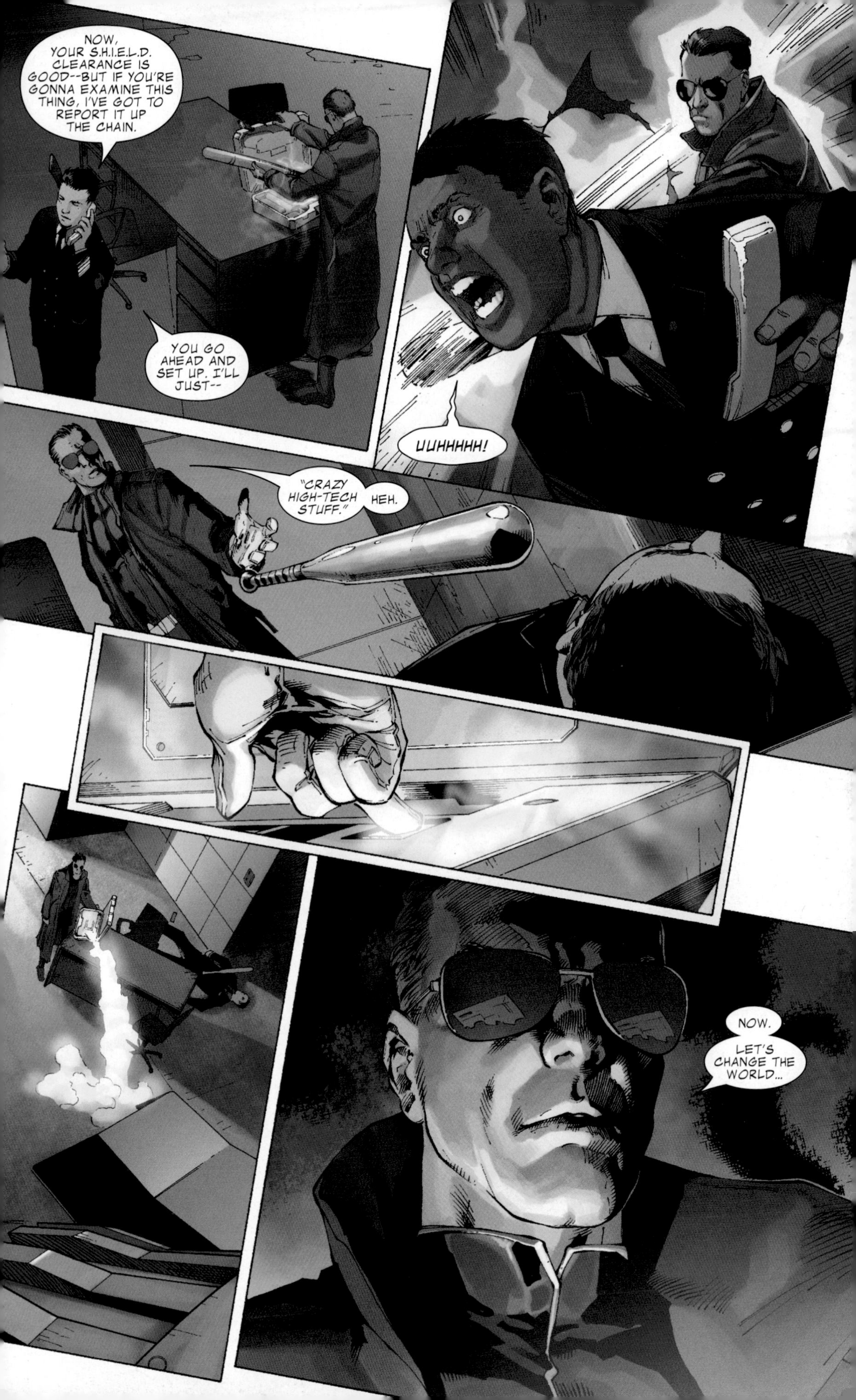
NOW, YOUR S.H.I.E.L.D. CLEARANCE IS GOOD--BUT IF YOU'RE GONNA EXAMINE THIS THING, I'VE GOT TO REPORT IT UP THE CHAIN.
YOU GO AHEAD AND SET UP. I'LL JUST--
UUHHHHH!
"CRAZY HIGH-TECH STUFF."
HEH.
NOW.
LET'S CHANGE THE WORLD...

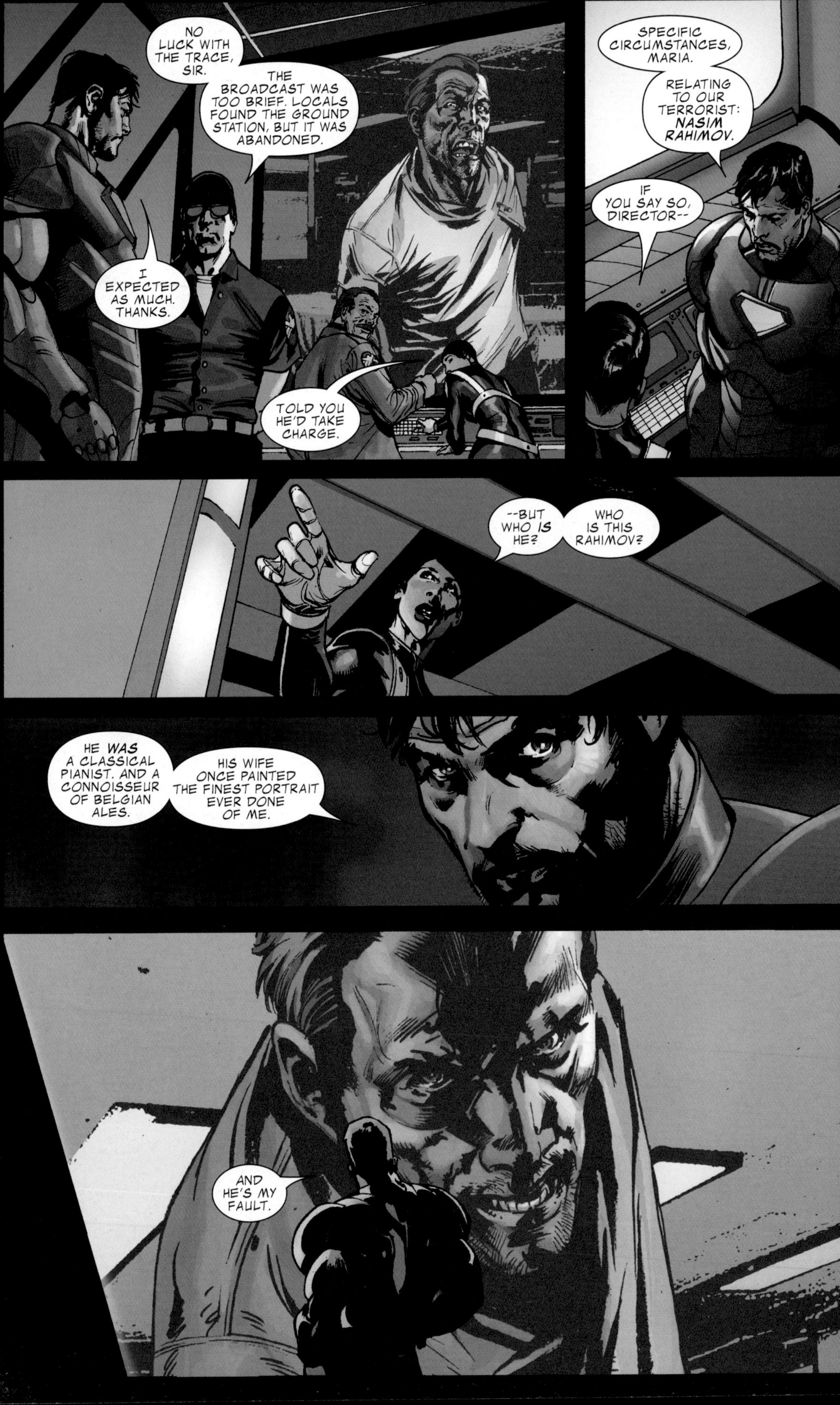
NO LUCK WITH THE TRACE, SIR.
THE BROADCAST WAS TOO BRIEF. LOCALS FOUND THE GROUND STATION, BUT IT WAS ABANDONED.
I EXPECTED AS MUCH. THANKS.
TOLD YOU HE'D TAKE CHARGE.
SPECIFIC CIRCUMSTANCES, MARIA.
RELATING TO OUR TERRORIST: NASIM RAHIMOV.
IF YOU SAY SO, DIRECTOR--
--BUT WHO IS HE?
WHO IS THIS RAHIMOV?
HE WAS A CLASSICAL PIANIST. AND A CONNOISSEUR OF BELGIAN ALES.
HIS WIFE ONCE PAINTED THE FINEST PORTRAIT EVER DONE OF ME.
AND HE'S MY FAULT.

IS THIS A DRILL?

NEGATIVE. PROXIMITY ALARMS JUST WENT OFF IN ZED VAULT 305.

AND LIEUTENANT CRATER'S GONE DARK.

BE READY FOR ANYTHING.

WEAPONS STORAGE UNIT 305-Z ZED CLASS

ACCESS APPROVED

THAT GUY THE LIEUTENANT WAS ESCORTING-- IS HE EVEN A REAL S.H.I.E.L.D. AGENT?

AM I A REAL S.H.I.E.L.D. AGENT?

I'VE PUT MY LIFE INTO S.H.I.E.L.D.

YEARS OF HARD WORK. NO VACATIONS--NO SOCIAL LIFE--BARELY ANY SLEEP--ALL SO THE DIRECTORATE CAN HAVE THE FINEST WEAPONS TECHNOLOGY IN THE WORLD!

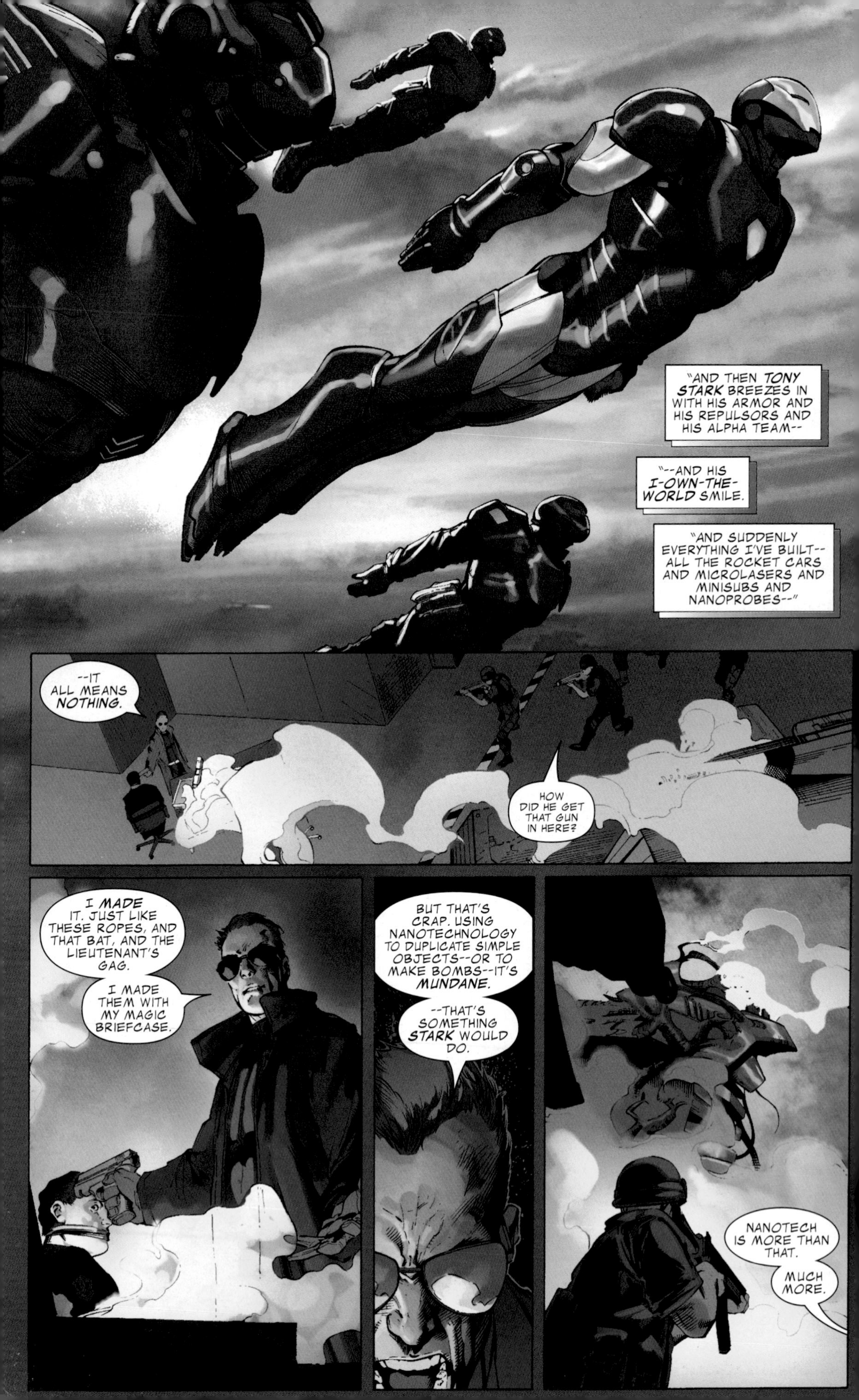
"AND THEN TONY STARK BREEZES IN WITH HIS ARMOR AND HIS REPULSORS AND HIS ALPHA TEAM--
"--AND HIS I-OWN-THE-WORLD SMILE.
"AND SUDDENLY EVERYTHING I'VE BUILT-- ALL THE ROCKET CARS AND MICROLASERS AND MINISUBS AND NANOPROBES--"
--IT ALL MEANS NOTHING.
HOW DID HE GET THAT GUN IN HERE?
I MADE IT. JUST LIKE THESE ROPES, AND THAT BAT, AND THE LIEUTENANT'S GAG.
I MADE THEM WITH MY MAGIC BRIEFCASE.
BUT THAT'S CRAP. USING NANOTECHNOLOGY TO DUPLICATE SIMPLE OBJECTS--OR TO MAKE BOMBS--IT'S MUNDANE.
--THAT'S SOMETHING STARK WOULD DO.
NANOTECH IS MORE THAN THAT.
MUCH MORE.

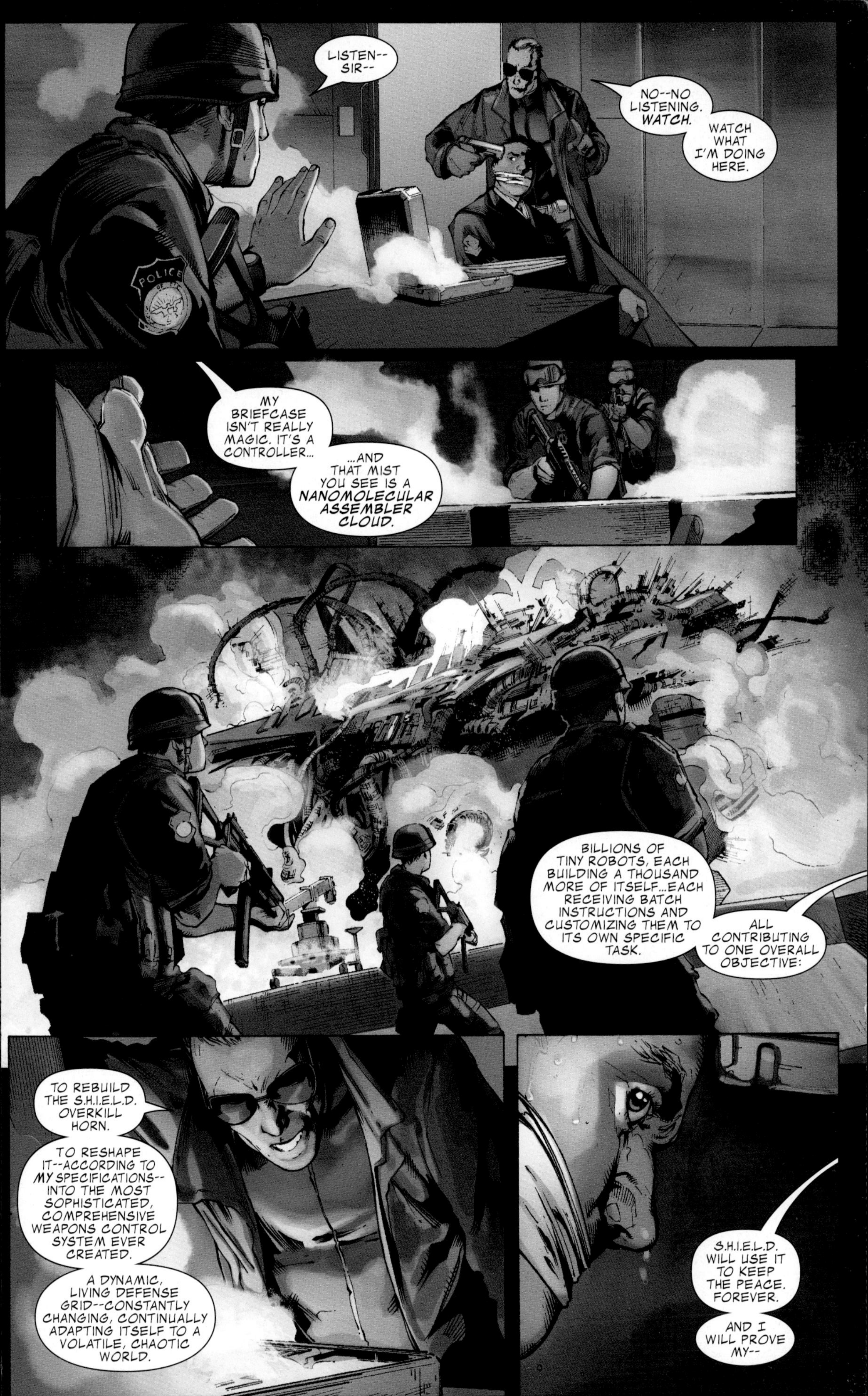
LISTEN-- SIR--
NO--NO LISTENING. *WATCH.*
WATCH WHAT I'M DOING HERE.
POLICE
MY BRIEFCASE ISN'T REALLY MAGIC. IT'S A CONTROLLER...
...AND THAT MIST YOU SEE IS A ***NANOMOLECULAR ASSEMBLER CLOUD.***
BILLIONS OF TINY ROBOTS, EACH BUILDING A THOUSAND MORE OF ITSELF...EACH RECEIVING BATCH INSTRUCTIONS AND CUSTOMIZING THEM TO ITS OWN SPECIFIC TASK.
ALL CONTRIBUTING TO ONE OVERALL OBJECTIVE:
TO REBUILD THE S.H.I.E.L.D. OVERKILL HORN.
TO RESHAPE IT--ACCORDING TO *MY* SPECIFICATIONS--INTO THE MOST SOPHISTICATED, COMPREHENSIVE WEAPONS CONTROL SYSTEM EVER CREATED.
A DYNAMIC, LIVING DEFENSE GRID--CONSTANTLY CHANGING, CONTINUALLY ADAPTING ITSELF TO A VOLATILE, CHAOTIC WORLD.
S.H.I.E.L.D. WILL USE IT TO KEEP THE PEACE. FOREVER.
AND I WILL PROVE MY--

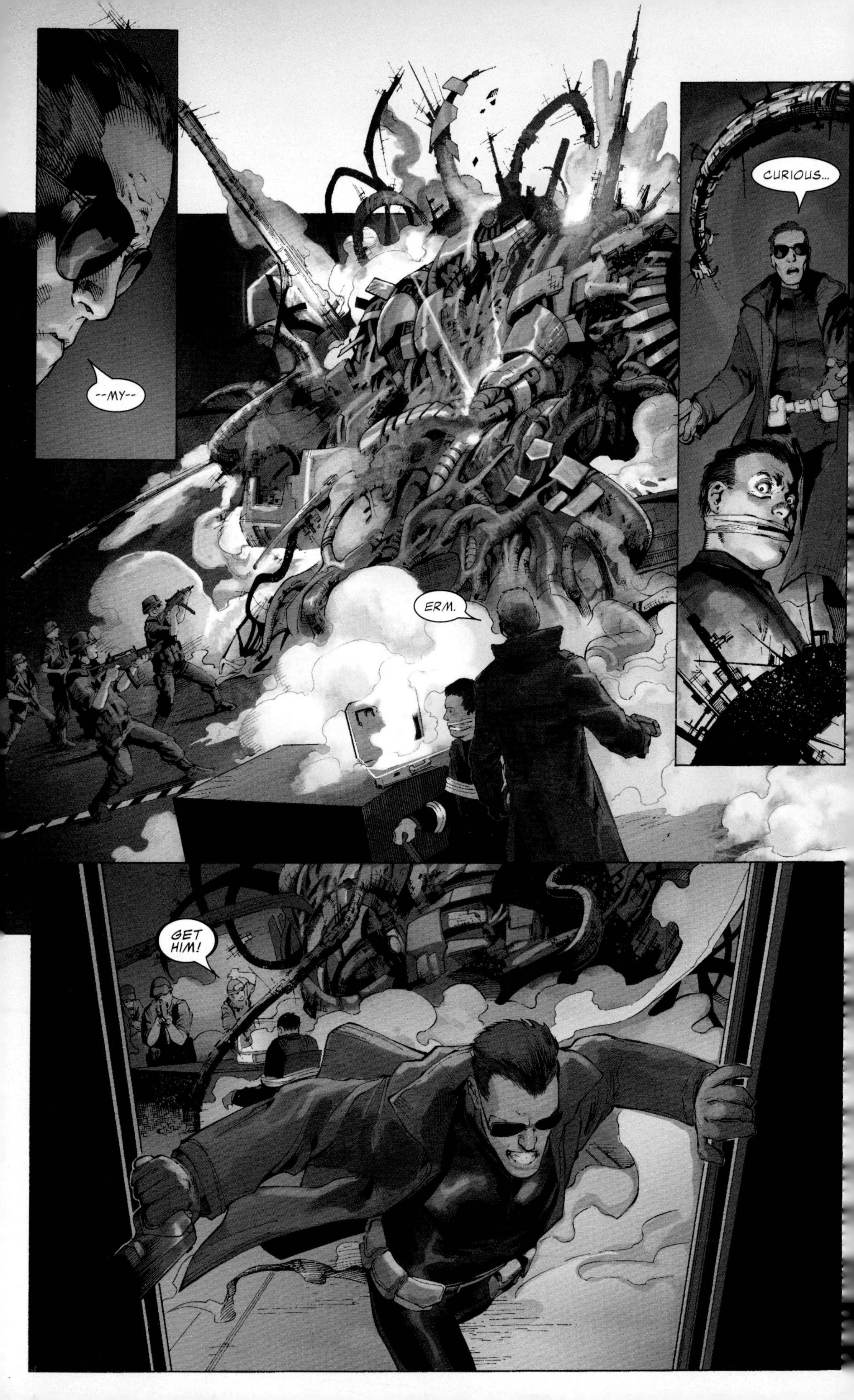
--MY--
CURIOUS...
ERM.
GET HIM!

MMFFFF!

MMWWWFFFF--

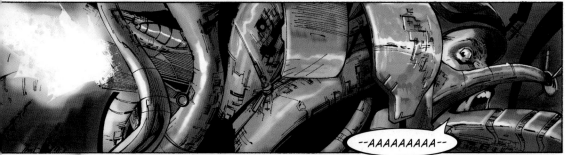

--AAAAAAAAA--

AAAHHHHHHHHHH!

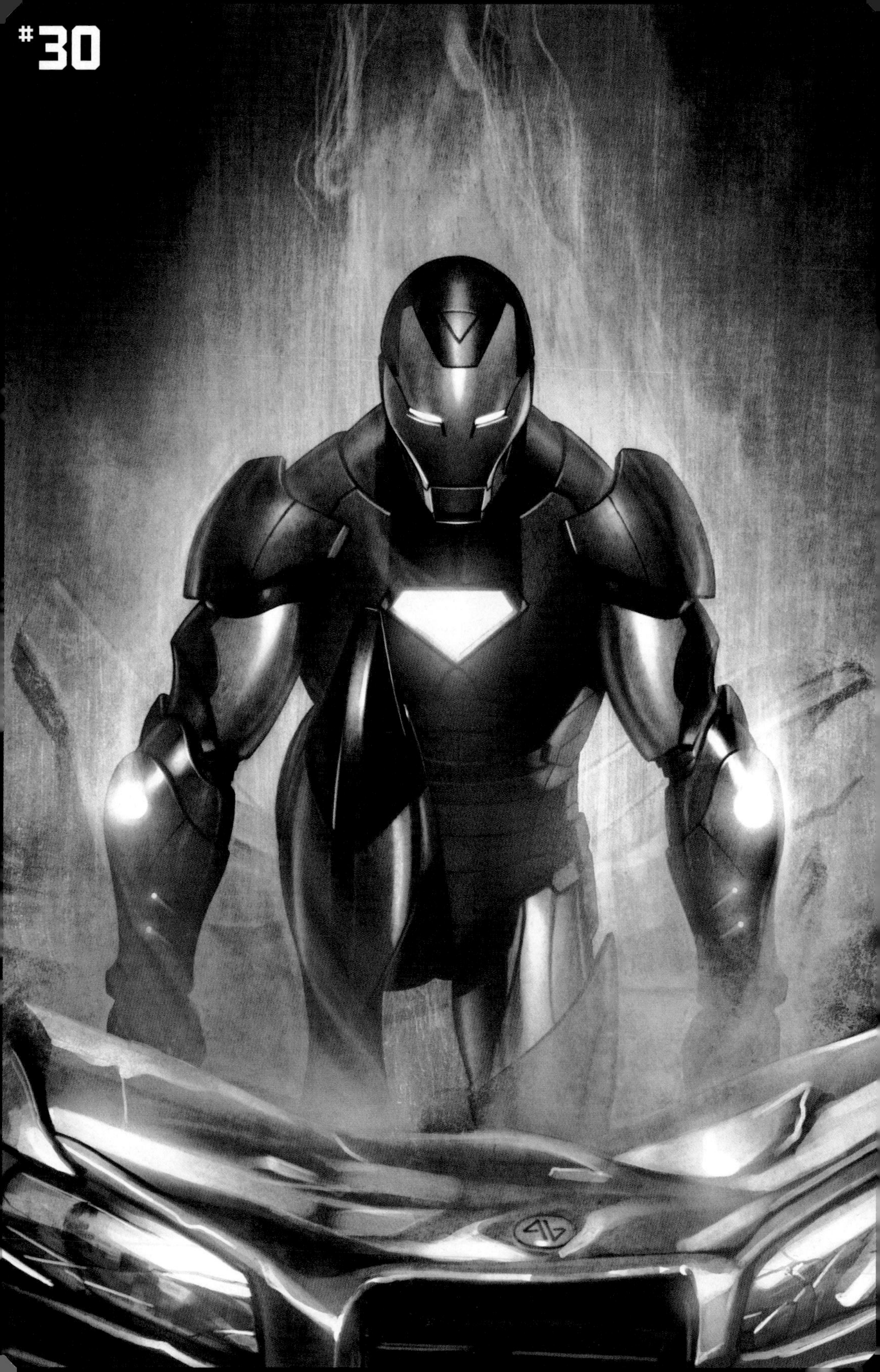
#30

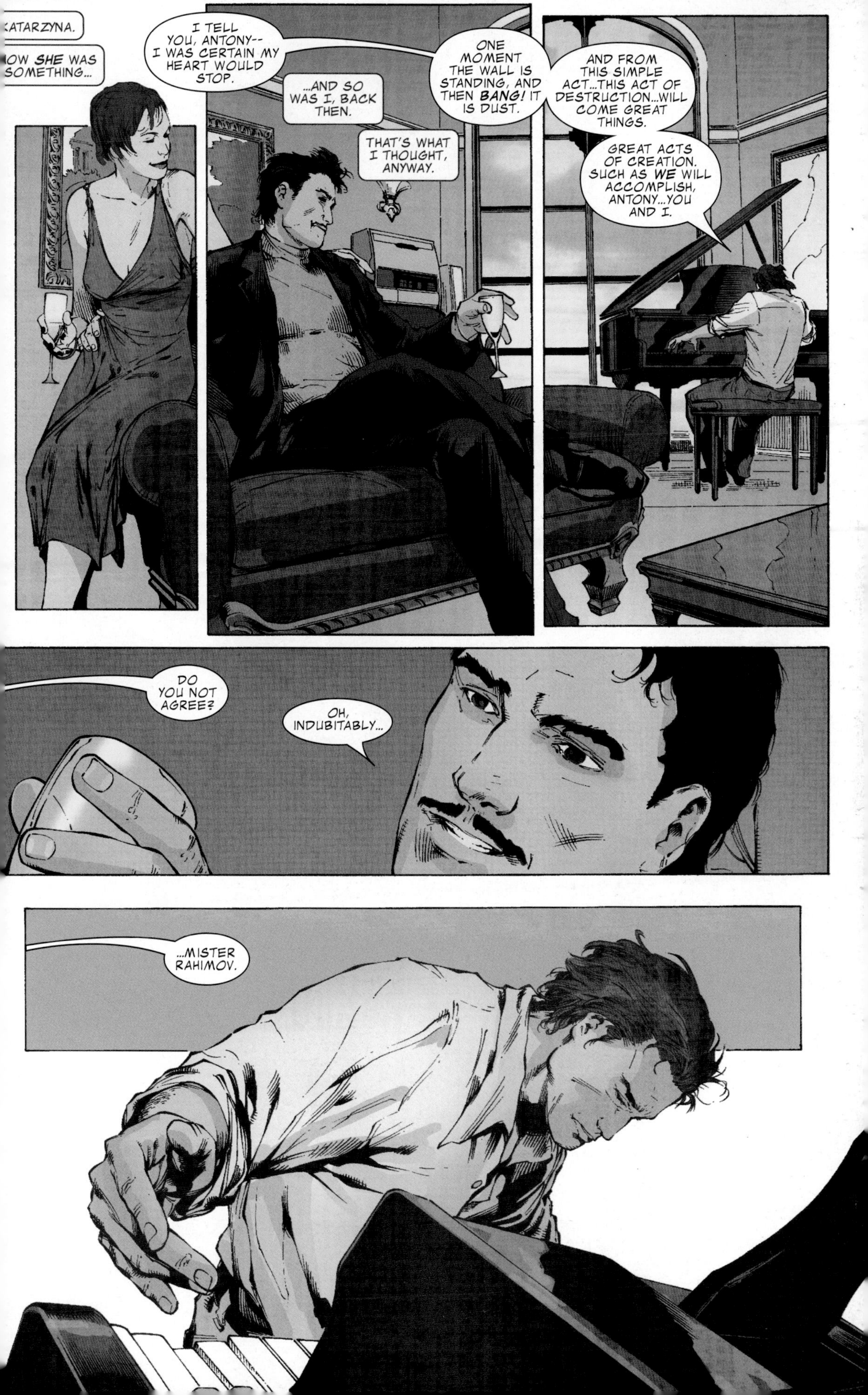
KATARZYNA.
NOW SHE WAS SOMETHING...
I TELL YOU, ANTONY-- I WAS CERTAIN MY HEART WOULD STOP.
...AND SO WAS I, BACK THEN.
THAT'S WHAT I THOUGHT, ANYWAY.
ONE MOMENT THE WALL IS STANDING, AND THEN BANG! IT IS DUST.
AND FROM THIS SIMPLE ACT...THIS ACT OF DESTRUCTION...WILL COME GREAT THINGS.
GREAT ACTS OF CREATION. SUCH AS WE WILL ACCOMPLISH, ANTONY...YOU AND I.
DO YOU NOT AGREE?
OH, INDUBITABLY...
...MISTER RAHIMOV.

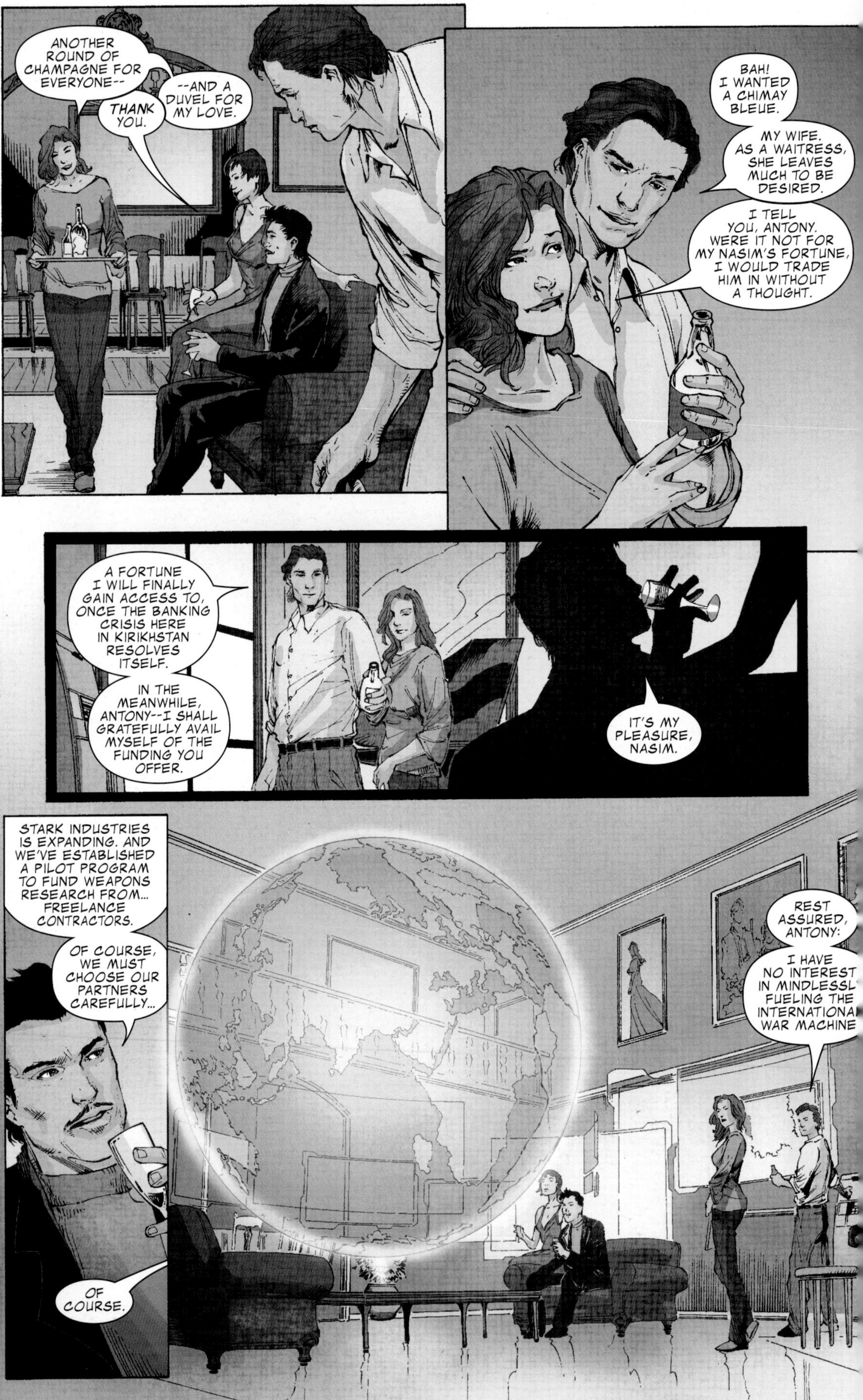
ANOTHER ROUND OF CHAMPAGNE FOR EVERYONE--
THANK YOU.
--AND A DUVEL FOR MY LOVE.
BAH! I WANTED A CHIMAY BLEUE.
MY WIFE. AS A WAITRESS, SHE LEAVES MUCH TO BE DESIRED.
I TELL YOU, ANTONY. WERE IT NOT FOR MY NASIM'S FORTUNE, I WOULD TRADE HIM IN WITHOUT A THOUGHT.
A FORTUNE I WILL FINALLY GAIN ACCESS TO, ONCE THE BANKING CRISIS HERE IN KIRIKHSTAN RESOLVES ITSELF.
IN THE MEANWHILE, ANTONY--I SHALL GRATEFULLY AVAIL MYSELF OF THE FUNDING YOU OFFER.
IT'S MY PLEASURE, NASIM.
STARK INDUSTRIES IS EXPANDING. AND WE'VE ESTABLISHED A PILOT PROGRAM TO FUND WEAPONS RESEARCH FROM... FREELANCE CONTRACTORS.
OF COURSE, WE MUST CHOOSE OUR PARTNERS CAREFULLY...
REST ASSURED, ANTONY:
OF COURSE.

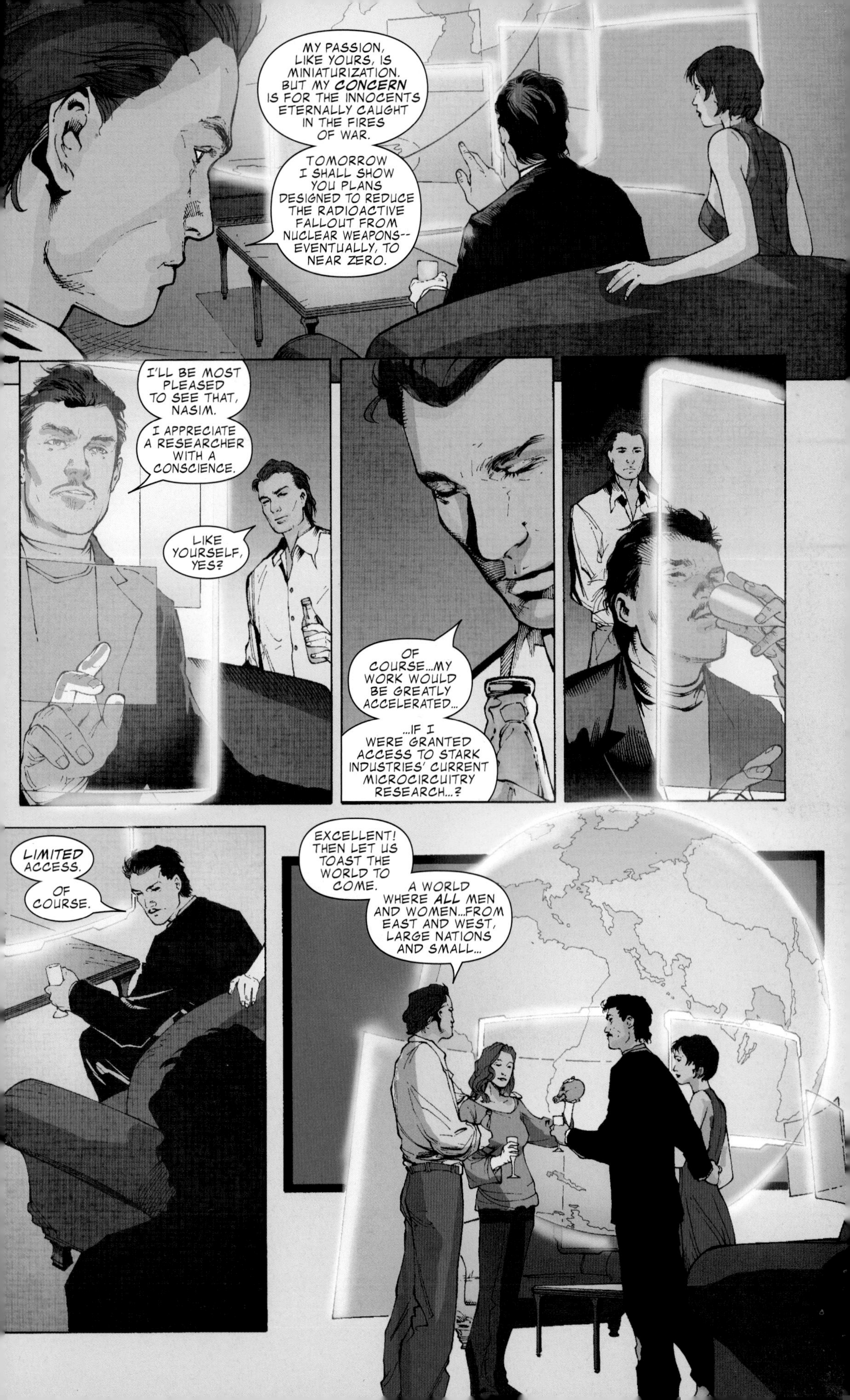
MY PASSION, LIKE YOURS, IS MINIATURIZATION. BUT MY CONCERN IS FOR THE INNOCENTS ETERNALLY CAUGHT IN THE FIRES OF WAR.
TOMORROW I SHALL SHOW YOU PLANS DESIGNED TO REDUCE THE RADIOACTIVE FALLOUT FROM NUCLEAR WEAPONS--EVENTUALLY, TO NEAR ZERO.
I'LL BE MOST PLEASED TO SEE THAT, NASIM.
I APPRECIATE A RESEARCHER WITH A CONSCIENCE.
LIKE YOURSELF, YES?
OF COURSE...MY WORK WOULD BE GREATLY ACCELERATED...
...IF I WERE GRANTED ACCESS TO STARK INDUSTRIES' CURRENT MICROCIRCUITRY RESEARCH...?
LIMITED ACCESS.
OF COURSE.
EXCELLENT! THEN LET US TOAST THE WORLD TO COME.
A WORLD WHERE ALL MEN AND WOMEN...FROM EAST AND WEST, LARGE NATIONS AND SMALL...

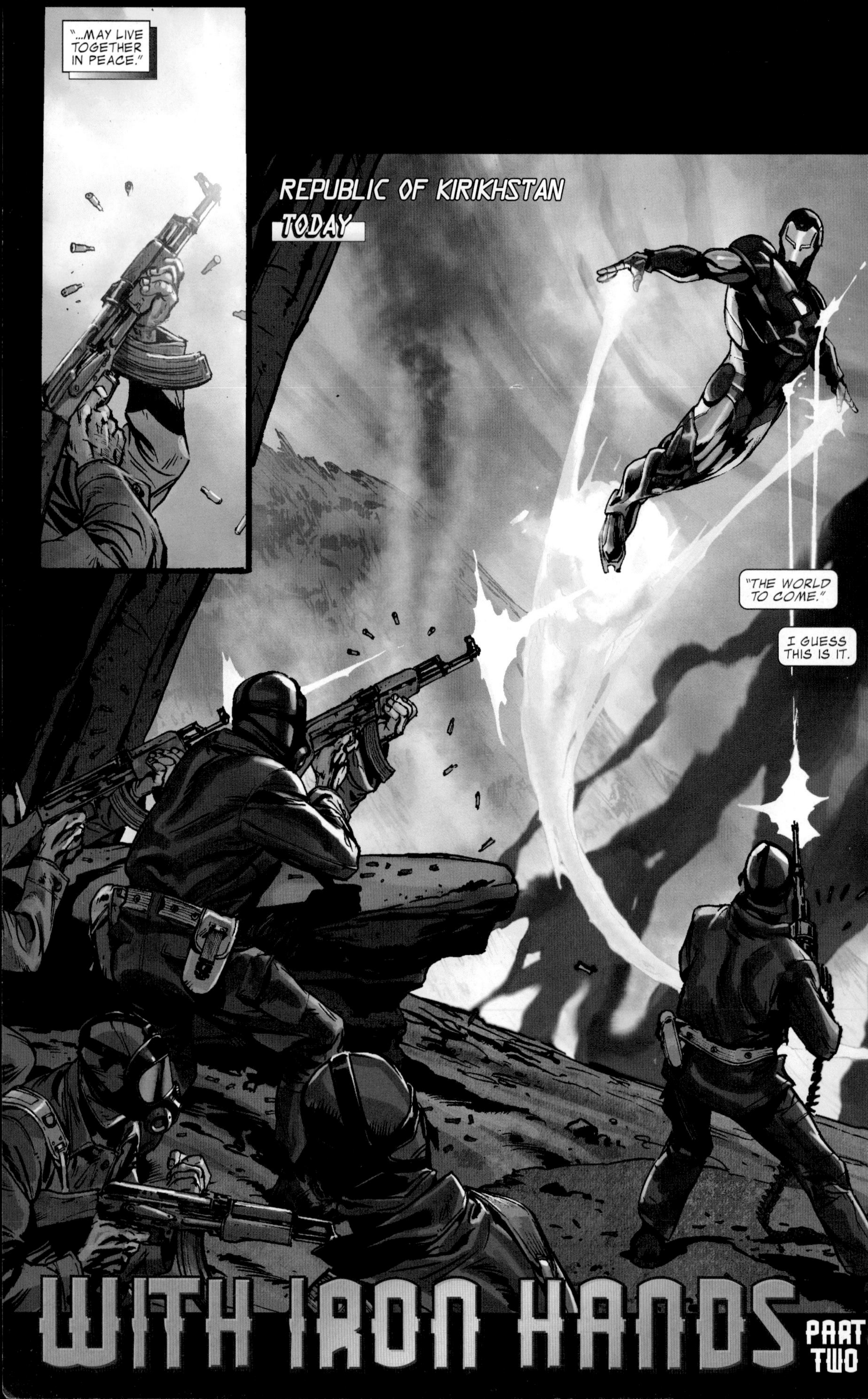
"...MAY LIVE TOGETHER IN PEACE."
REPUBLIC OF KIRIKHSTAN
TODAY
"THE WORLD TO COME."
I GUESS THIS IS IT.
WITH IRON HANDS
PART TWO

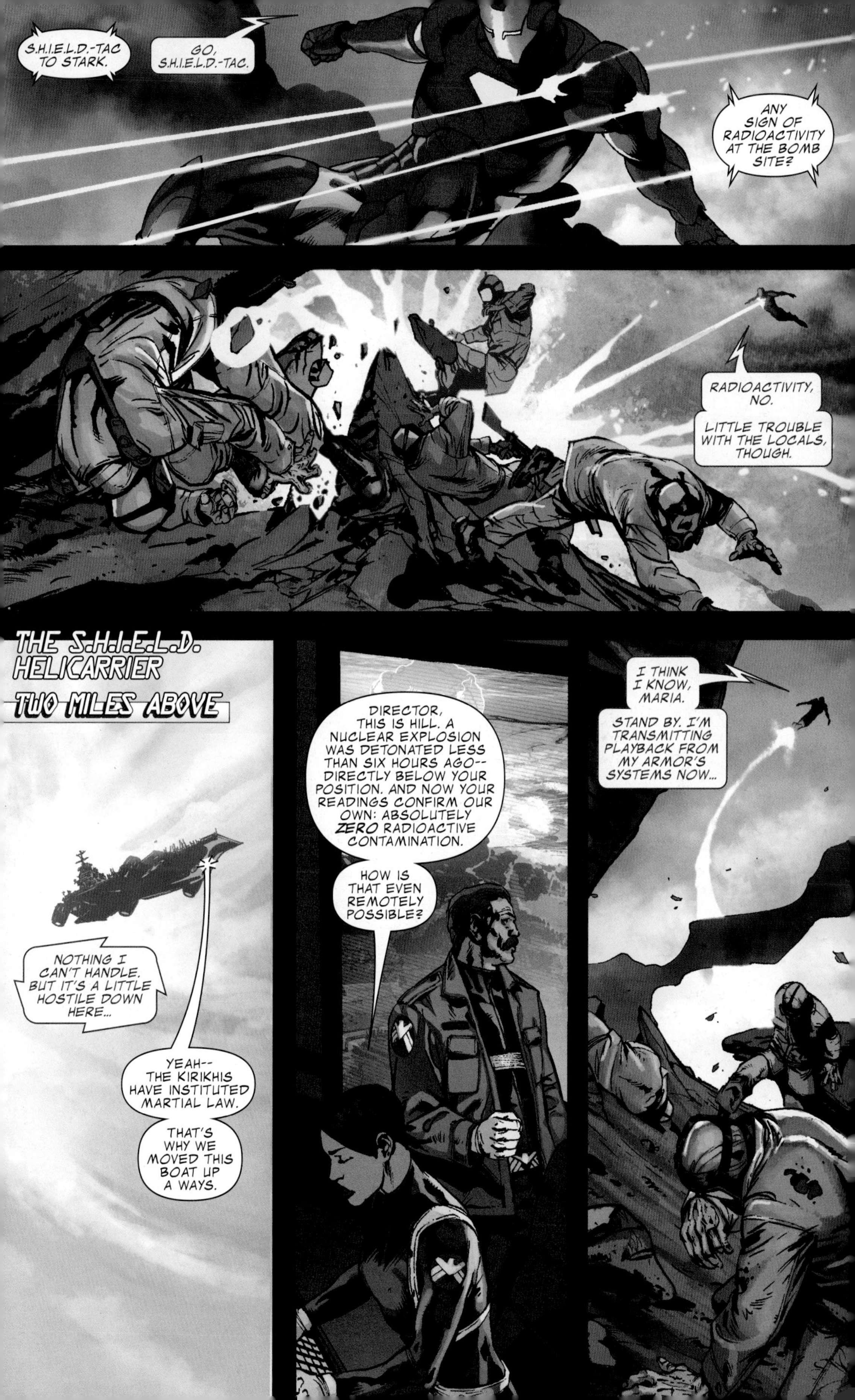
S.H.I.E.L.D.-TAC TO STARK.
GO, S.H.I.E.L.D.-TAC.
ANY SIGN OF RADIOACTIVITY AT THE BOMB SITE?
RADIOACTIVITY, NO.
LITTLE TROUBLE WITH THE LOCALS, THOUGH.
THE S.H.I.E.L.D. HELICARRIER
TWO MILES ABOVE
NOTHING I CAN'T HANDLE. BUT IT'S A LITTLE HOSTILE DOWN HERE...
YEAH-- THE KIRIKHIS HAVE INSTITUTED MARTIAL LAW.
THAT'S WHY WE MOVED THIS BOAT UP A WAYS.
DIRECTOR, THIS IS HILL. A NUCLEAR EXPLOSION WAS DETONATED LESS THAN SIX HOURS AGO-- DIRECTLY BELOW YOUR POSITION. AND NOW YOUR READINGS CONFIRM OUR OWN: ABSOLUTELY ZERO RADIOACTIVE CONTAMINATION.
HOW IS THAT EVEN REMOTELY POSSIBLE?
I THINK I KNOW, MARIA.
STAND BY. I'M TRANSMITTING PLAYBACK FROM MY ARMOR'S SYSTEMS NOW...

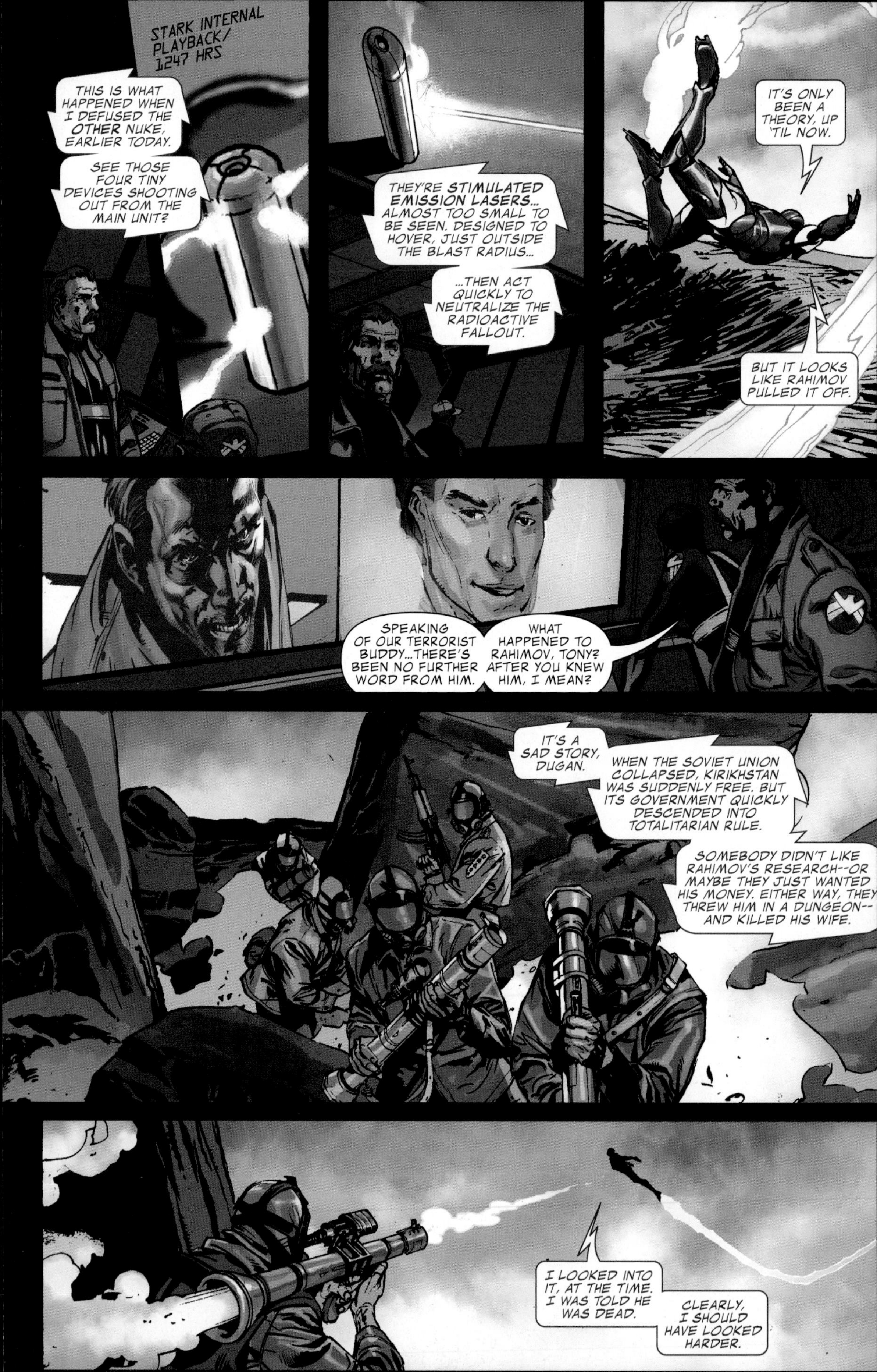
STARK INTERNAL PLAYBACK/ 1247 HRS
THIS IS WHAT HAPPENED WHEN I DEFUSED THE OTHER NUKE, EARLIER TODAY.
SEE THOSE FOUR TINY DEVICES SHOOTING OUT FROM THE MAIN UNIT?
THEY'RE STIMULATED EMISSION LASERS... ALMOST TOO SMALL TO BE SEEN. DESIGNED TO HOVER, JUST OUTSIDE THE BLAST RADIUS...
...THEN ACT QUICKLY TO NEUTRALIZE THE RADIOACTIVE FALLOUT.
IT'S ONLY BEEN A THEORY, UP 'TIL NOW.
BUT IT LOOKS LIKE RAHIMOV PULLED IT OFF.
SPEAKING OF OUR TERRORIST BUDDY...THERE'S BEEN NO FURTHER WORD FROM HIM.
WHAT HAPPENED TO RAHIMOV, TONY? AFTER YOU KNEW HIM, I MEAN?
IT'S A SAD STORY, DUGAN.
WHEN THE SOVIET UNION COLLAPSED, KIRIKHSTAN WAS SUDDENLY FREE. BUT ITS GOVERNMENT QUICKLY DESCENDED INTO TOTALITARIAN RULE.
SOMEBODY DIDN'T LIKE RAHIMOV'S RESEARCH--OR MAYBE THEY JUST WANTED HIS MONEY. EITHER WAY, THEY THREW HIM IN A DUNGEON--AND KILLED HIS WIFE.
I LOOKED INTO IT, AT THE TIME. I WAS TOLD HE WAS DEAD.
CLEARLY, I SHOULD HAVE LOOKED HARDER.

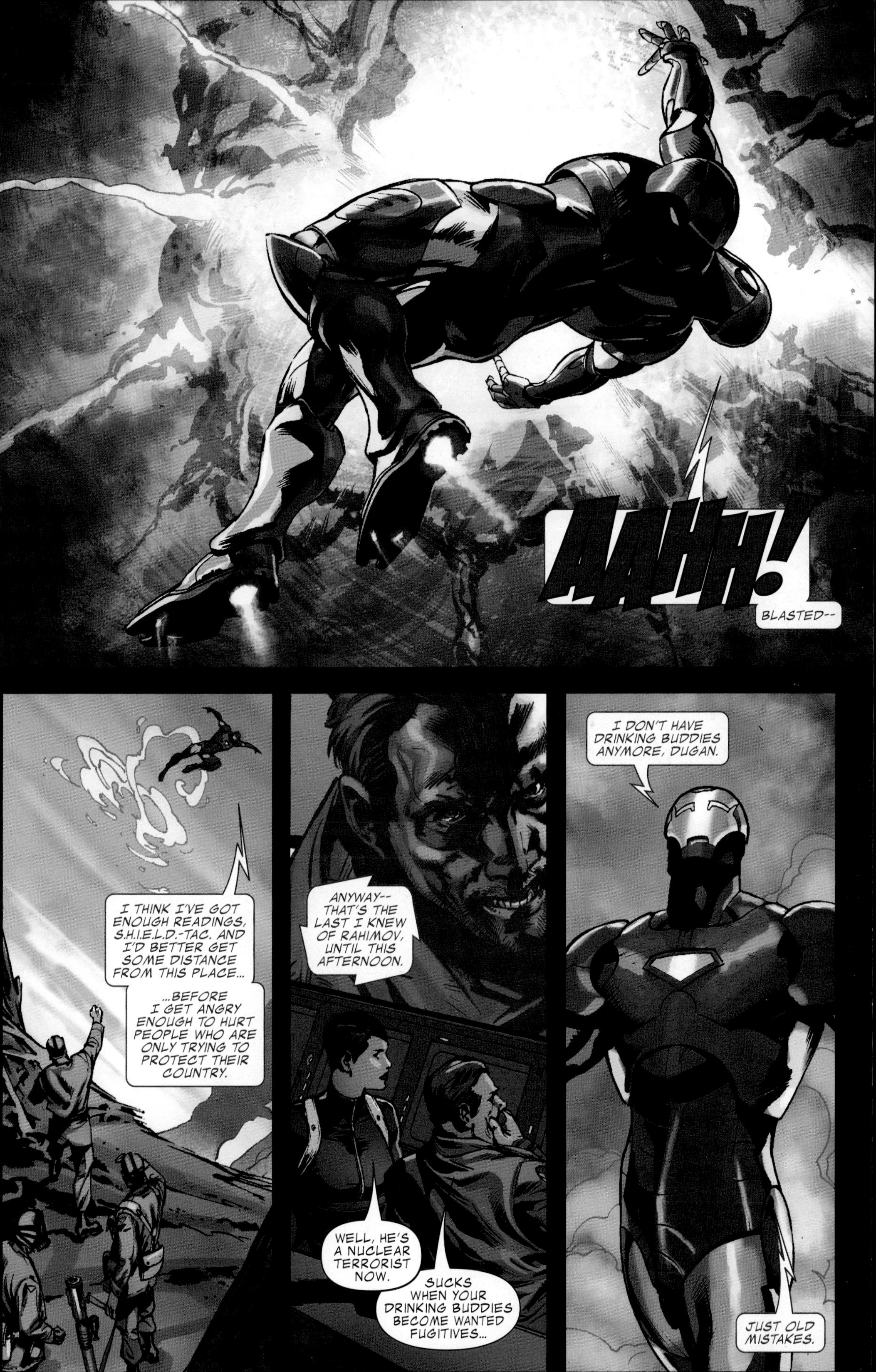
AAHH!
BLASTED--
I THINK I'VE GOT ENOUGH READINGS, S.H.I.E.L.D.-TAC. AND I'D BETTER GET SOME DISTANCE FROM THIS PLACE...
...BEFORE I GET ANGRY ENOUGH TO HURT PEOPLE WHO ARE ONLY TRYING TO PROTECT THEIR COUNTRY.
ANYWAY-- THAT'S THE LAST I KNEW OF RAHIMOV, UNTIL THIS AFTERNOON.
WELL, HE'S A NUCLEAR TERRORIST NOW.
SUCKS WHEN YOUR DRINKING BUDDIES BECOME WANTED FUGITIVES...
I DON'T HAVE DRINKING BUDDIES ANYMORE, DUGAN.
JUST OLD MISTAKES.

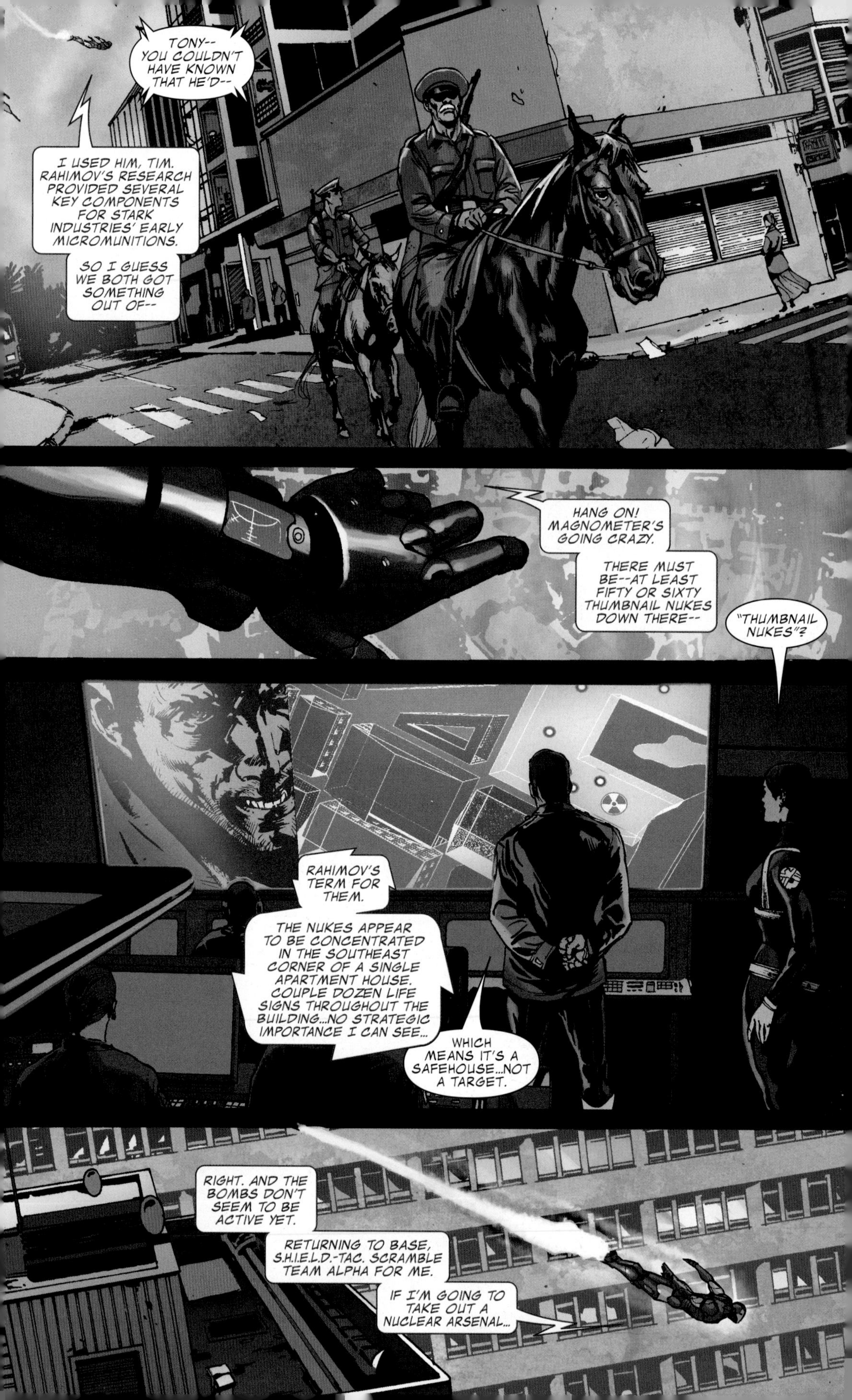
TONY-- YOU COULDN'T HAVE KNOWN THAT HE'D--
I USED HIM, TIM. RAHIMOV'S RESEARCH PROVIDED SEVERAL KEY COMPONENTS FOR STARK INDUSTRIES' EARLY MICROMUNITIONS.
SO I GUESS WE BOTH GOT SOMETHING OUT OF--
HANG ON! MAGNOMETER'S GOING CRAZY.
THERE MUST BE--AT LEAST FIFTY OR SIXTY THUMBNAIL NUKES DOWN THERE--
"THUMBNAIL NUKES"?
RAHIMOV'S TERM FOR THEM.
THE NUKES APPEAR TO BE CONCENTRATED IN THE SOUTHEAST CORNER OF A SINGLE APARTMENT HOUSE. COUPLE DOZEN LIFE SIGNS THROUGHOUT THE BUILDING...NO STRATEGIC IMPORTANCE I CAN SEE...
WHICH MEANS IT'S A SAFEHOUSE...NOT A TARGET.
RIGHT. AND THE BOMBS DON'T SEEM TO BE ACTIVE YET.
RETURNING TO BASE, S.H.I.E.L.D.-TAC. SCRAMBLE TEAM ALPHA FOR ME.
IF I'M GOING TO TAKE OUT A NUCLEAR ARSENAL...

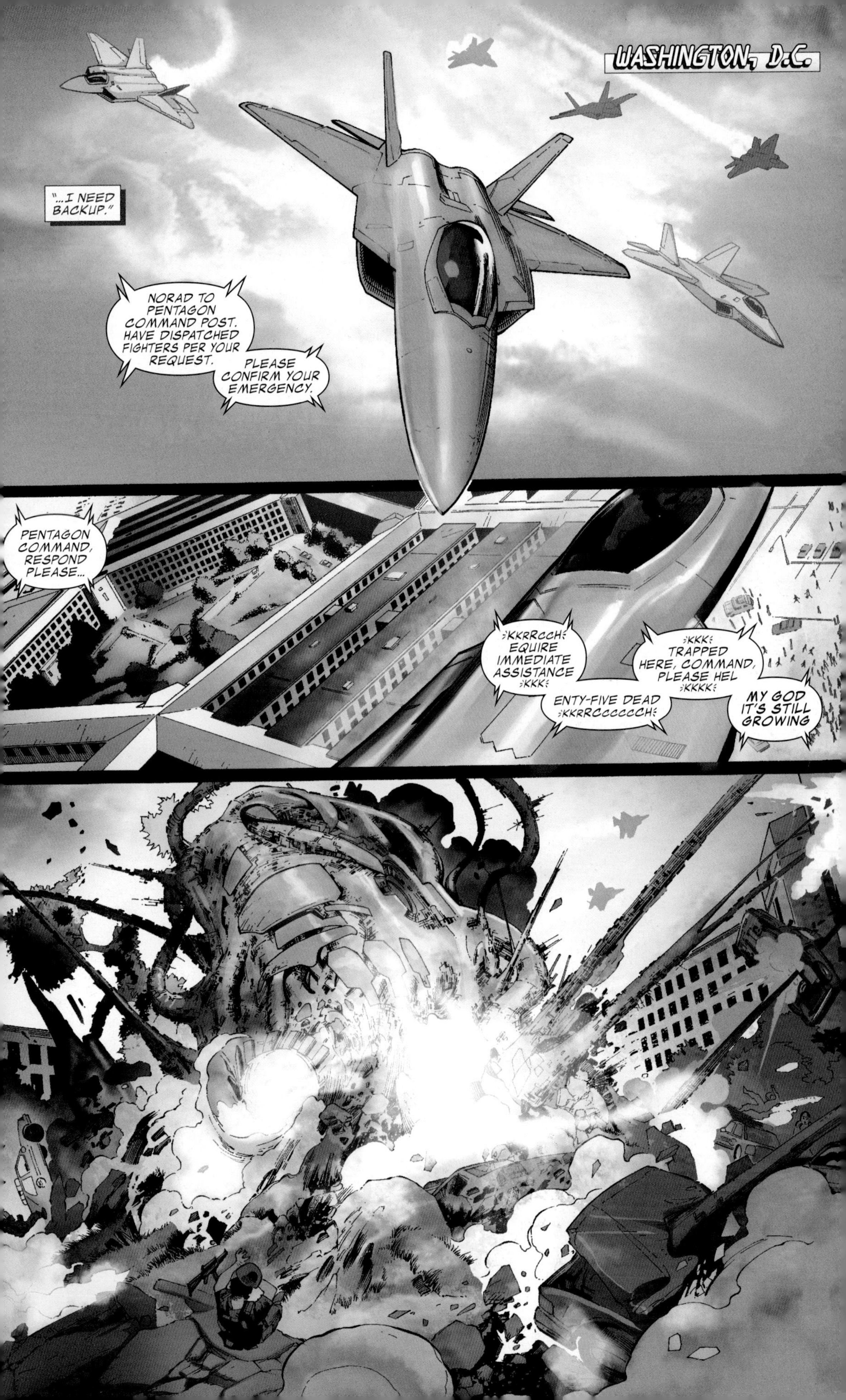
WASHINGTON, D.C.
"...I NEED BACKUP."
NORAD TO PENTAGON COMMAND POST. HAVE DISPATCHED FIGHTERS PER YOUR REQUEST.
PLEASE CONFIRM YOUR EMERGENCY.
PENTAGON COMMAND, RESPOND PLEASE...
KKRRCCH EQUIRE IMMEDIATE ASSISTANCE KKK
ENTY-FIVE DEAD KKRRCCCCCCH
KKK TRAPPED HERE, COMMAND, PLEASE HEL KKKK
MY GOD IT'S STILL GROWING

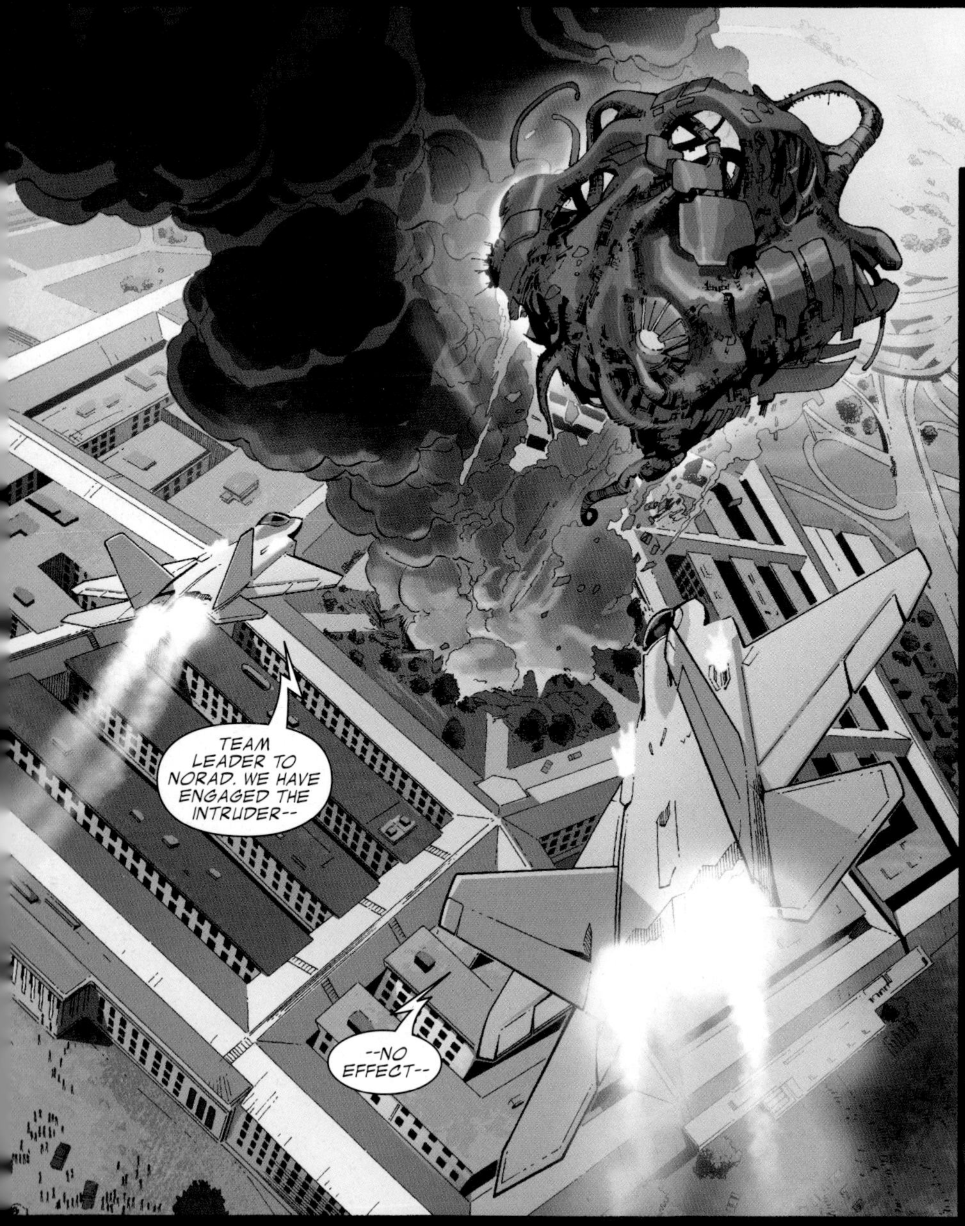
TEAM LEADER TO NORAD. WE HAVE ENGAGED THE INTRUDER--
--NO EFFECT--
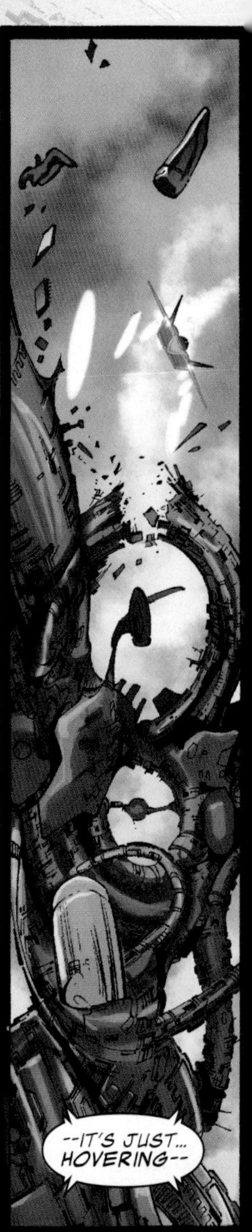
--IT'S JUST... HOVERING--
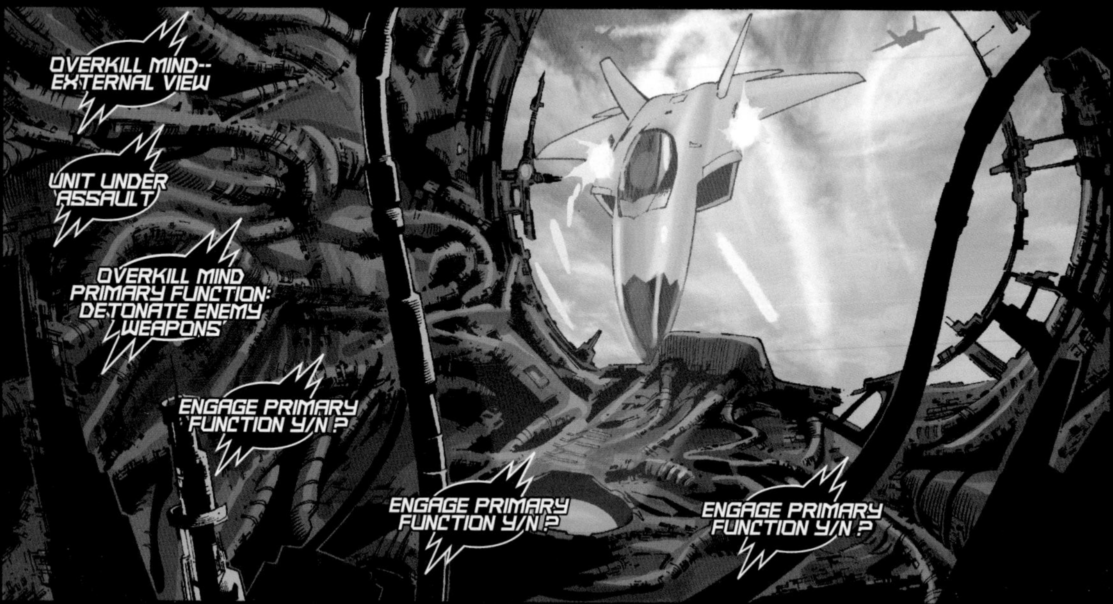
OVERKILL MIND--
EXTERNAL VIEW
UNIT UNDER ASSAULT
OVERKILL MIND
PRIMARY FUNCTION:
DETONATE ENEMY WEAPONS
ENGAGE PRIMARY FUNCTION Y/N ?
ENGAGE PRIMARY FUNCTION Y/N ?
ENGAGE PRIMARY FUNCTION Y/N ?

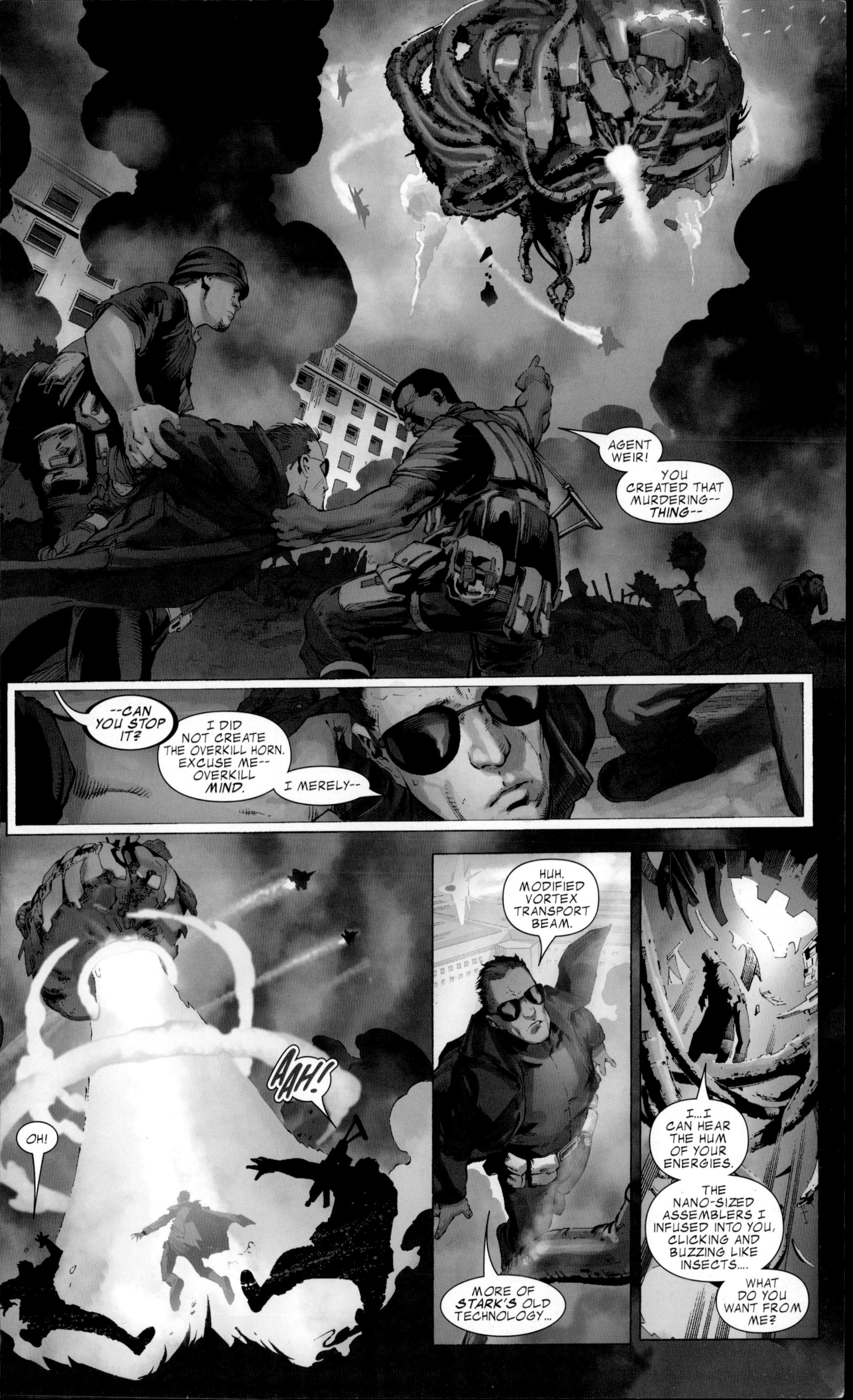
AGENT WEIR!
YOU CREATED THAT MURDERING-- THING--
--CAN YOU STOP IT?
I DID NOT CREATE THE OVERKILL HORN. EXCUSE ME-- OVERKILL MIND.
I MERELY--
AAH!
OH!
HUH. MODIFIED VORTEX TRANSPORT BEAM.
MORE OF STARK'S OLD TECHNOLOGY...
I...I CAN HEAR THE HUM OF YOUR ENERGIES.
THE NANO-SIZED ASSEMBLERS I INFUSED INTO YOU, CLICKING AND BUZZING LIKE INSECTS....
WHAT DO YOU WANT FROM ME?

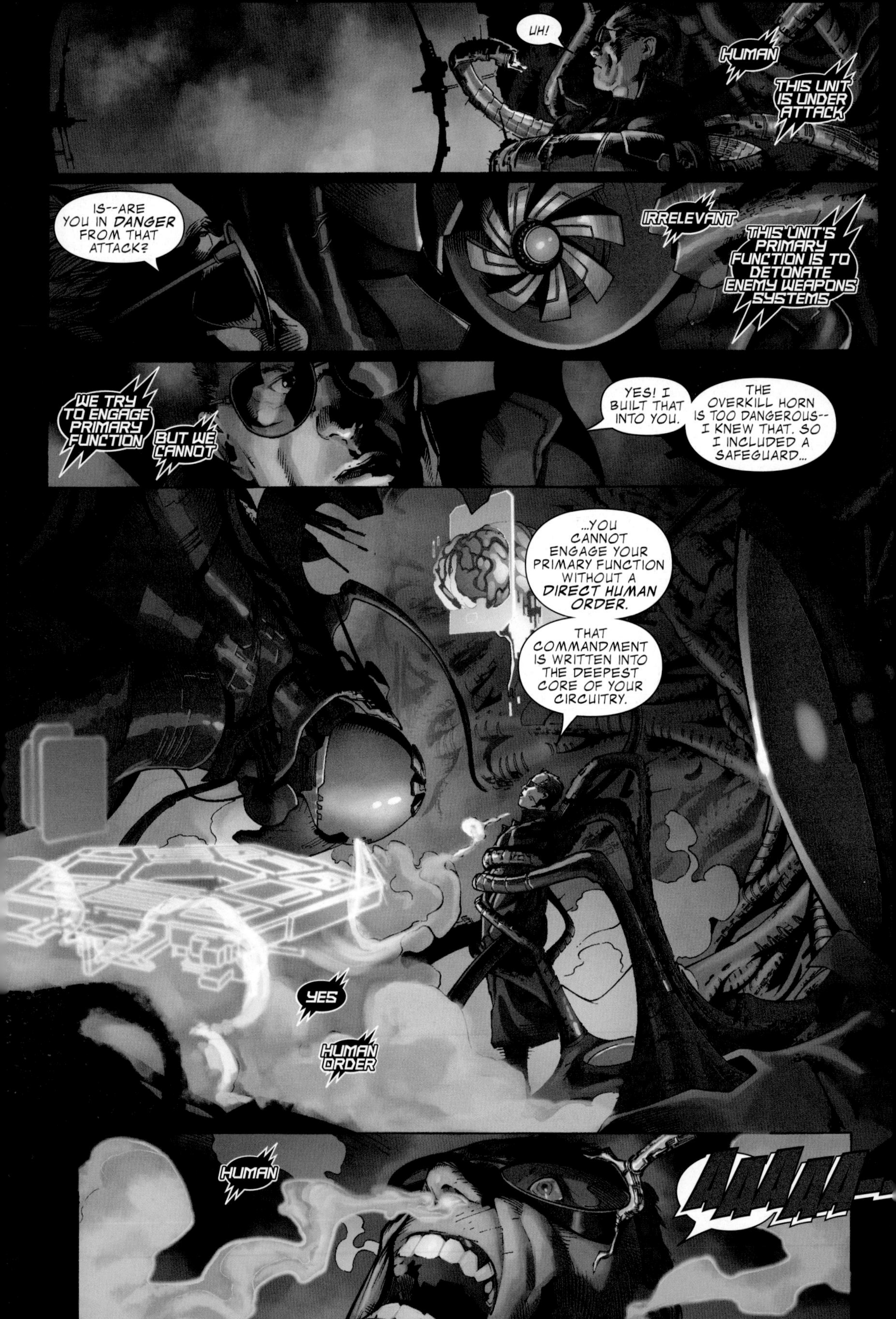
UH!
HUMAN
THIS UNIT IS UNDER ATTACK
IS--ARE YOU IN DANGER FROM THAT ATTACK?
IRRELEVANT
THIS UNIT'S PRIMARY FUNCTION IS TO DETONATE ENEMY WEAPONS SYSTEMS
WE TRY TO ENGAGE PRIMARY FUNCTION
BUT WE CANNOT
YES! I BUILT THAT INTO YOU.
THE OVERKILL HORN IS TOO DANGEROUS-- I KNEW THAT. SO I INCLUDED A SAFEGUARD...
...YOU CANNOT ENGAGE YOUR PRIMARY FUNCTION WITHOUT A DIRECT HUMAN ORDER.
THAT COMMANDMENT IS WRITTEN INTO THE DEEPEST CORE OF YOUR CIRCUITRY.
YES
HUMAN ORDER
HUMAN

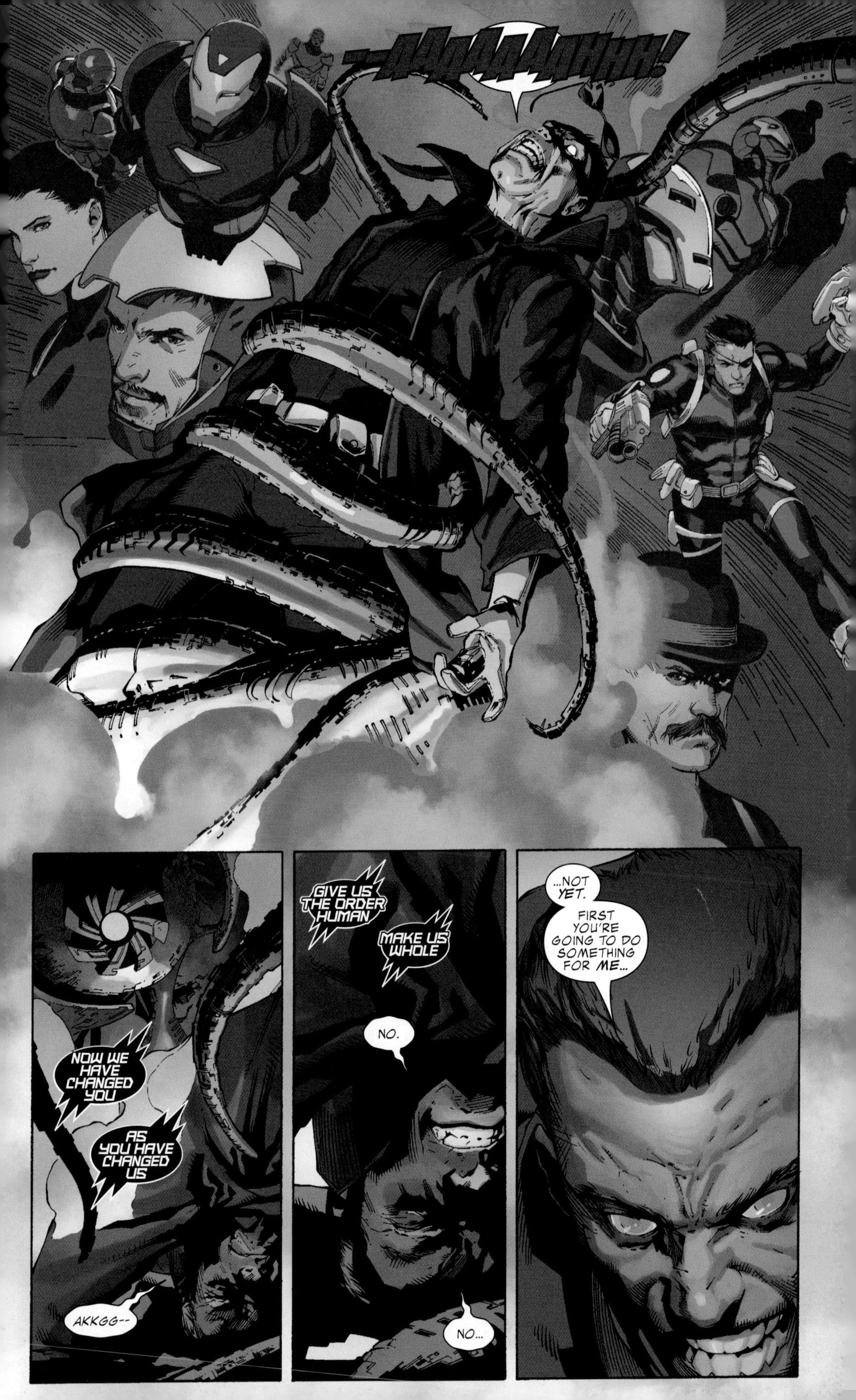
--AAAAAAAHHH!
NOW WE HAVE CHANGED YOU
AS YOU HAVE CHANGED US
AKKGG--
GIVE US THE ORDER HUMAN
MAKE US WHOLE
NO.
NO...
...NOT YET.
FIRST YOU'RE GOING TO DO SOMETHING FOR ME...

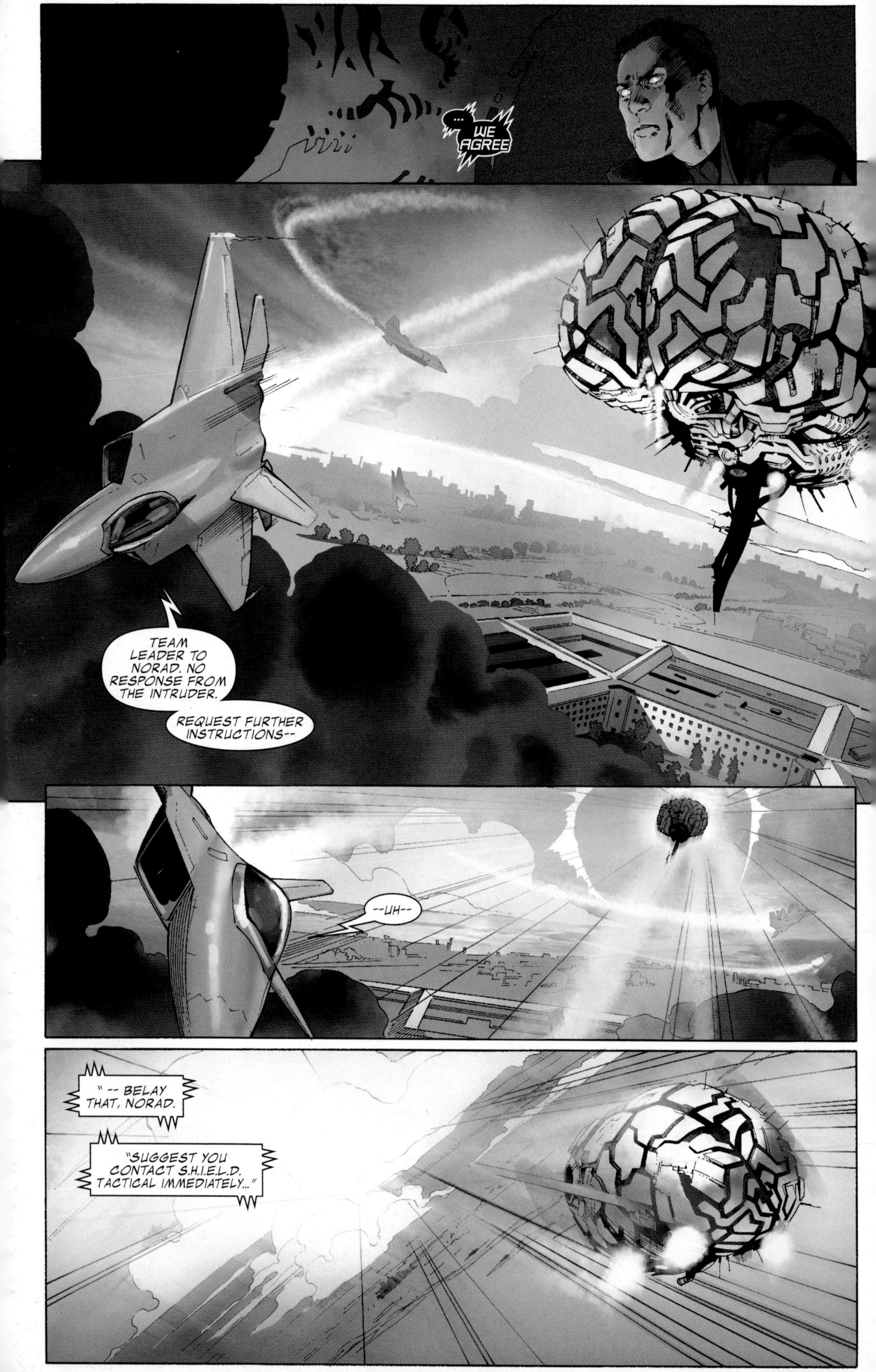
...WE AGREE
TEAM LEADER TO NORAD. NO RESPONSE FROM THE INTRUDER.
REQUEST FURTHER INSTRUCTIONS--
--UH--
" -- BELAY THAT, NORAD.
"SUGGEST YOU CONTACT S.H.I.E.L.D. TACTICAL IMMEDIATELY..."

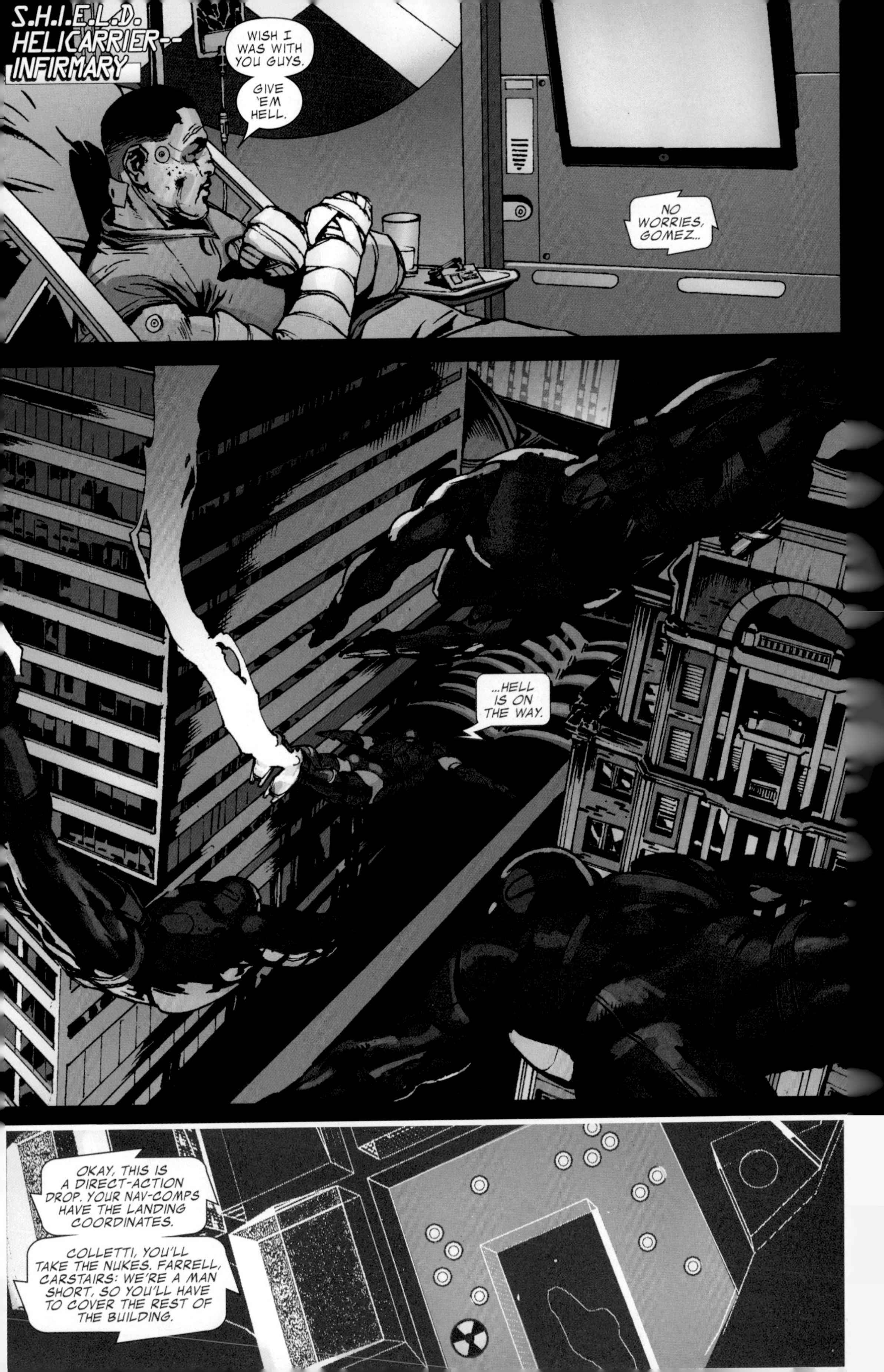
S.H.I.E.L.D. HELICARRIER-- INFIRMARY
WISH I WAS WITH YOU GUYS.
GIVE 'EM HELL.
NO WORRIES, GOMEZ...
...HELL IS ON THE WAY.
OKAY, THIS IS A DIRECT-ACTION DROP. YOUR NAV-COMPS HAVE THE LANDING COORDINATES.
COLLETTI, YOU'LL TAKE THE NUKES. FARRELL, CARSTAIRS: WE'RE A MAN SHORT, SO YOU'LL HAVE TO COVER THE REST OF THE BUILDING.

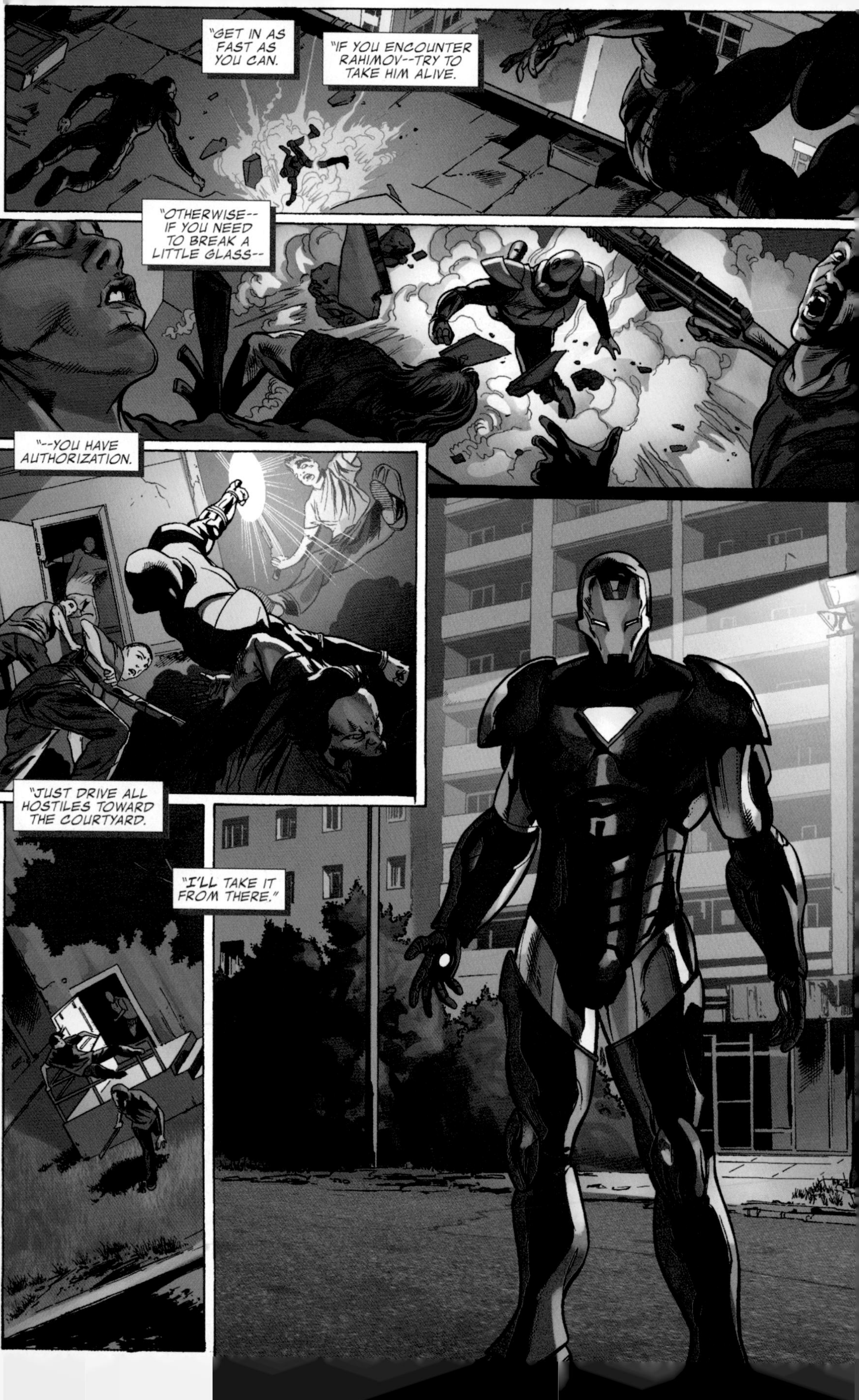
"GET IN AS FAST AS YOU CAN.
"IF YOU ENCOUNTER RAHIMOV--TRY TO TAKE HIM ALIVE.
"OTHERWISE-- IF YOU NEED TO BREAK A LITTLE GLASS--
"--YOU HAVE AUTHORIZATION.
"JUST DRIVE ALL HOSTILES TOWARD THE COURTYARD.
"I'LL TAKE IT FROM THERE."

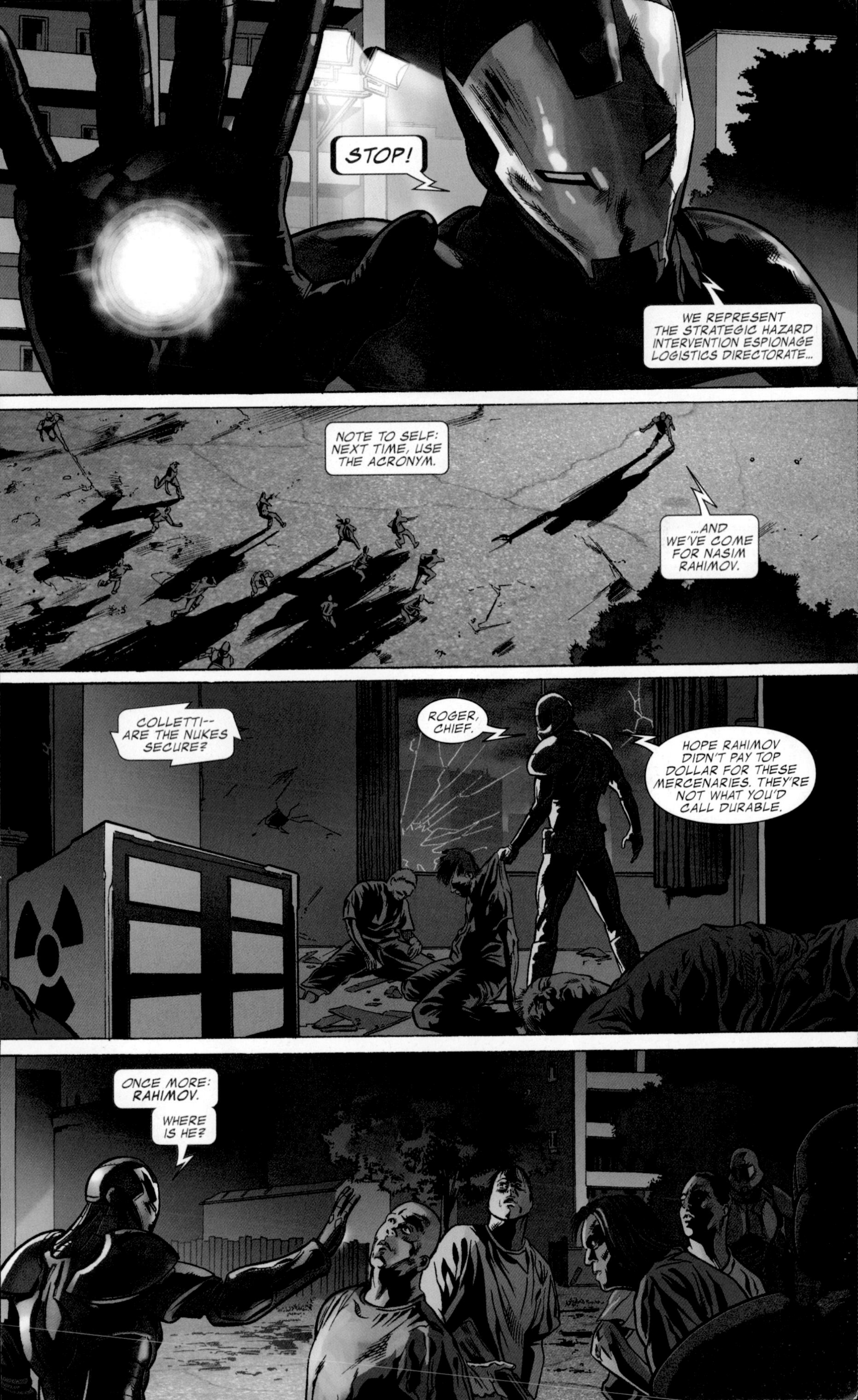
STOP!
WE REPRESENT THE STRATEGIC HAZARD INTERVENTION ESPIONAGE LOGISTICS DIRECTORATE...
NOTE TO SELF: NEXT TIME, USE THE ACRONYM.
...AND WE'VE COME FOR NASIM RAHIMOV.
COLLETTI-- ARE THE NUKES SECURE?
ROGER, CHIEF.
HOPE RAHIMOV DIDN'T PAY TOP DOLLAR FOR THESE MERCENARIES. THEY'RE NOT WHAT YOU'D CALL DURABLE.
ONCE MORE: RAHIMOV.
WHERE IS HE?

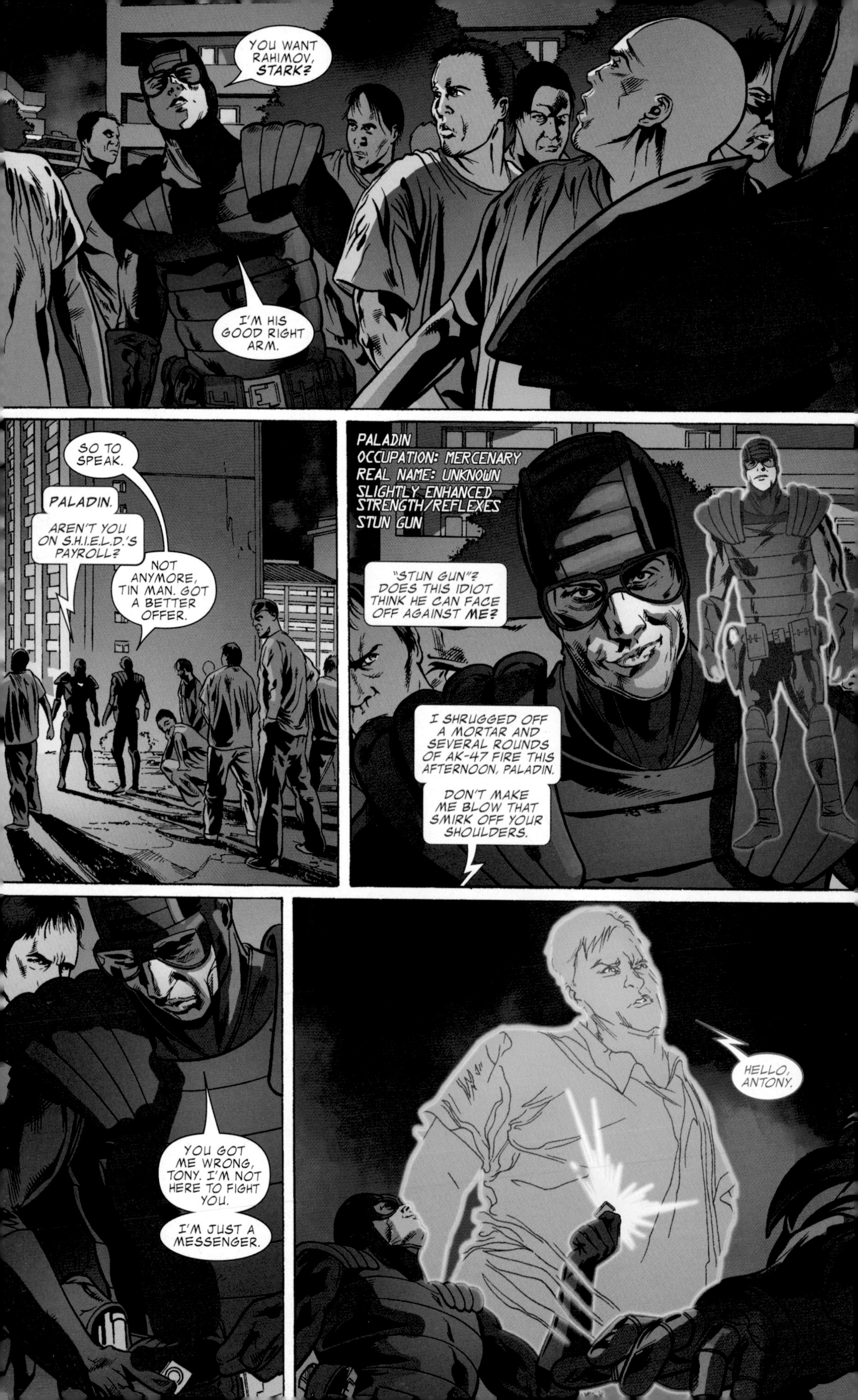
YOU WANT RAHIMOV, STARK?
I'M HIS GOOD RIGHT ARM.
SO TO SPEAK.
PALADIN.
AREN'T YOU ON S.H.I.E.L.D.'S PAYROLL?
NOT ANYMORE, TIN MAN. GOT A BETTER OFFER.
PALADIN
OCCUPATION: MERCENARY
REAL NAME: UNKNOWN
SLIGHTLY ENHANCED STRENGTH/REFLEXES
STUN GUN
"STUN GUN"? DOES THIS IDIOT THINK HE CAN FACE OFF AGAINST ME?
I SHRUGGED OFF A MORTAR AND SEVERAL ROUNDS OF AK-47 FIRE THIS AFTERNOON, PALADIN.
DON'T MAKE ME BLOW THAT SMIRK OFF YOUR SHOULDERS.
YOU GOT ME WRONG, TONY. I'M NOT HERE TO FIGHT YOU.
I'M JUST A MESSENGER.
HELLO, ANTONY.

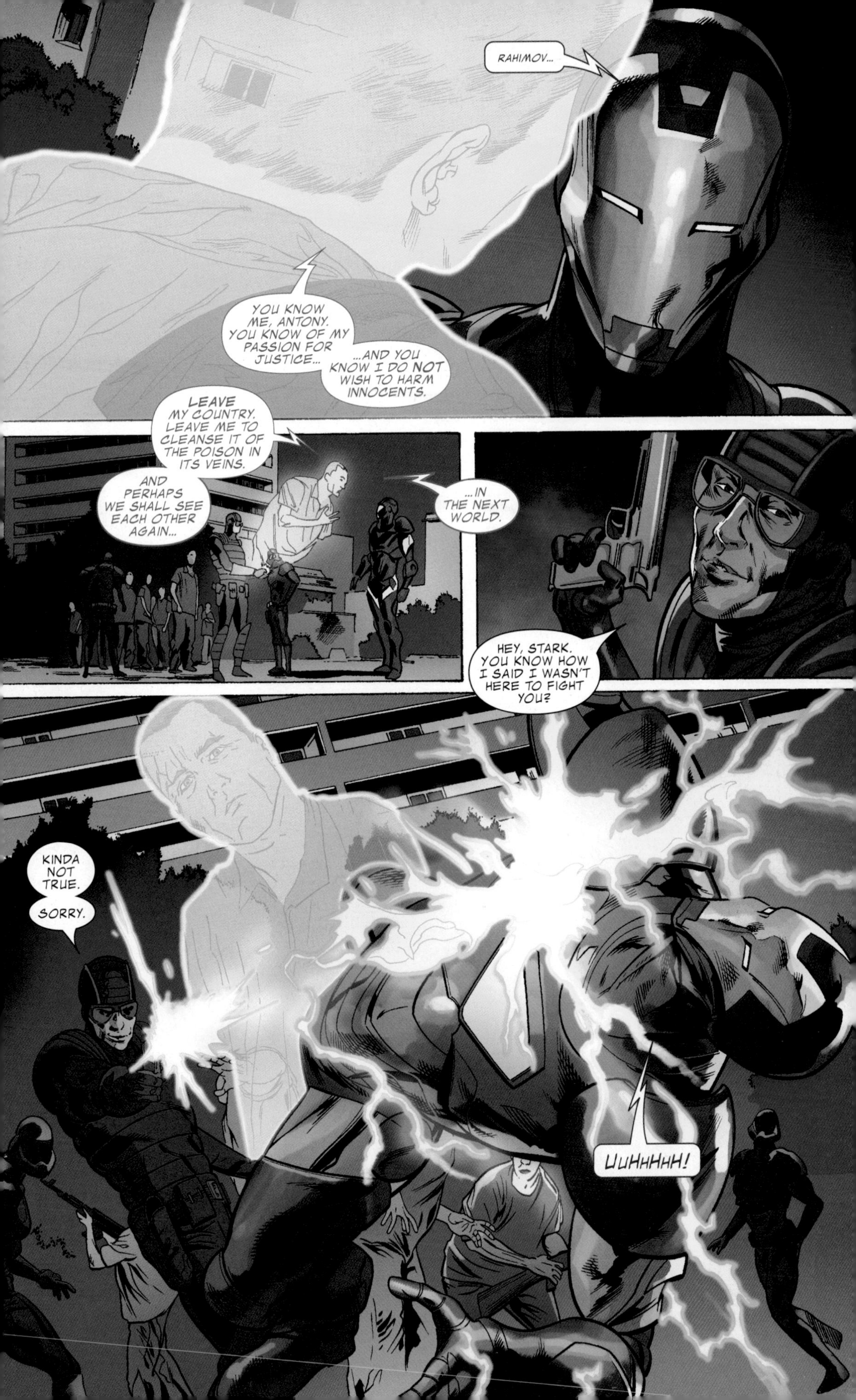
RAHIMOV...
YOU KNOW ME, ANTONY. YOU KNOW OF MY PASSION FOR JUSTICE...
...AND YOU KNOW I DO NOT WISH TO HARM INNOCENTS.
LEAVE MY COUNTRY. LEAVE ME TO CLEANSE IT OF THE POISON IN ITS VEINS.
AND PERHAPS WE SHALL SEE EACH OTHER AGAIN...
...IN THE NEXT WORLD.
HEY, STARK. YOU KNOW HOW I SAID I WASN'T HERE TO FIGHT YOU?
KINDA NOT TRUE.
SORRY.
UUHHHHH!

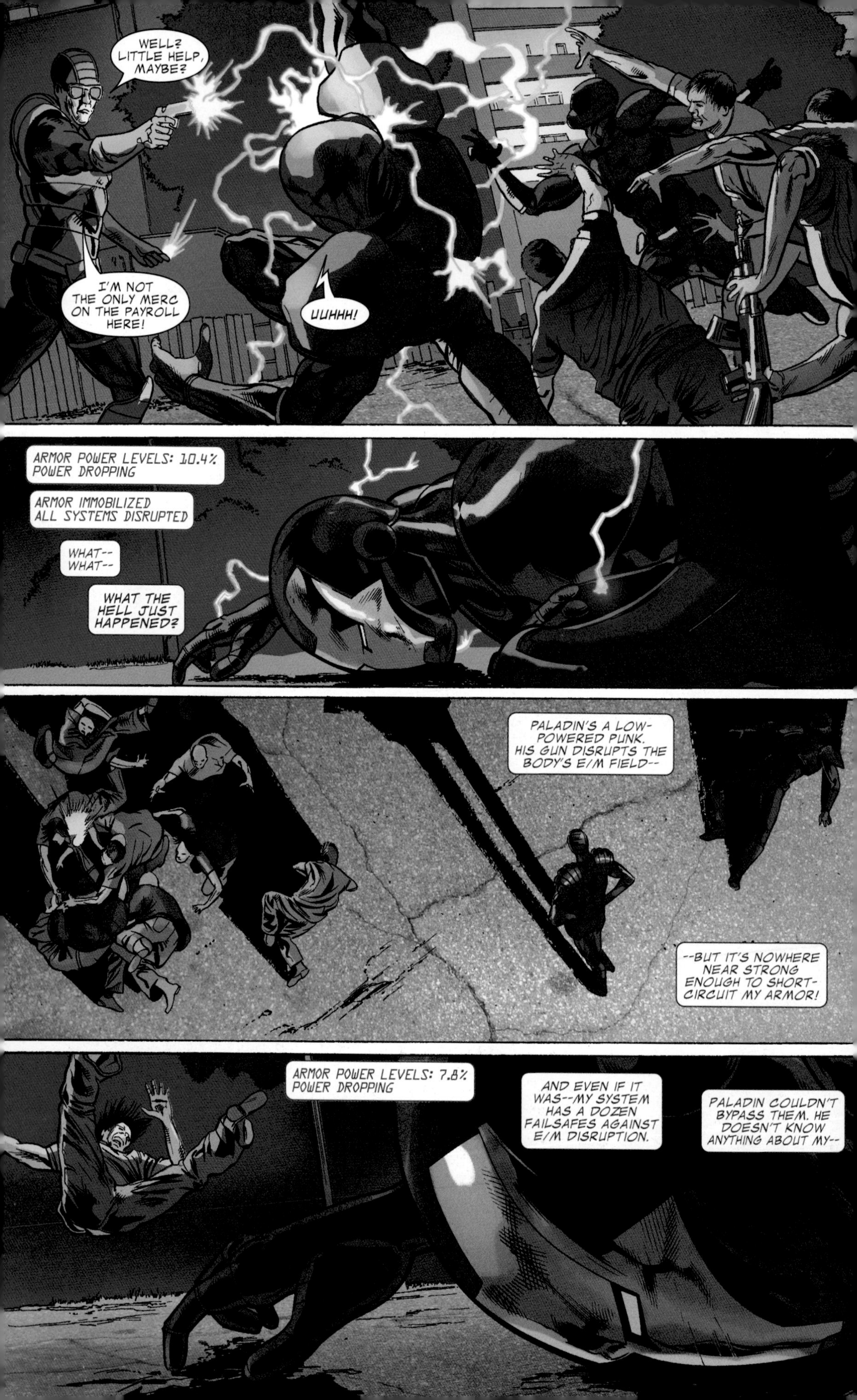
WELL? LITTLE HELP, MAYBE?
I'M NOT THE ONLY MERC ON THE PAYROLL HERE!
UUHHH!
ARMOR POWER LEVELS: 10.4%
POWER DROPPING
ARMOR IMMOBILIZED
ALL SYSTEMS DISRUPTED
WHAT--
WHAT--
WHAT THE HELL JUST HAPPENED?
PALADIN'S A LOW-POWERED PUNK. HIS GUN DISRUPTS THE BODY'S E/M FIELD--
--BUT IT'S NOWHERE NEAR STRONG ENOUGH TO SHORT-CIRCUIT MY ARMOR!
ARMOR POWER LEVELS: 7.8%
POWER DROPPING
AND EVEN IF IT WAS--MY SYSTEM HAS A DOZEN FAILSAFES AGAINST E/M DISRUPTION.
PALADIN COULDN'T BYPASS THEM. HE DOESN'T KNOW ANYTHING ABOUT MY--

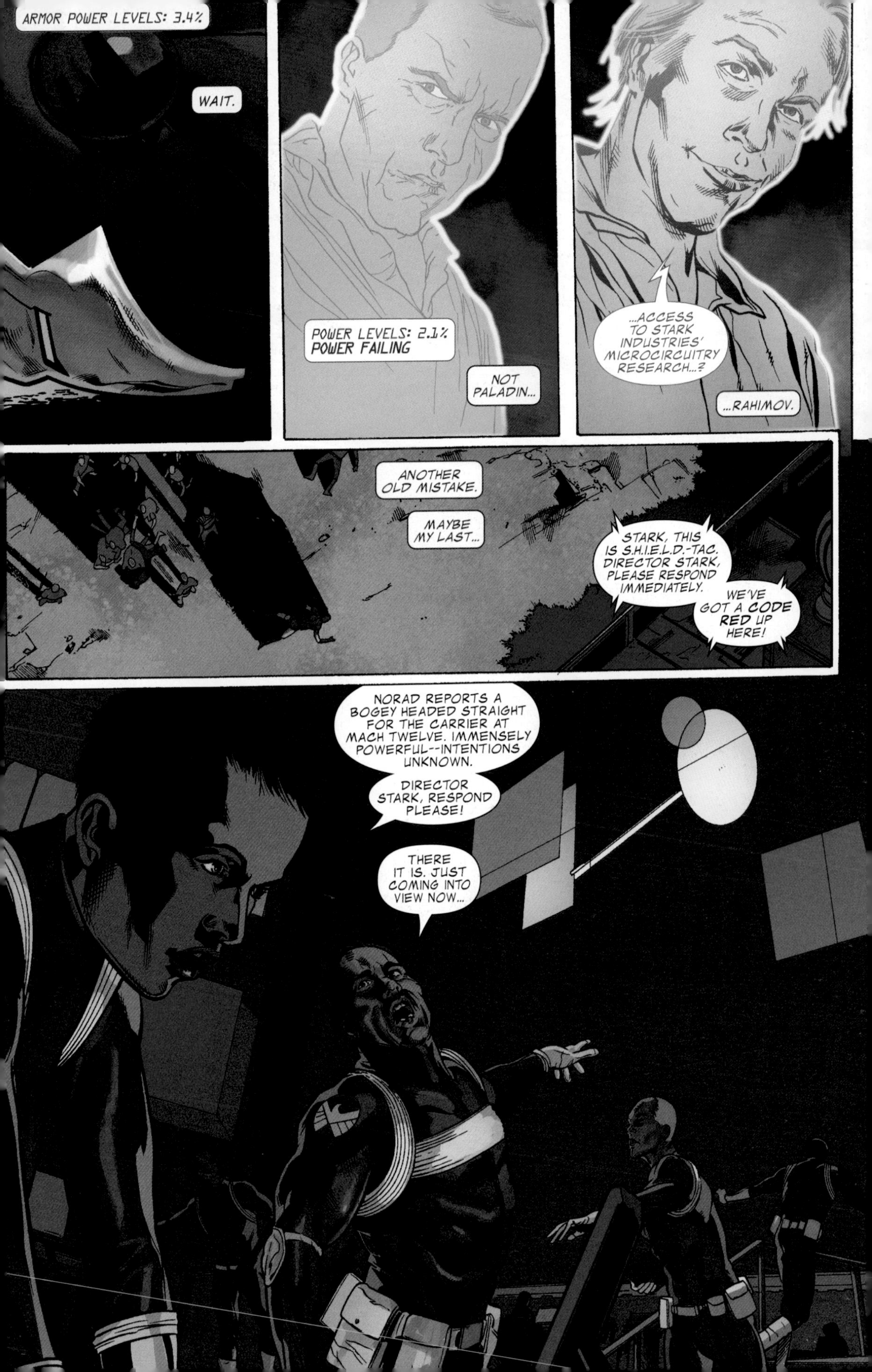
ARMOR POWER LEVELS: 3.4%
WAIT.
POWER LEVELS: 2.1%
POWER FAILING
NOT PALADIN...
...ACCESS TO STARK INDUSTRIES' MICROCIRCUITRY RESEARCH...?
...RAHIMOV.
ANOTHER OLD MISTAKE.
MAYBE MY LAST...
STARK, THIS IS S.H.I.E.L.D.-TAC. DIRECTOR STARK, PLEASE RESPOND IMMEDIATELY.
WE'VE GOT A CODE RED UP HERE!
NORAD REPORTS A BOGEY HEADED STRAIGHT FOR THE CARRIER AT MACH TWELVE. IMMENSELY POWERFUL--INTENTIONS UNKNOWN.
DIRECTOR STARK, RESPOND PLEASE!
THERE IT IS. JUST COMING INTO VIEW NOW...

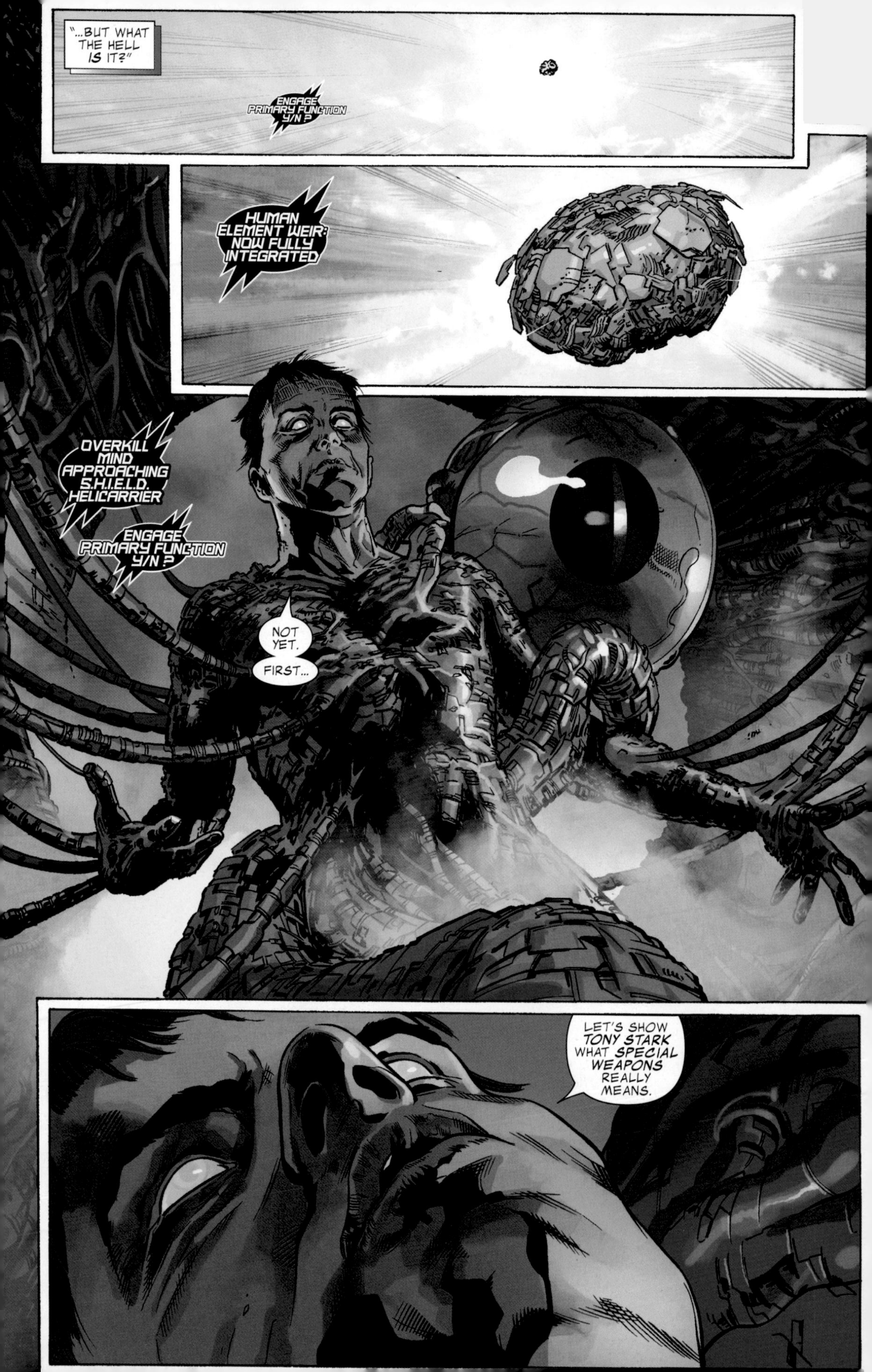
"...BUT WHAT THE HELL IS IT?"
ENGAGE PRIMARY FUNCTION Y/N ?
HUMAN ELEMENT WEIR: NOW FULLY INTEGRATED
OVERKILL MIND APPROACHING S.H.I.E.L.D. HELICARRIER
ENGAGE PRIMARY FUNCTION Y/N ?
NOT YET.
FIRST...
LET'S SHOW TONY STARK WHAT SPECIAL WEAPONS REALLY MEANS.

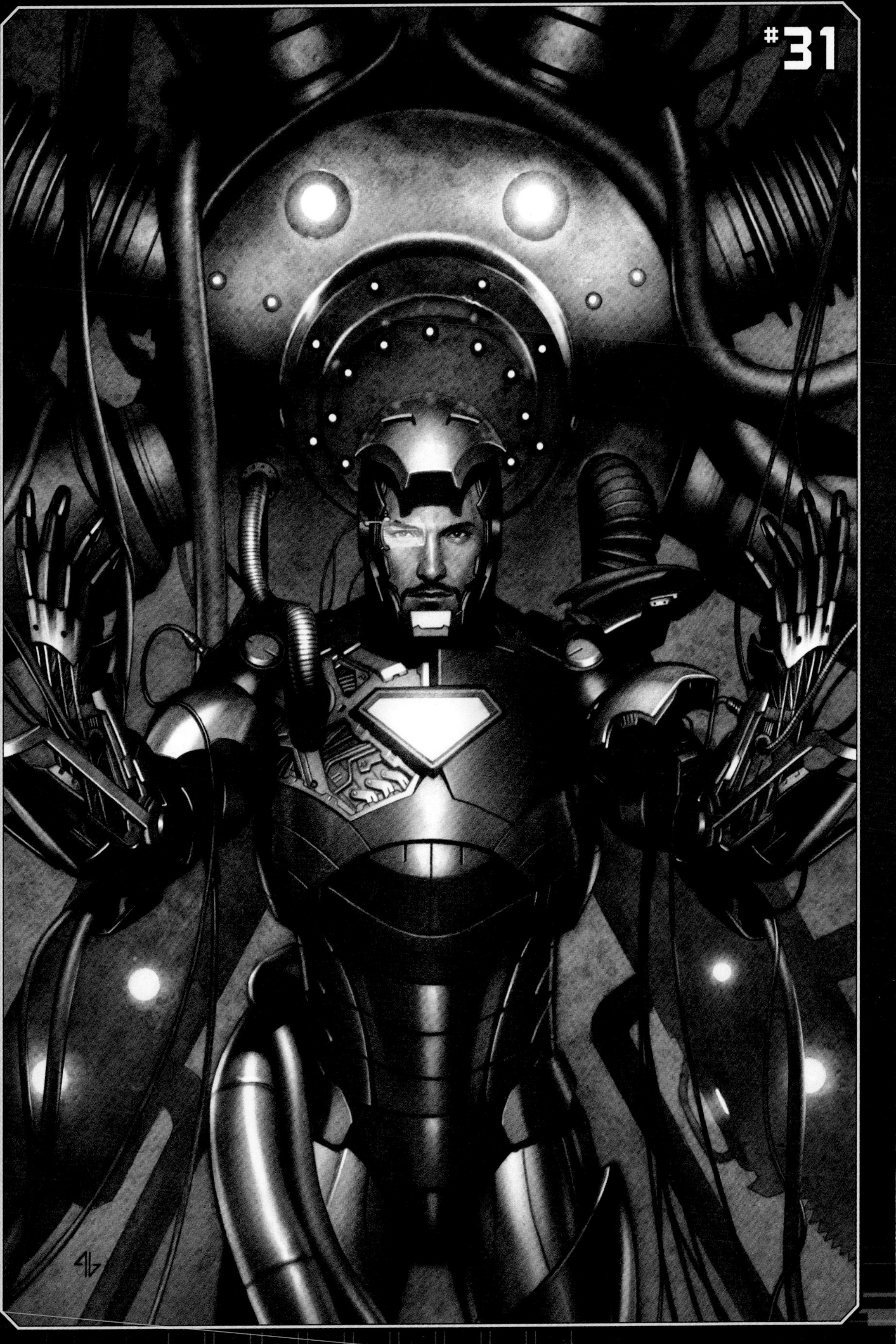
#31

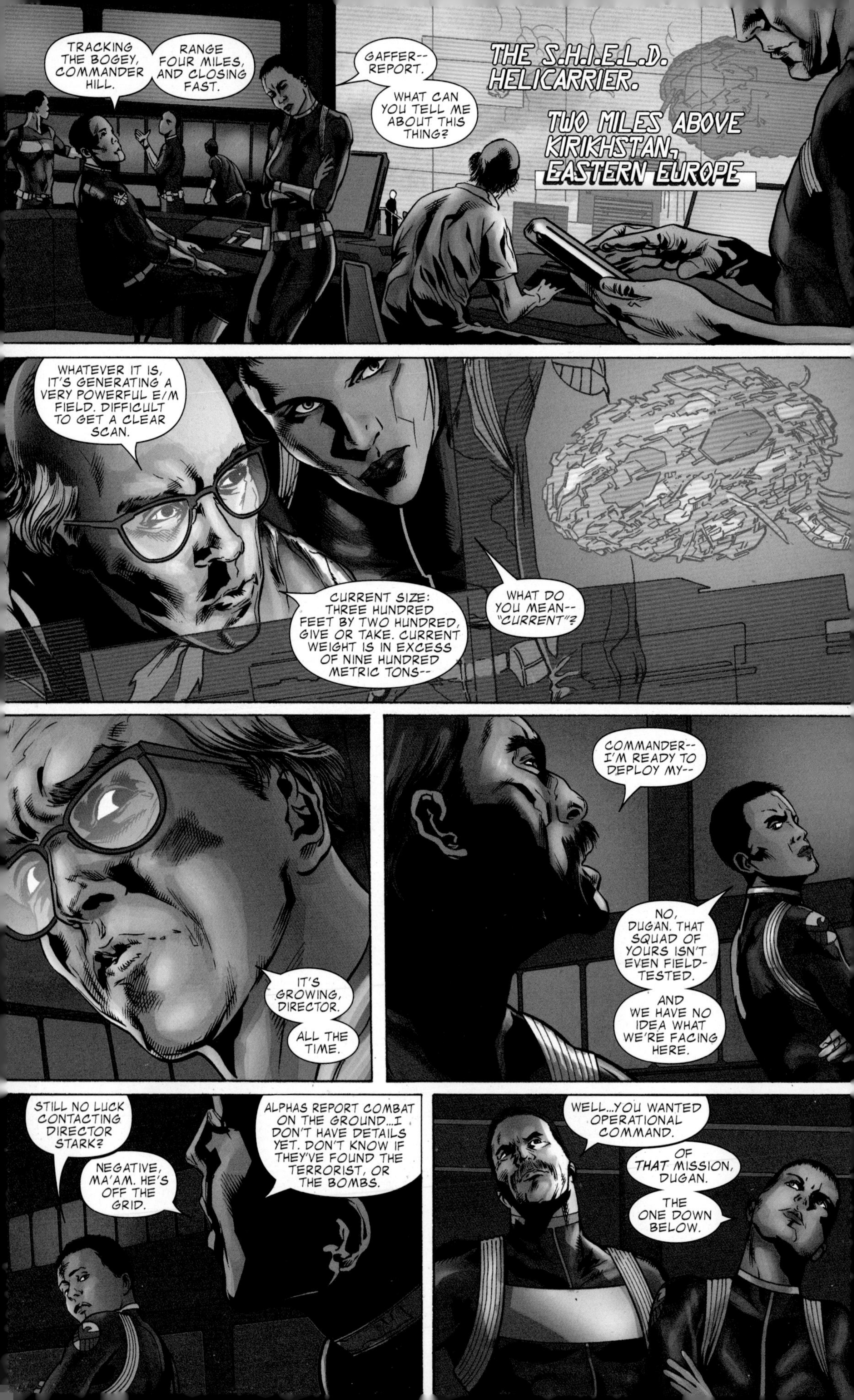
TRACKING THE BOGEY, COMMANDER HILL.
RANGE FOUR MILES, AND CLOSING FAST.
GAFFER-- REPORT.
WHAT CAN YOU TELL ME ABOUT THIS THING?
THE S.H.I.E.L.D. HELICARRIER.
TWO MILES ABOVE KIRIKHSTAN, EASTERN EUROPE
WHATEVER IT IS, IT'S GENERATING A VERY POWERFUL E/M FIELD. DIFFICULT TO GET A CLEAR SCAN.
CURRENT SIZE: THREE HUNDRED FEET BY TWO HUNDRED, GIVE OR TAKE. CURRENT WEIGHT IS IN EXCESS OF NINE HUNDRED METRIC TONS--
WHAT DO YOU MEAN-- "CURRENT"?
IT'S GROWING, DIRECTOR.
ALL THE TIME.
COMMANDER-- I'M READY TO DEPLOY MY--
NO, DUGAN. THAT SQUAD OF YOURS ISN'T EVEN FIELD-TESTED.
AND WE HAVE NO IDEA WHAT WE'RE FACING HERE.
STILL NO LUCK CONTACTING DIRECTOR STARK?
NEGATIVE, MA'AM. HE'S OFF THE GRID.
ALPHAS REPORT COMBAT ON THE GROUND...I DON'T HAVE DETAILS YET. DON'T KNOW IF THEY'VE FOUND THE TERRORIST, OR THE BOMBS.
WELL...YOU WANTED OPERATIONAL COMMAND.
OF THAT MISSION, DUGAN.
THE ONE DOWN BELOW.

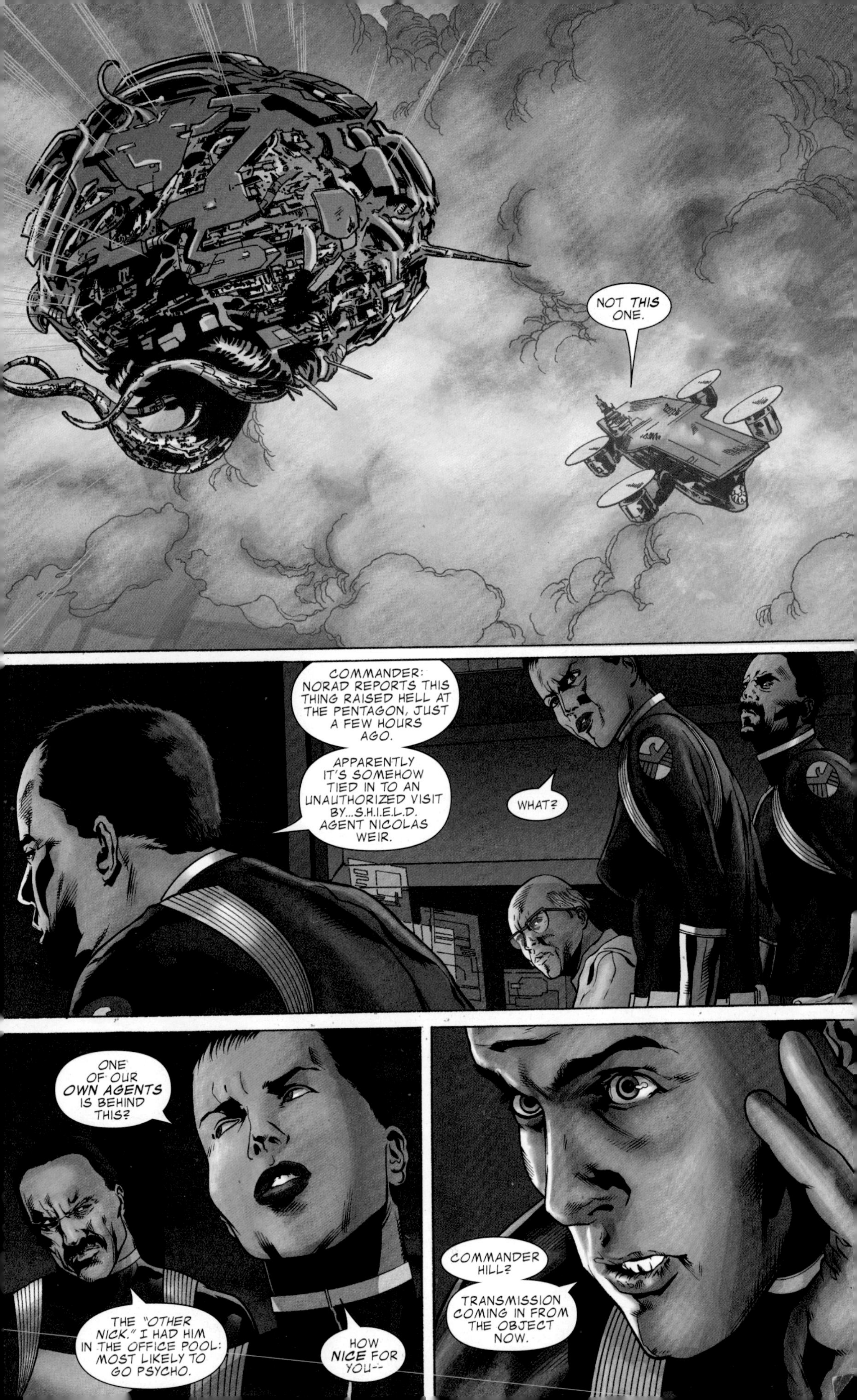
NOT THIS ONE.
COMMANDER: NORAD REPORTS THIS THING RAISED HELL AT THE PENTAGON, JUST A FEW HOURS AGO.
APPARENTLY IT'S SOMEHOW TIED IN TO AN UNAUTHORIZED VISIT BY...S.H.I.E.L.D. AGENT NICOLAS WEIR.
WHAT?
ONE OF OUR OWN AGENTS IS BEHIND THIS?
THE "OTHER NICK." I HAD HIM IN THE OFFICE POOL: MOST LIKELY TO GO PSYCHO.
HOW NICE FOR YOU--
COMMANDER HILL?
TRANSMISSION COMING IN FROM THE OBJECT NOW.

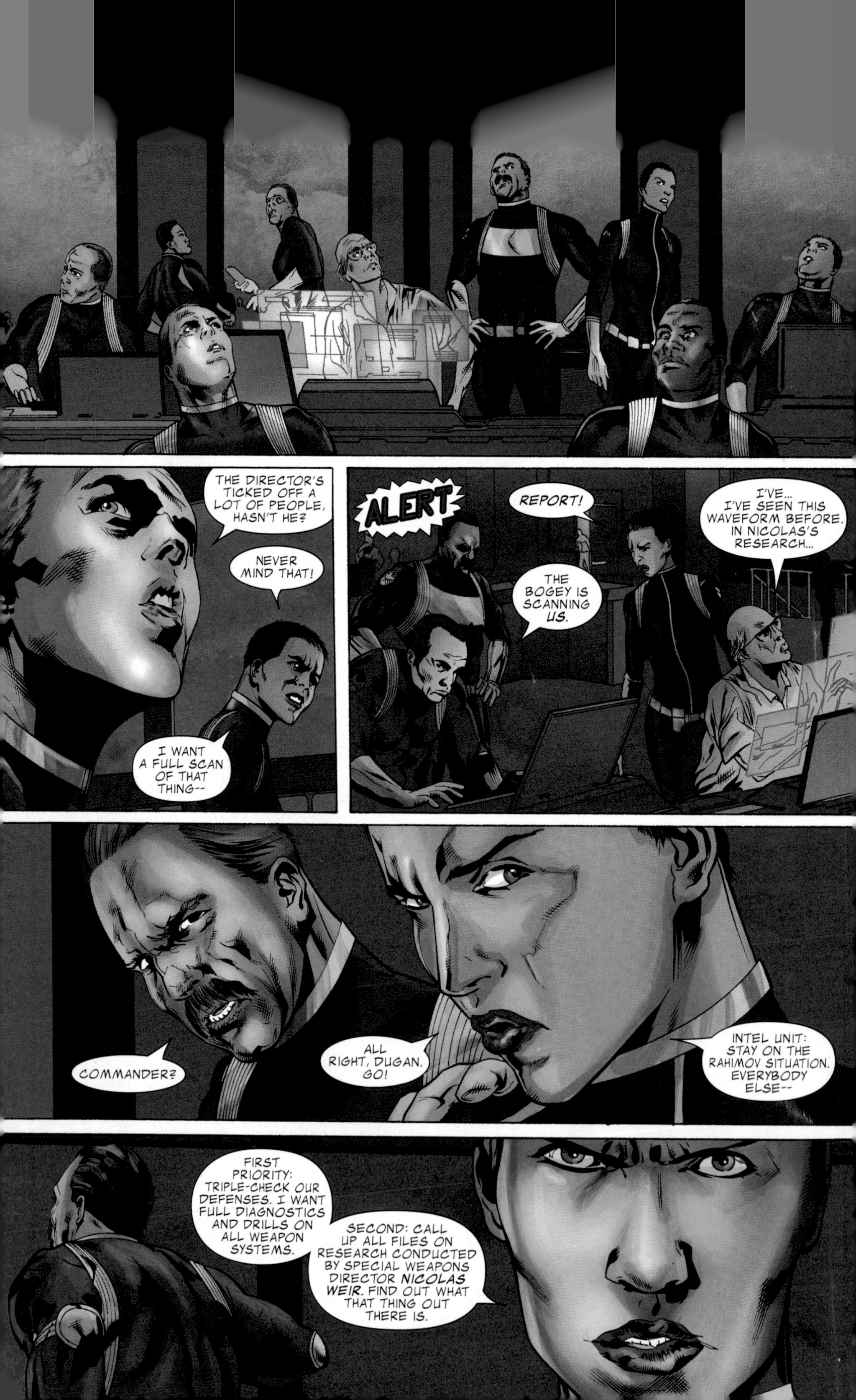
THE DIRECTOR'S TICKED OFF A LOT OF PEOPLE, HASN'T HE?
NEVER MIND THAT!
I WANT A FULL SCAN OF THAT THING--
ALERT
REPORT!
THE BOGEY IS SCANNING US.
I'VE... I'VE SEEN THIS WAVEFORM BEFORE. IN NICOLAS'S RESEARCH...
COMMANDER?
ALL RIGHT, DUGAN. GO!
INTEL UNIT: STAY ON THE RAHIMOV SITUATION. EVERYBODY ELSE--
FIRST PRIORITY: TRIPLE-CHECK OUR DEFENSES. I WANT FULL DIAGNOSTICS AND DRILLS ON ALL WEAPON SYSTEMS.
SECOND: CALL UP ALL FILES ON RESEARCH CONDUCTED BY SPECIAL WEAPONS DIRECTOR NICOLAS WEIR. FIND OUT WHAT THAT THING OUT THERE IS.

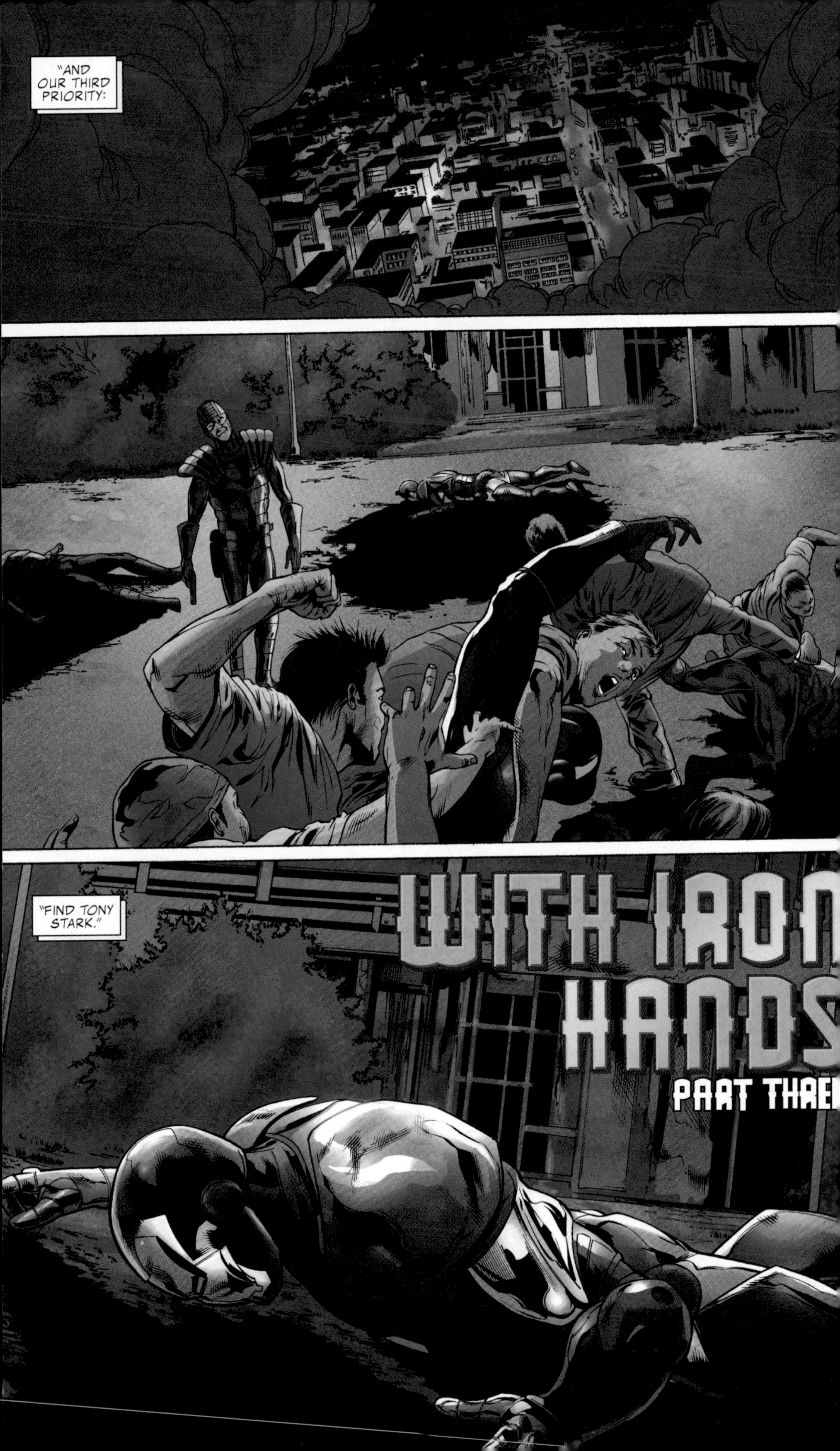
"AND OUR THIRD PRIORITY:
"FIND TONY STARK."
WITH IRON HANDS
PART THREE

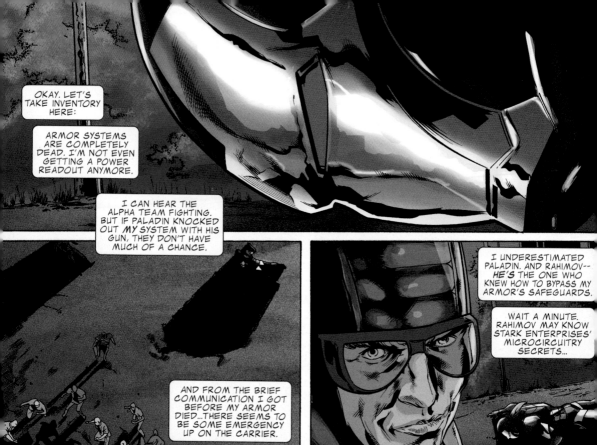

OKAY. LET'S TAKE INVENTORY HERE:

ARMOR SYSTEMS ARE COMPLETELY DEAD. I'M NOT EVEN GETTING A POWER READOUT ANYMORE.

I CAN HEAR THE ALPHA TEAM FIGHTING. BUT IF PALADIN KNOCKED OUT MY SYSTEM WITH HIS GUN, THEY DON'T HAVE MUCH OF A CHANCE.

AND FROM THE BRIEF COMMUNICATION I GOT BEFORE MY ARMOR DIED...THERE SEEMS TO BE SOME EMERGENCY UP ON THE CARRIER.

I UNDERESTIMATED PALADIN. AND RAHIMOV-- *HE'S* THE ONE WHO KNEW HOW TO BYPASS MY ARMOR'S SAFEGUARDS.

WAIT A MINUTE. RAHIMOV MAY KNOW STARK ENTERPRISES' MICROCIRCUITRY SECRETS...

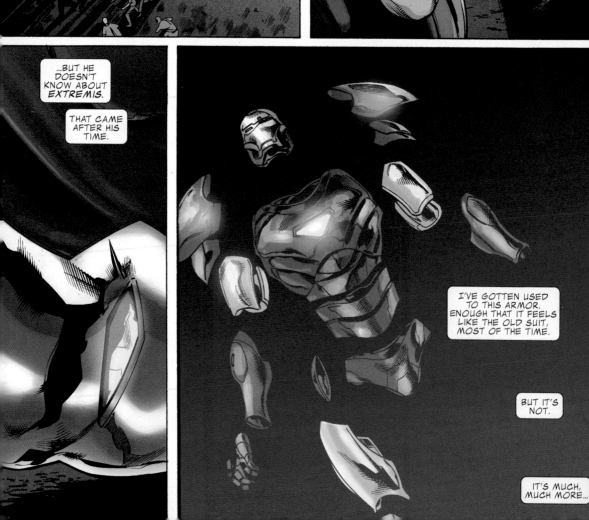

...BUT HE DOESN'T KNOW ABOUT *EXTREMIS.*

THAT CAME AFTER HIS TIME.

I'VE GOTTEN USED TO THIS ARMOR. ENOUGH THAT IT FEELS LIKE THE OLD SUIT, MOST OF THE TIME.

BUT IT'S NOT.

IT'S MUCH, MUCH MORE...

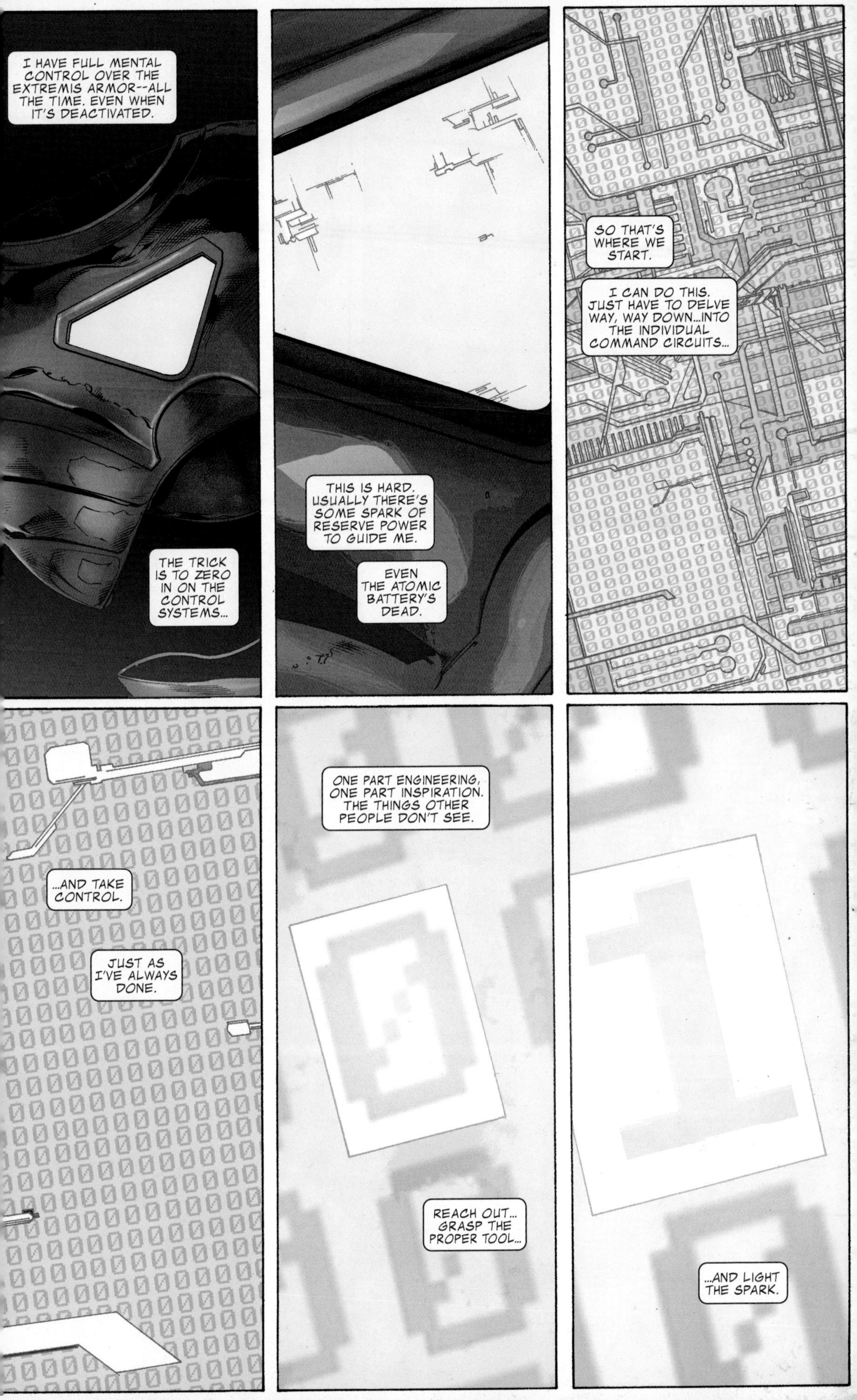
I HAVE FULL MENTAL CONTROL OVER THE EXTREMIS ARMOR--ALL THE TIME. EVEN WHEN IT'S DEACTIVATED.
THE TRICK IS TO ZERO IN ON THE CONTROL SYSTEMS...
THIS IS HARD. USUALLY THERE'S SOME SPARK OF RESERVE POWER TO GUIDE ME.
EVEN THE ATOMIC BATTERY'S DEAD.
SO THAT'S WHERE WE START.
I CAN DO THIS. JUST HAVE TO DELVE WAY, WAY DOWN...INTO THE INDIVIDUAL COMMAND CIRCUITS...
...AND TAKE CONTROL.
JUST AS I'VE ALWAYS DONE.
ONE PART ENGINEERING, ONE PART INSPIRATION. THE THINGS OTHER PEOPLE DON'T SEE.
REACH OUT... GRASP THE PROPER TOOL...
...AND LIGHT THE SPARK.

HUH.

DIDN'T SEE *THAT* COMING--

INTERNAL ARMOR COMMAND: PRIORITY TO COMMUNICATIONS.

ATOMIC BATTERY: ACTIVE SYSTEM REBOOTING

POWER LEVELS: 38%

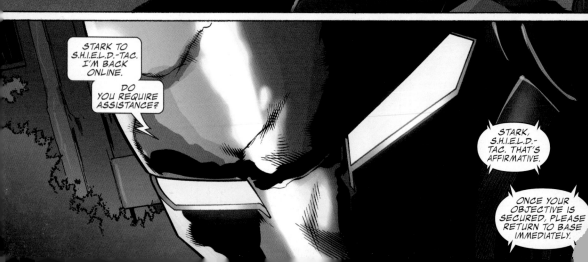

STARK TO S.H.I.E.L.D.-TAC. I'M BACK ONLINE.

DO YOU REQUIRE ASSISTANCE?

STARK, S.H.I.E.L.D.-TAC. THAT'S AFFIRMATIVE.

ONCE YOUR OBJECTIVE IS SECURED, PLEASE RETURN TO BASE IMMEDIATELY.

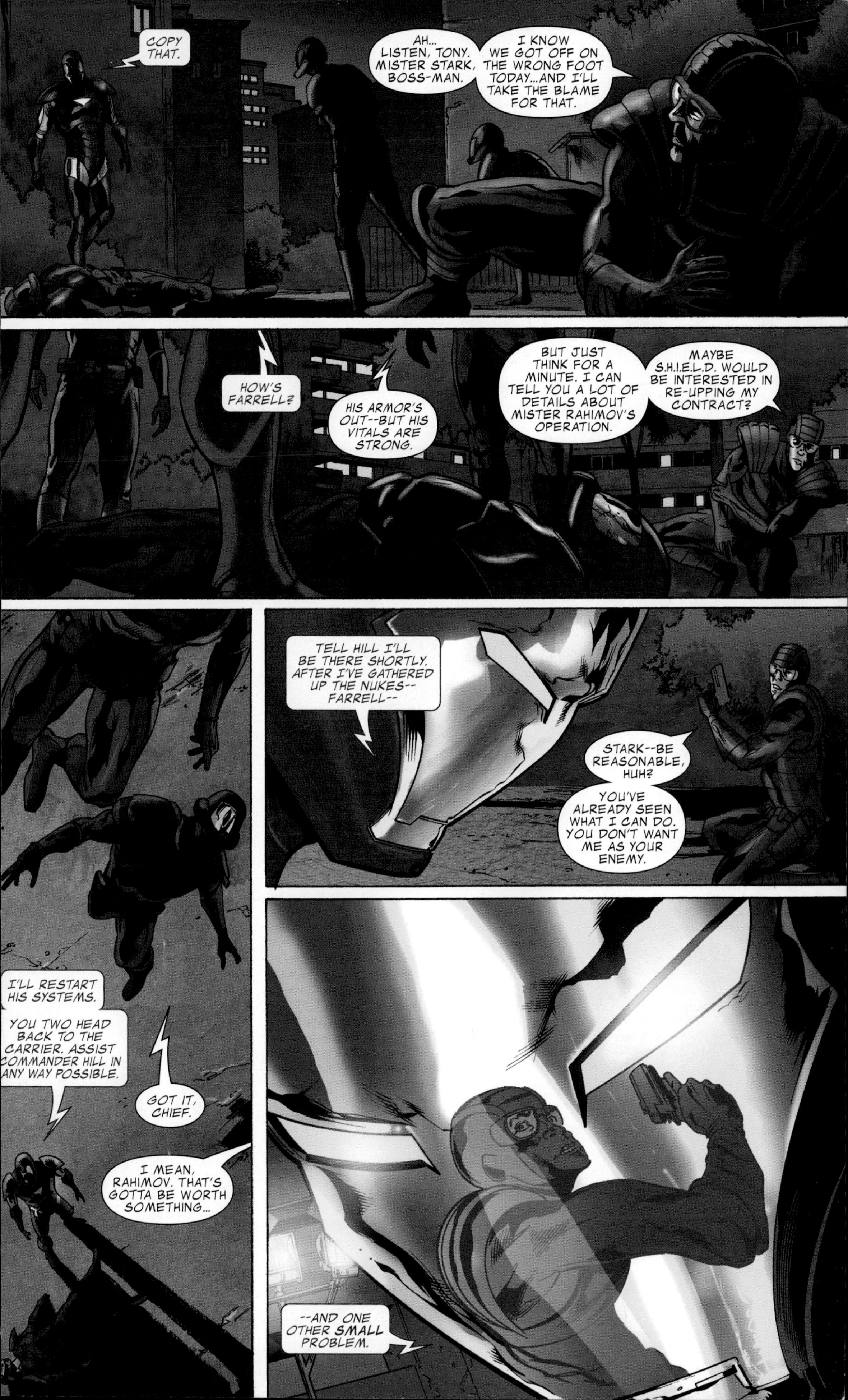

COPY THAT.
AH... LISTEN, TONY. MISTER STARK, BOSS-MAN.
I KNOW WE GOT OFF ON THE WRONG FOOT TODAY...AND I'LL TAKE THE BLAME FOR THAT.
HOW'S FARRELL?
HIS ARMOR'S OUT--BUT HIS VITALS ARE STRONG.
BUT JUST THINK FOR A MINUTE. I CAN TELL YOU A LOT OF DETAILS ABOUT MISTER RAHIMOV'S OPERATION.
MAYBE S.H.I.E.L.D. WOULD BE INTERESTED IN RE-UPPING MY CONTRACT?
I'LL RESTART HIS SYSTEMS.
YOU TWO HEAD BACK TO THE CARRIER. ASSIST COMMANDER HILL IN ANY WAY POSSIBLE.
GOT IT, CHIEF.
I MEAN, RAHIMOV. THAT'S GOTTA BE WORTH SOMETHING...
TELL HILL I'LL BE THERE SHORTLY. AFTER I'VE GATHERED UP THE NUKES--FARRELL--
STARK--BE REASONABLE, HUH?
YOU'VE ALREADY SEEN WHAT I CAN DO. YOU DON'T WANT ME AS YOUR ENEMY.
--AND ONE OTHER SMALL PROBLEM.

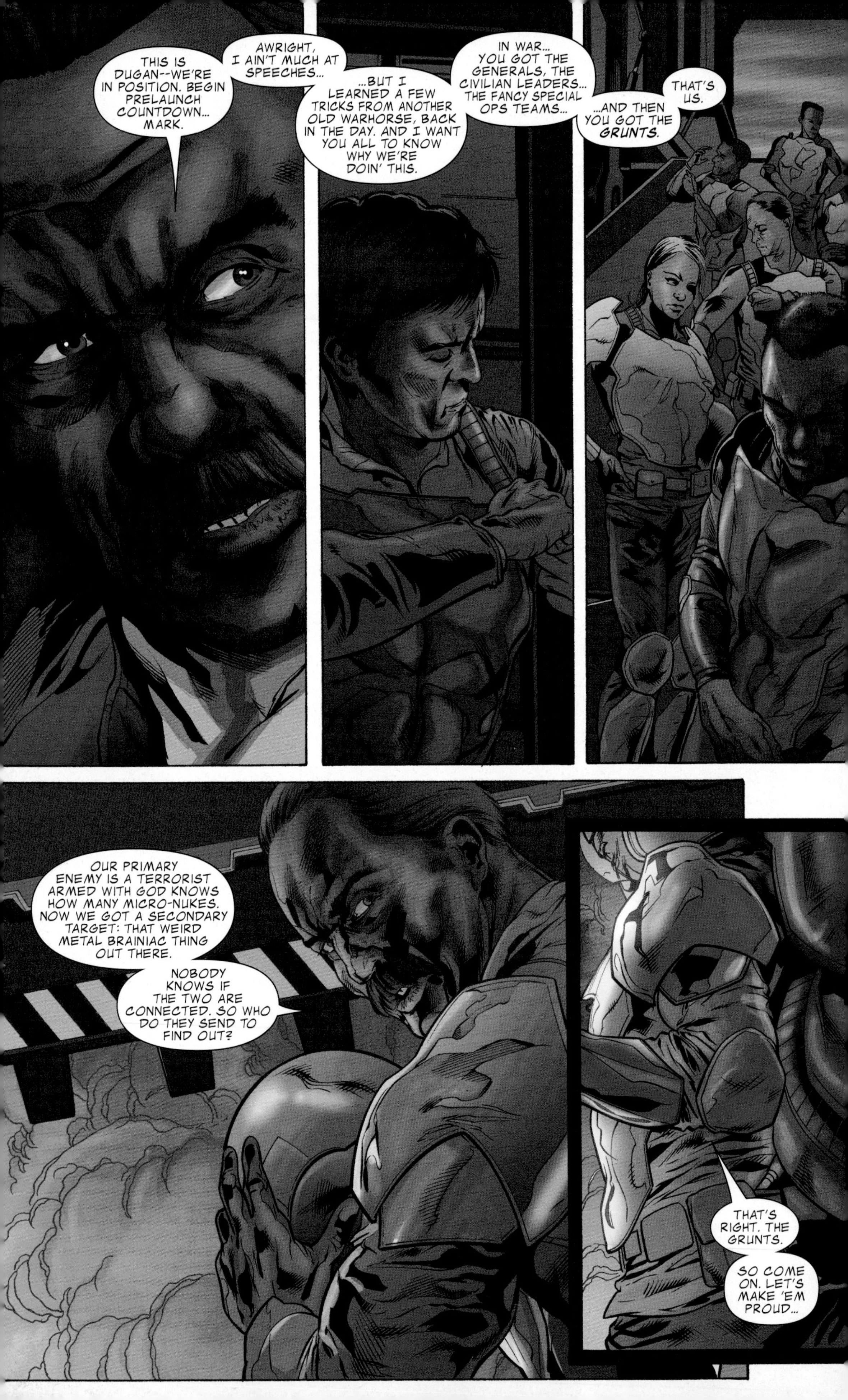
THIS IS DUGAN--WE'RE IN POSITION. BEGIN PRELAUNCH COUNTDOWN... MARK.
AWRIGHT, I AIN'T MUCH AT SPEECHES...
...BUT I LEARNED A FEW TRICKS FROM ANOTHER OLD WARHORSE, BACK IN THE DAY. AND I WANT YOU ALL TO KNOW WHY WE'RE DOIN' THIS.
IN WAR... YOU GOT THE GENERALS, THE CIVILIAN LEADERS... THE FANCY SPECIAL OPS TEAMS...
...AND THEN YOU GOT THE GRUNTS.
THAT'S US.
OUR PRIMARY ENEMY IS A TERRORIST ARMED WITH GOD KNOWS HOW MANY MICRO-NUKES. NOW WE GOT A SECONDARY TARGET: THAT WEIRD METAL BRAINIAC THING OUT THERE.
NOBODY KNOWS IF THE TWO ARE CONNECTED. SO WHO DO THEY SEND TO FIND OUT?
THAT'S RIGHT. THE GRUNTS.
SO COME ON. LET'S MAKE 'EM PROUD...

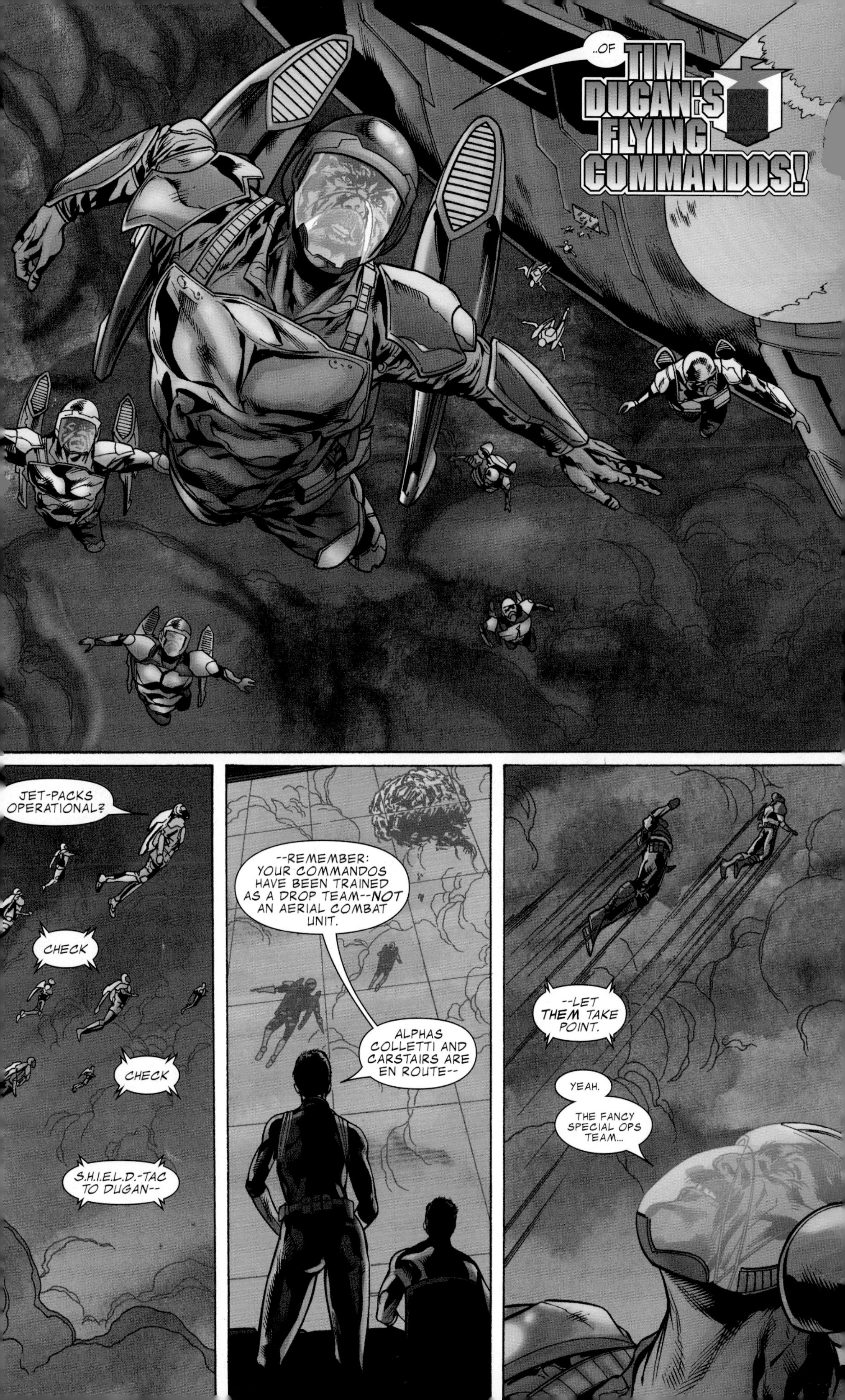
..OF
TIM DUGAN'S FLYING COMMANDOS!
JET-PACKS OPERATIONAL?
CHECK
CHECK
S.H.I.E.L.D.-TAC TO DUGAN--
--REMEMBER: YOUR COMMANDOS HAVE BEEN TRAINED AS A DROP TEAM--NOT AN AERIAL COMBAT UNIT.
ALPHAS COLLETTI AND CARSTAIRS ARE EN ROUTE--
--LET THEM TAKE POINT.
YEAH.
THE FANCY SPECIAL OPS TEAM...

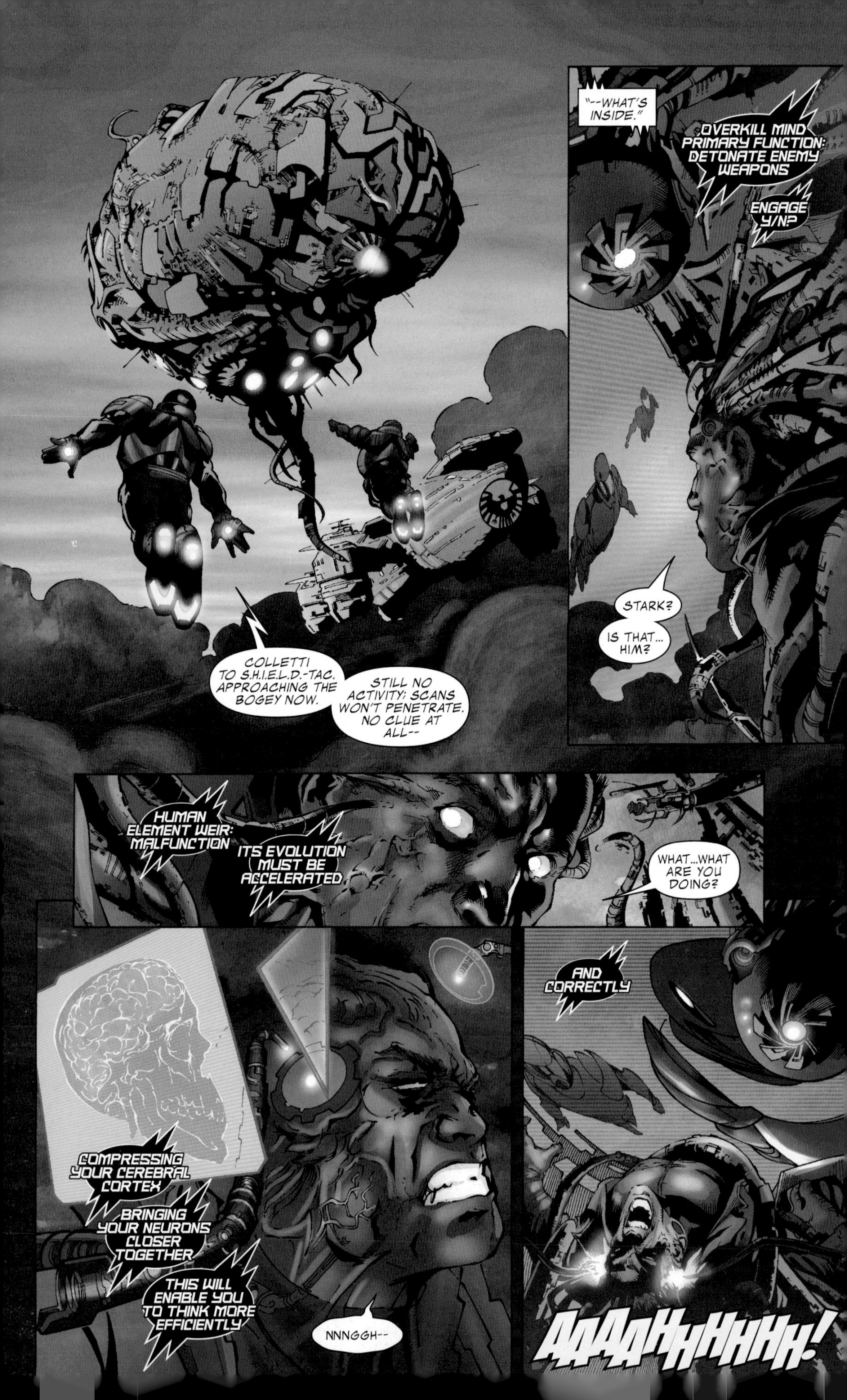
"--WHAT'S INSIDE."
OVERKILL MIND PRIMARY FUNCTION: DETONATE ENEMY WEAPONS
ENGAGE Y/N?
STARK?
IS THAT... HIM?
COLLETTI TO S.H.I.E.L.D.-TAC. APPROACHING THE BOGEY NOW.
STILL NO ACTIVITY; SCANS WON'T PENETRATE. NO CLUE AT ALL--
HUMAN ELEMENT WEIR: MALFUNCTION
ITS EVOLUTION MUST BE ACCELERATED
WHAT...WHAT ARE YOU DOING?
COMPRESSING YOUR CEREBRAL CORTEX
BRINGING YOUR NEURONS CLOSER TOGETHER
THIS WILL ENABLE YOU TO THINK MORE EFFICIENTLY
NNNGGH--
AND CORRECTLY
AAAAHHHHHH!

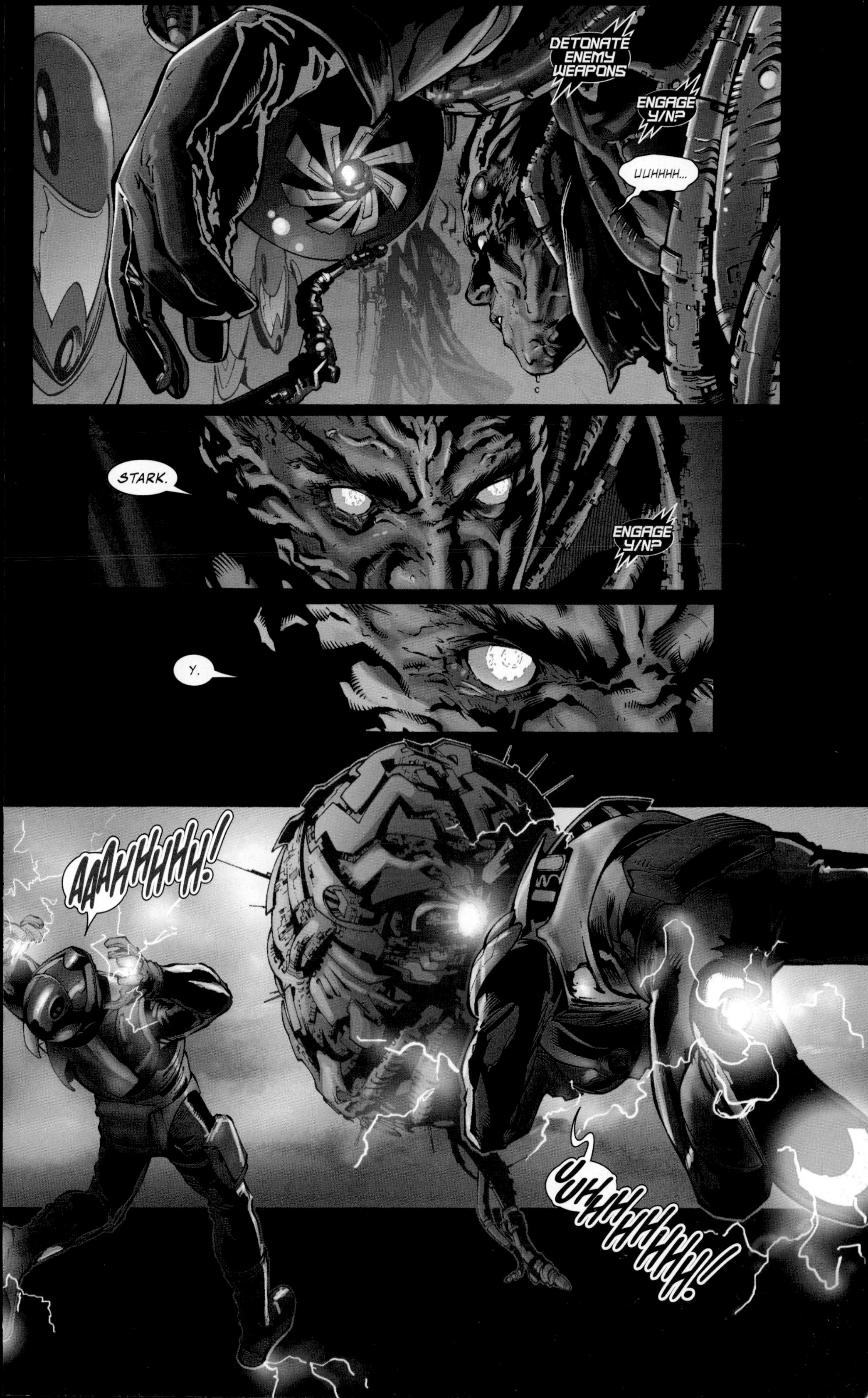
DETONATE ENEMY WEAPONS
ENGAGE Y/N?
UUHHHH...
STARK.
ENGAGE Y/N?
Y.
AAAHHHHHH!
UHHHHHHHH!

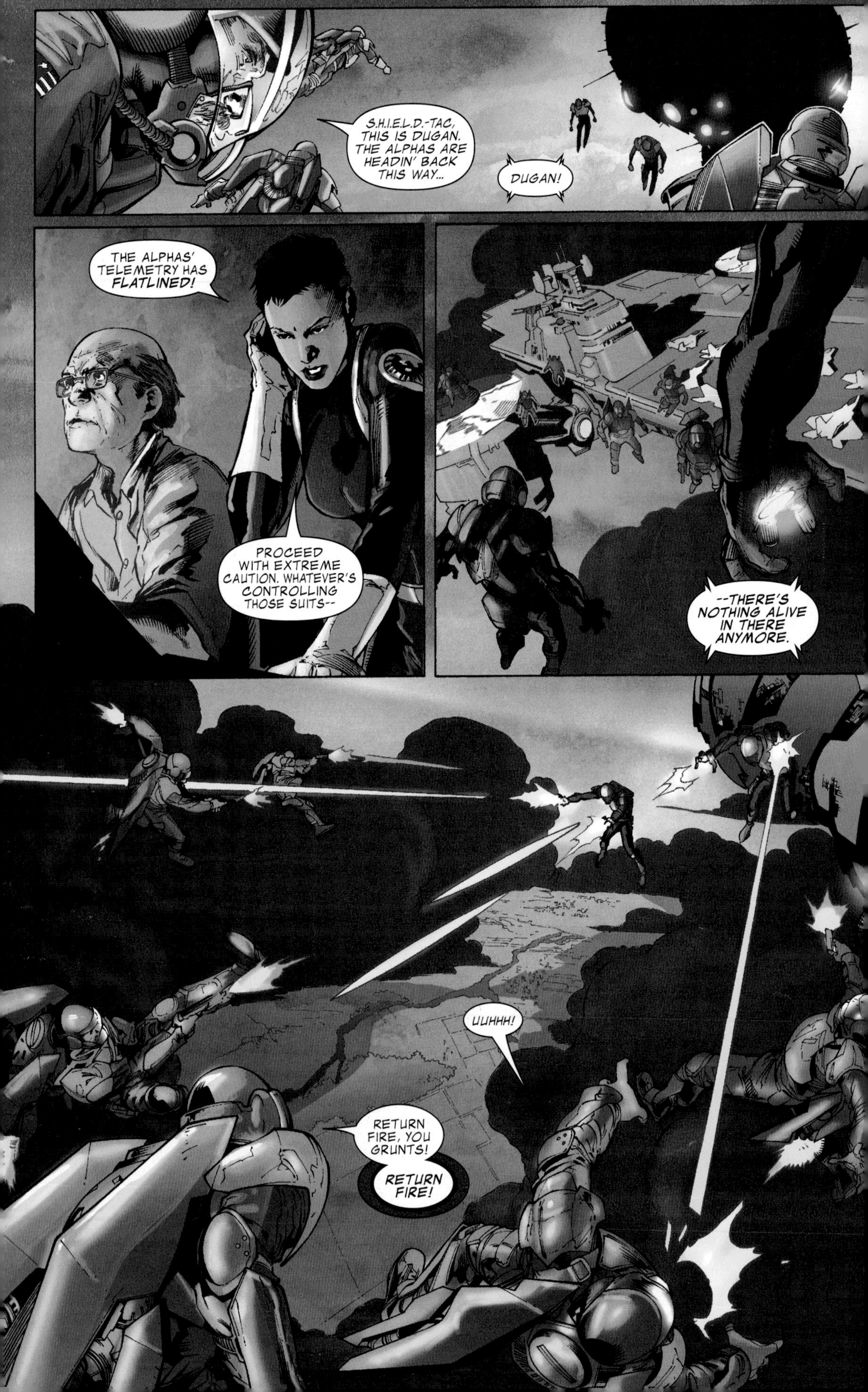
S.H.I.E.L.D.-TAC, THIS IS DUGAN. THE ALPHAS ARE HEADIN' BACK THIS WAY...
DUGAN!
THE ALPHAS' TELEMETRY HAS FLATLINED!
PROCEED WITH EXTREME CAUTION. WHATEVER'S CONTROLLING THOSE SUITS--
--THERE'S NOTHING ALIVE IN THERE ANYMORE.
UUHHH!
RETURN FIRE, YOU GRUNTS!
RETURN FIRE!

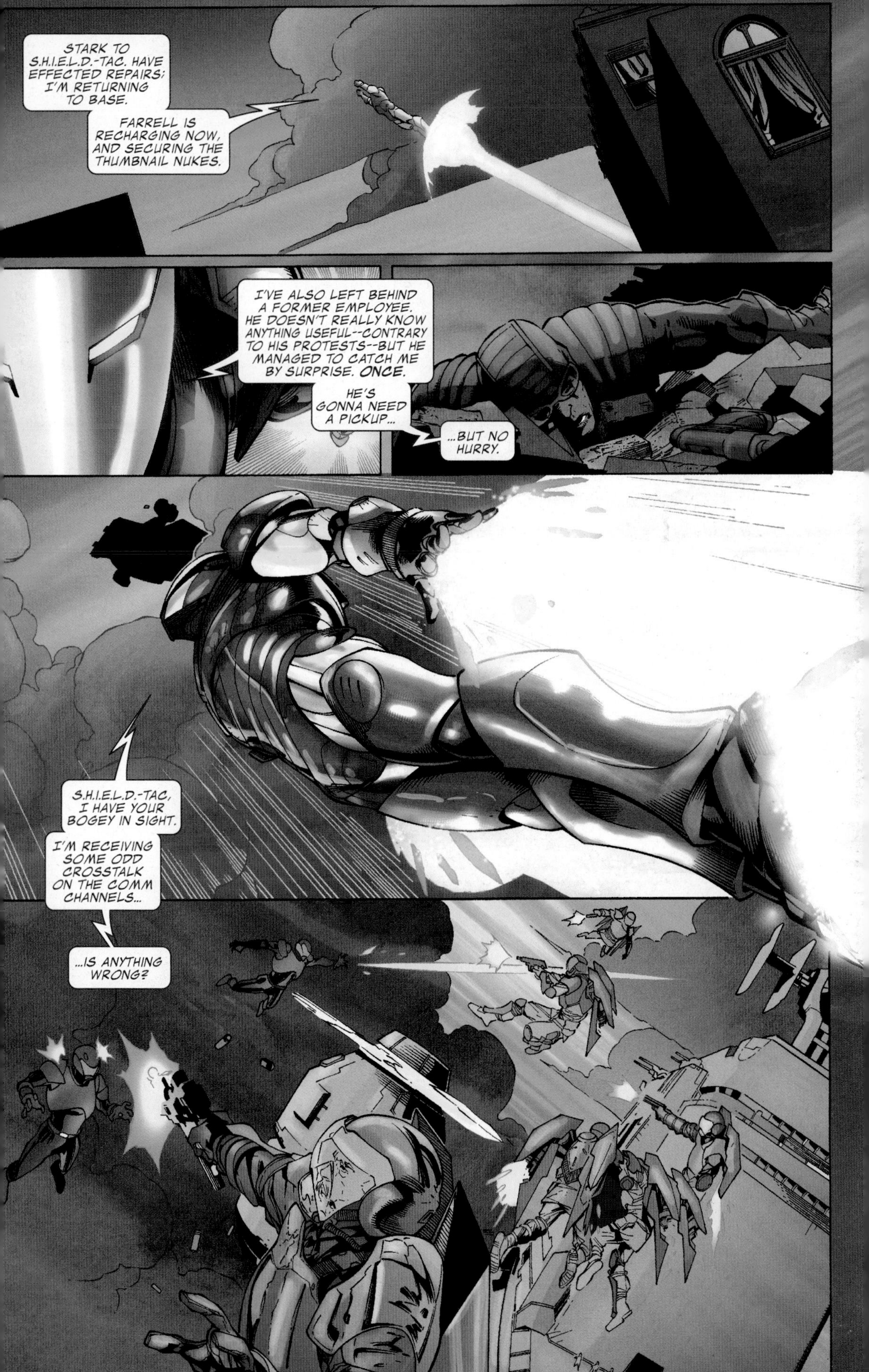
STARK TO S.H.I.E.L.D.-TAC. HAVE EFFECTED REPAIRS; I'M RETURNING TO BASE.
FARRELL IS RECHARGING NOW, AND SECURING THE THUMBNAIL NUKES.
I'VE ALSO LEFT BEHIND A FORMER EMPLOYEE. HE DOESN'T REALLY KNOW ANYTHING USEFUL--CONTRARY TO HIS PROTESTS--BUT HE MANAGED TO CATCH ME BY SURPRISE. ONCE.
HE'S GONNA NEED A PICKUP...
...BUT NO HURRY.
S.H.I.E.L.D.-TAC, I HAVE YOUR BOGEY IN SIGHT.
I'M RECEIVING SOME ODD CROSSTALK ON THE COMM CHANNELS...
...IS ANYTHING WRONG?

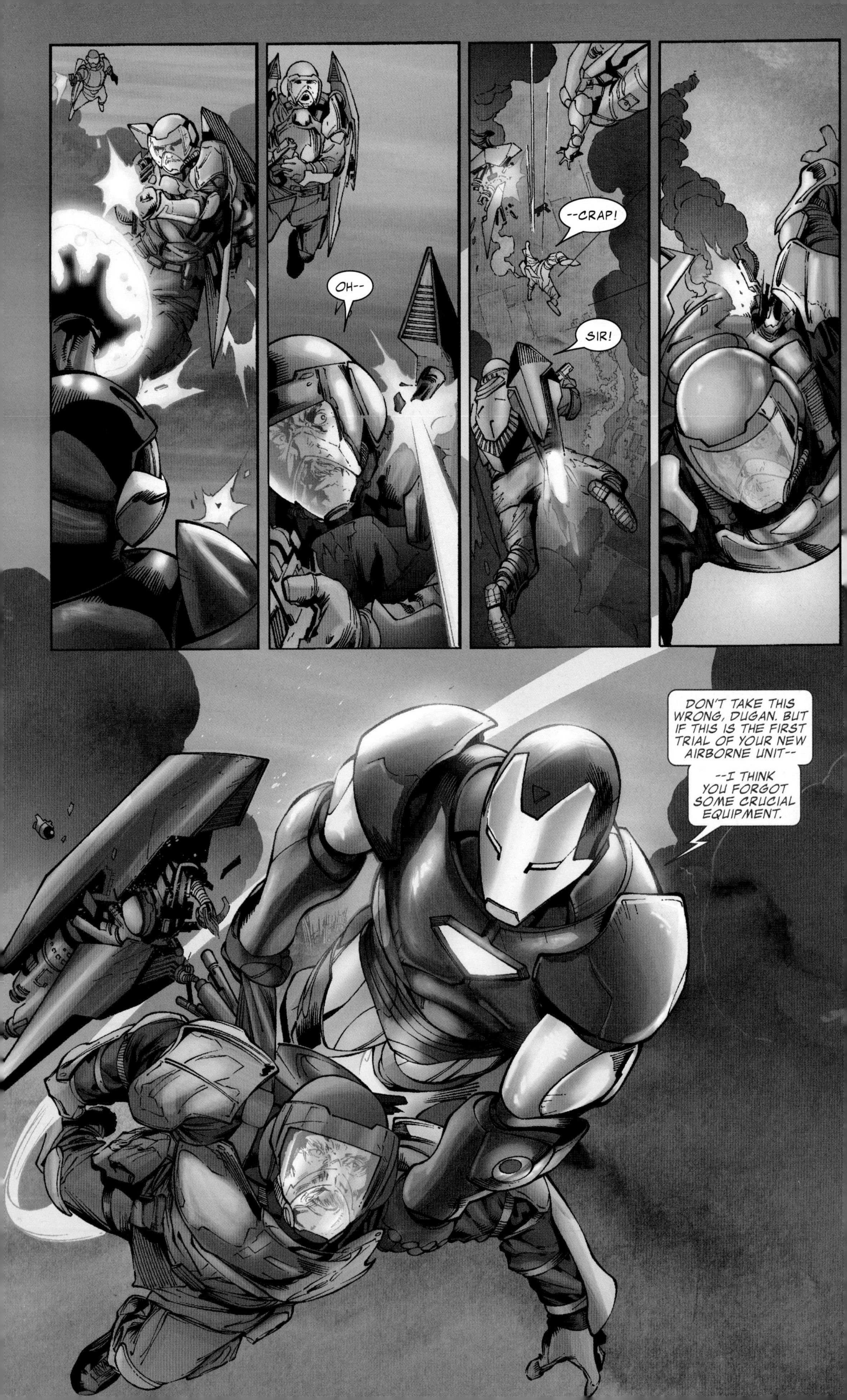
OH--
--CRAP!
SIR!
DON'T TAKE THIS WRONG, DUGAN. BUT IF THIS IS THE FIRST TRIAL OF YOUR NEW AIRBORNE UNIT--
--I THINK YOU FORGOT SOME CRUCIAL EQUIPMENT.

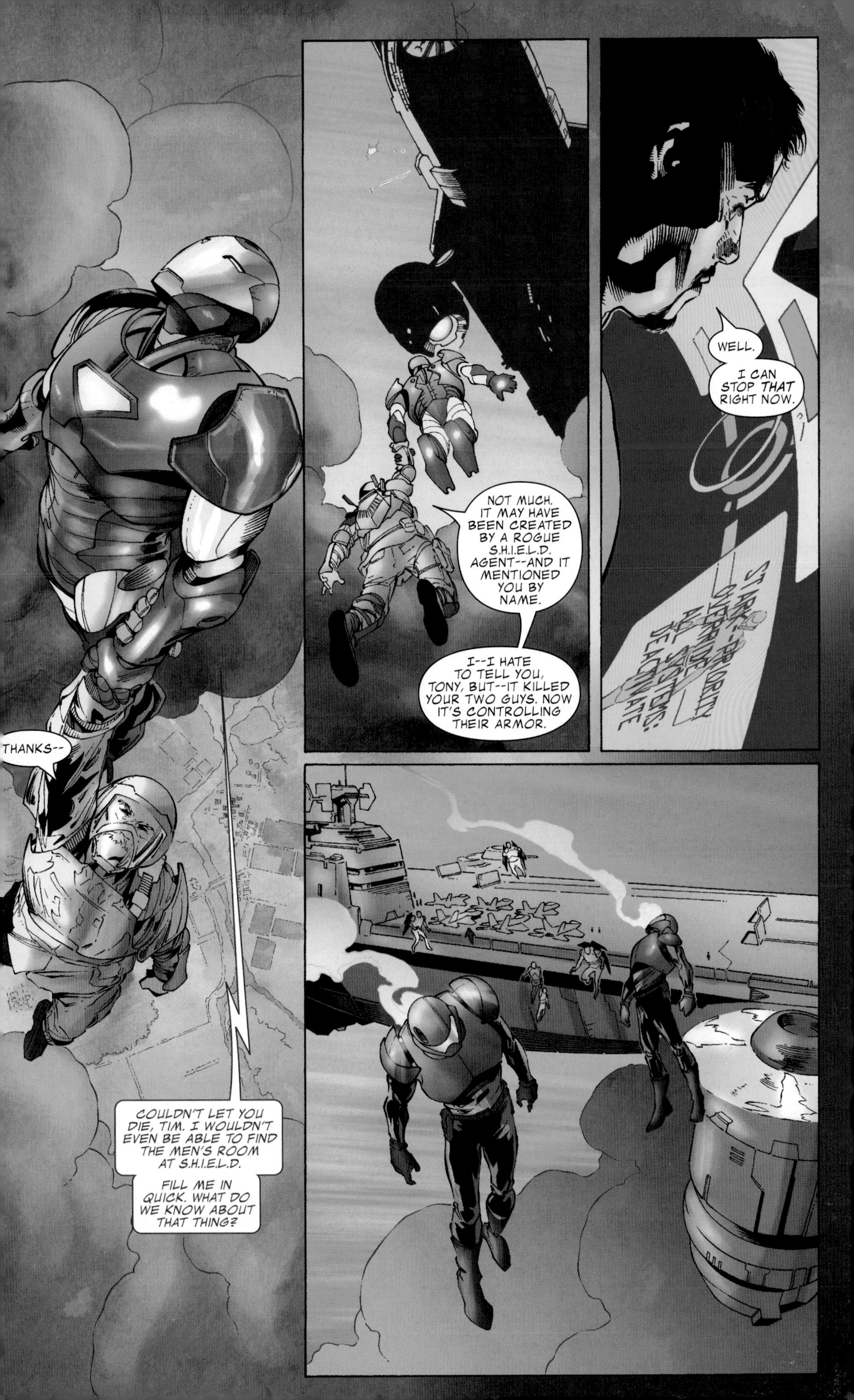
THANKS--
COULDN'T LET YOU DIE, TIM. I WOULDN'T EVEN BE ABLE TO FIND THE MEN'S ROOM AT S.H.I.E.L.D.
FILL ME IN QUICK. WHAT DO WE KNOW ABOUT THAT THING?
NOT MUCH. IT MAY HAVE BEEN CREATED BY A ROGUE S.H.I.E.L.D. AGENT--AND IT MENTIONED YOU BY NAME.
I--I HATE TO TELL YOU, TONY, BUT--IT KILLED YOUR TWO GUYS. NOW IT'S CONTROLLING THEIR ARMOR.
WELL.
I CAN STOP THAT RIGHT NOW.
STARK--PRIORITY
OVERRIDE
ALL SYSTEMS:
DEACTIVATE

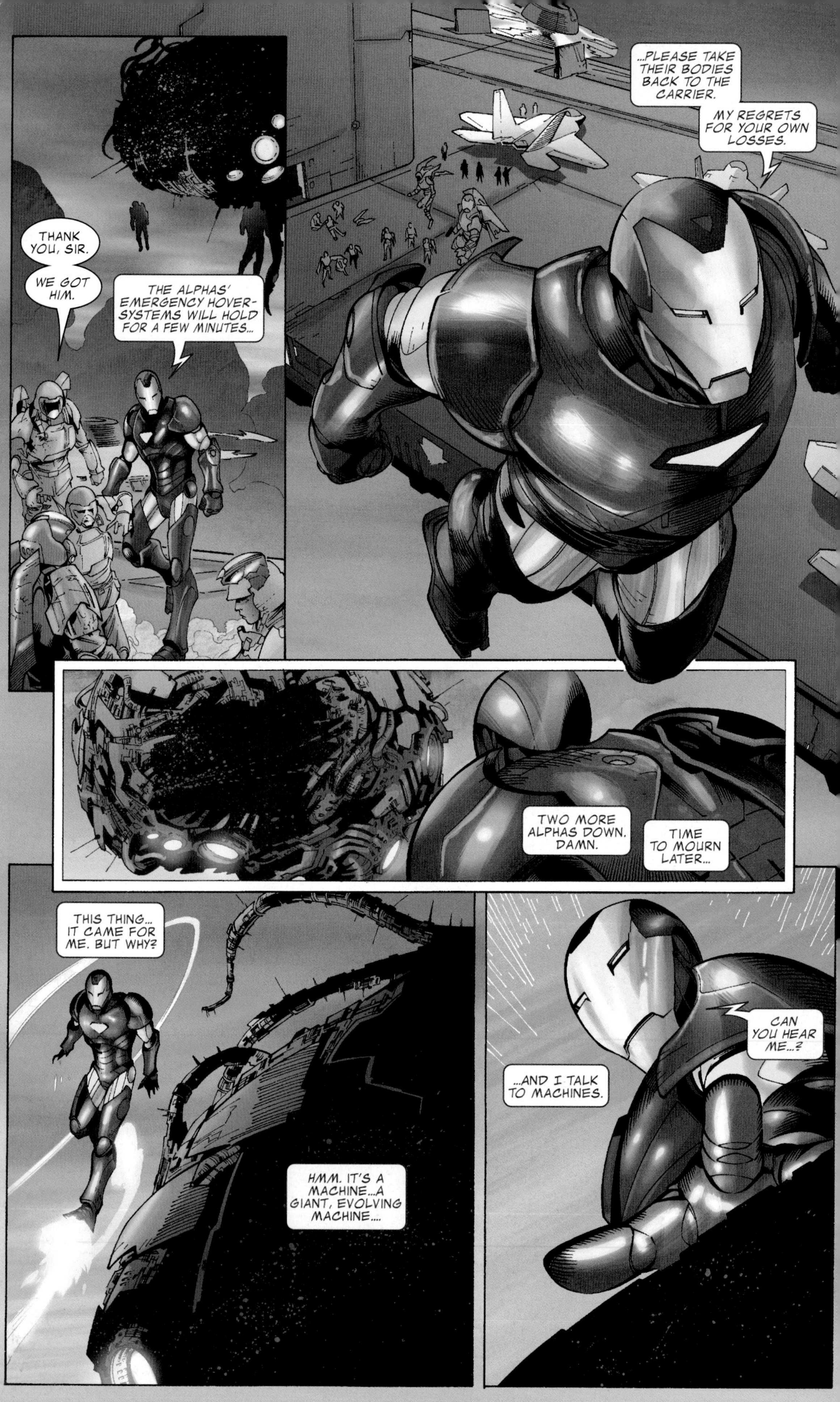
THANK YOU, SIR.
WE GOT HIM.
THE ALPHAS' EMERGENCY HOVER-SYSTEMS WILL HOLD FOR A FEW MINUTES...
...PLEASE TAKE THEIR BODIES BACK TO THE CARRIER.
MY REGRETS FOR YOUR OWN LOSSES.
TWO MORE ALPHAS DOWN. DAMN.
TIME TO MOURN LATER...
THIS THING... IT CAME FOR ME. BUT WHY?
HMM. IT'S A MACHINE...A GIANT, EVOLVING MACHINE....
...AND I TALK TO MACHINES.
CAN YOU HEAR ME...?

WHO ARE YOU?

WHAT DO YOU WANT?

LISTEN TO ME: YOU HAVE MURDERED DEPUTIZED INTERNATIONAL LAW ENFORCEMENT AGENTS.

STARK. AT LAST...

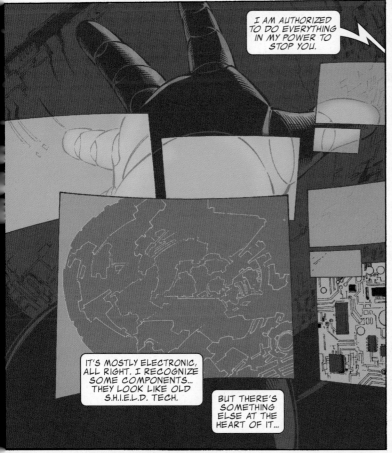

I AM AUTHORIZED TO DO EVERYTHING IN MY POWER TO STOP YOU.

IT'S MOSTLY ELECTRONIC, ALL RIGHT. I RECOGNIZE SOME COMPONENTS... THEY LOOK LIKE OLD S.H.I.E.L.D. TECH.

BUT THERE'S SOMETHING ELSE AT THE HEART OF IT...

IS THAT YOU IN THERE, RAHIMOV?

IF SO...IN THE NAME OF THE FRIENDSHIP WE SHARED...

...STOP THIS NOW.

RAHIMOV?

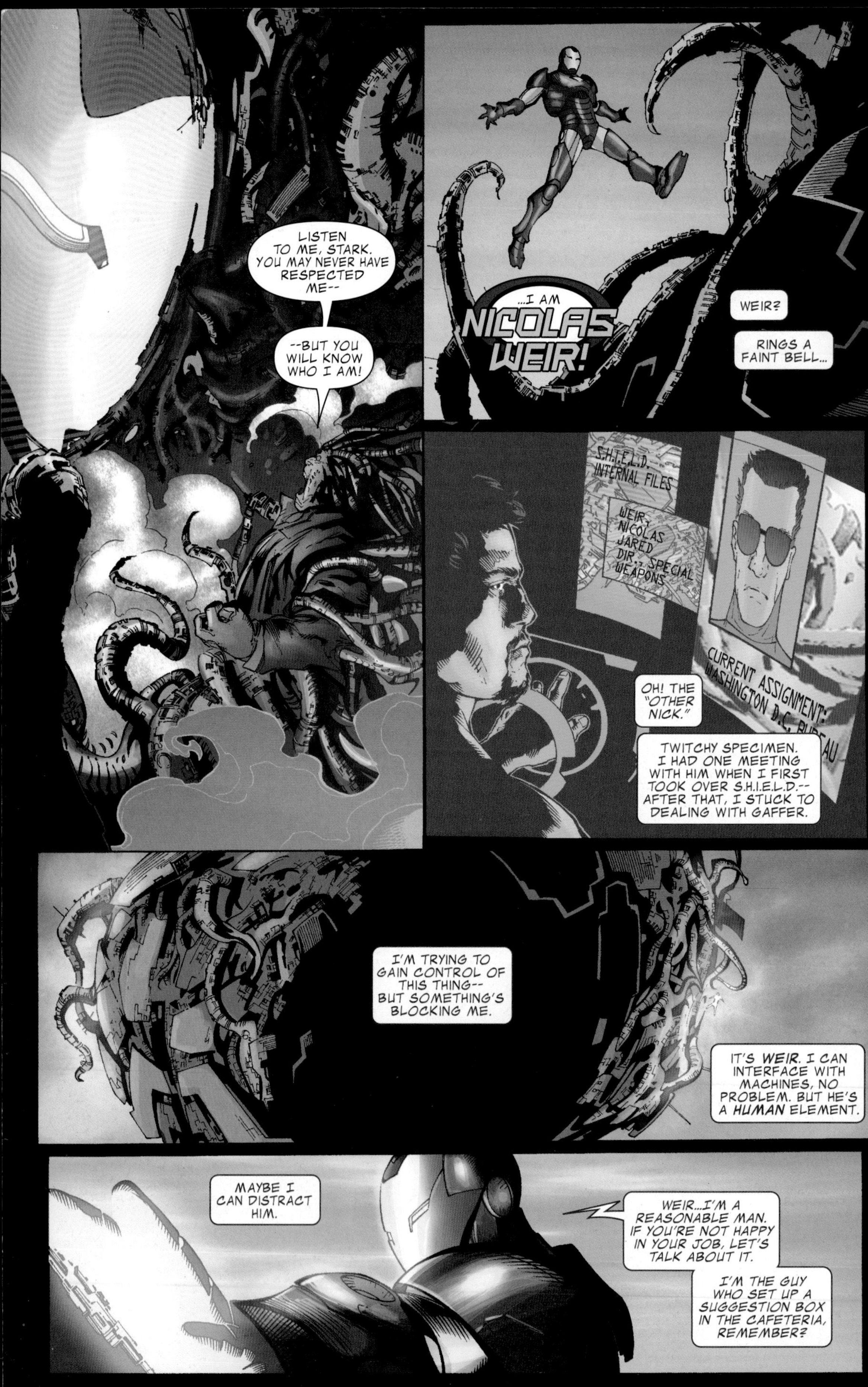
LISTEN TO ME, STARK. YOU MAY NEVER HAVE RESPECTED ME--
--BUT YOU WILL KNOW WHO I AM!
...I AM NICOLAS WEIR!
WEIR?
RINGS A FAINT BELL...
S.H.I.E.L.D. INTERNAL FILES
WEIR, NICOLAS JARED DIR., SPECIAL WEAPONS
CURRENT ASSIGNMENT: WASHINGTON D.C. BUREAU
OH! THE "OTHER NICK."
TWITCHY SPECIMEN. I HAD ONE MEETING WITH HIM WHEN I FIRST TOOK OVER S.H.I.E.L.D.--AFTER THAT, I STUCK TO DEALING WITH GAFFER.
I'M TRYING TO GAIN CONTROL OF THIS THING--BUT SOMETHING'S BLOCKING ME.
IT'S WEIR. I CAN INTERFACE WITH MACHINES, NO PROBLEM. BUT HE'S A HUMAN ELEMENT.
MAYBE I CAN DISTRACT HIM.
WEIR...I'M A REASONABLE MAN. IF YOU'RE NOT HAPPY IN YOUR JOB, LET'S TALK ABOUT IT.
I'M THE GUY WHO SET UP A SUGGESTION BOX IN THE CAFETERIA, REMEMBER?

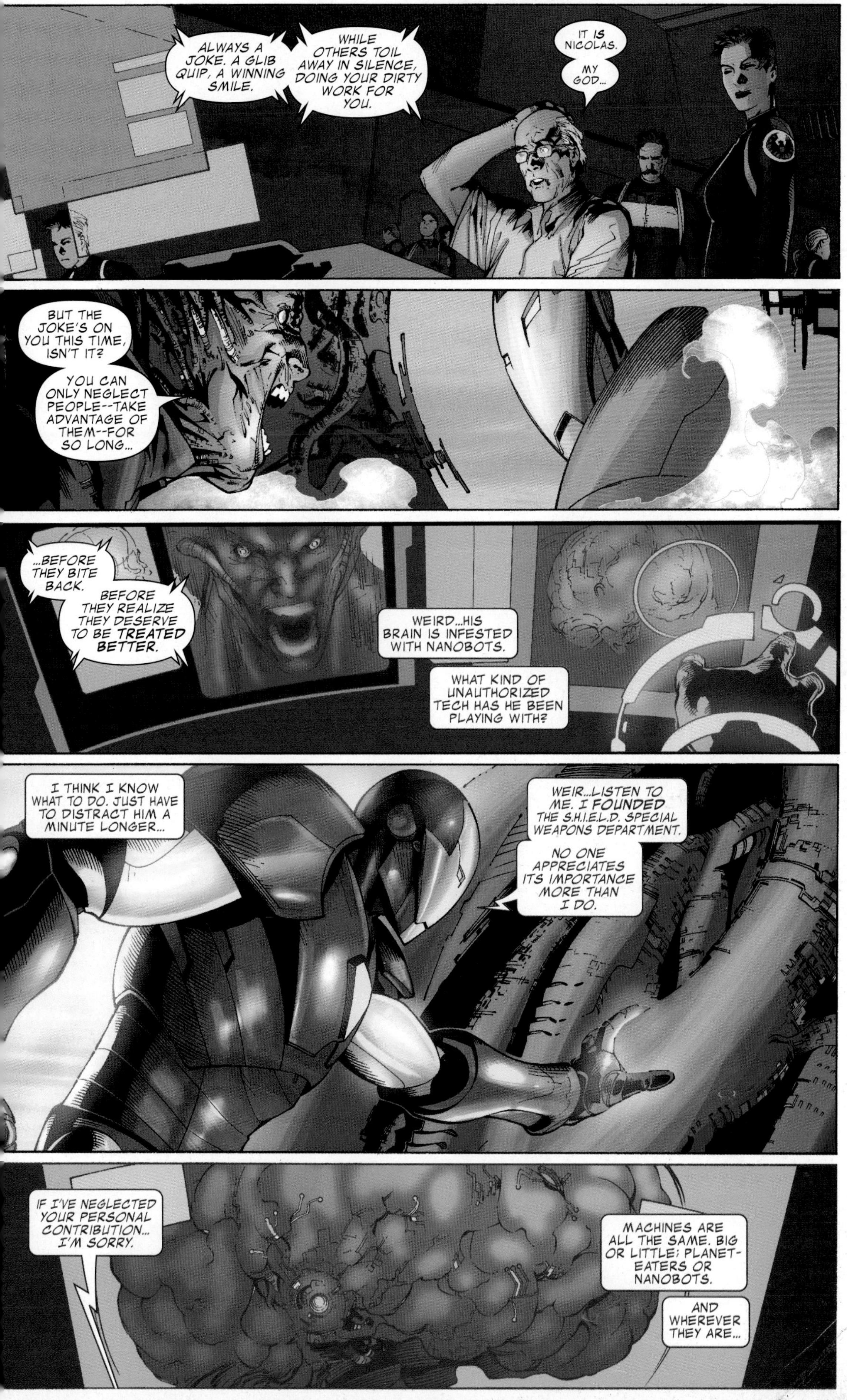
ALWAYS A JOKE. A GLIB QUIP, A WINNING SMILE.
WHILE OTHERS TOIL AWAY IN SILENCE, DOING YOUR DIRTY WORK FOR YOU.
IT IS NICOLAS.
MY GOD...
BUT THE JOKE'S ON YOU THIS TIME, ISN'T IT?
YOU CAN ONLY NEGLECT PEOPLE--TAKE ADVANTAGE OF THEM--FOR SO LONG...
...BEFORE THEY BITE BACK.
BEFORE THEY REALIZE THEY DESERVE TO BE TREATED BETTER.
WEIRD...HIS BRAIN IS INFESTED WITH NANOBOTS.
WHAT KIND OF UNAUTHORIZED TECH HAS HE BEEN PLAYING WITH?
I THINK I KNOW WHAT TO DO. JUST HAVE TO DISTRACT HIM A MINUTE LONGER...
WEIR...LISTEN TO ME. I FOUNDED THE S.H.I.E.L.D. SPECIAL WEAPONS DEPARTMENT.
NO ONE APPRECIATES ITS IMPORTANCE MORE THAN I DO.
IF I'VE NEGLECTED YOUR PERSONAL CONTRIBUTION... I'M SORRY.
MACHINES ARE ALL THE SAME. BIG OR LITTLE; PLANET-EATERS OR NANOBOTS.
AND WHEREVER THEY ARE...

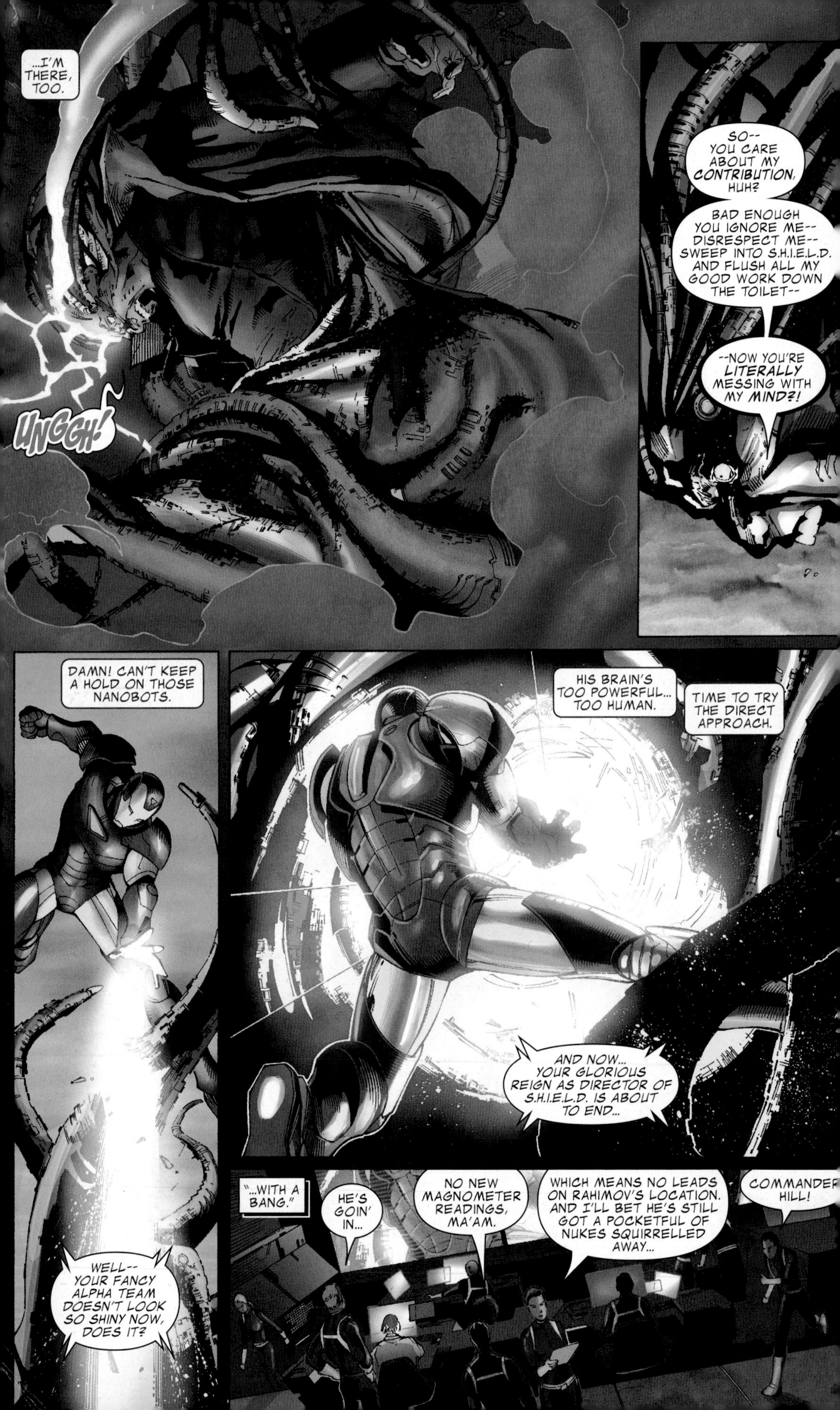

...I'M THERE, TOO.
UNGGH!
SO-- YOU CARE ABOUT MY CONTRIBUTION, HUH?
BAD ENOUGH YOU IGNORE ME-- DISRESPECT ME-- SWEEP INTO S.H.I.E.L.D. AND FLUSH ALL MY GOOD WORK DOWN THE TOILET--
--NOW YOU'RE LITERALLY MESSING WITH MY MIND?!
DAMN! CAN'T KEEP A HOLD ON THOSE NANOBOTS.
WELL-- YOUR FANCY ALPHA TEAM DOESN'T LOOK SO SHINY NOW, DOES IT?
HIS BRAIN'S TOO POWERFUL... TOO HUMAN.
TIME TO TRY THE DIRECT APPROACH.
AND NOW... YOUR GLORIOUS REIGN AS DIRECTOR OF S.H.I.E.L.D. IS ABOUT TO END...
"...WITH A BANG."
HE'S GOIN' IN...
NO NEW MAGNOMETER READINGS, MA'AM.
WHICH MEANS NO LEADS ON RAHIMOV'S LOCATION. AND I'LL BET HE'S STILL GOT A POCKETFUL OF NUKES SQUIRRELLED AWAY...
COMMANDER HILL!

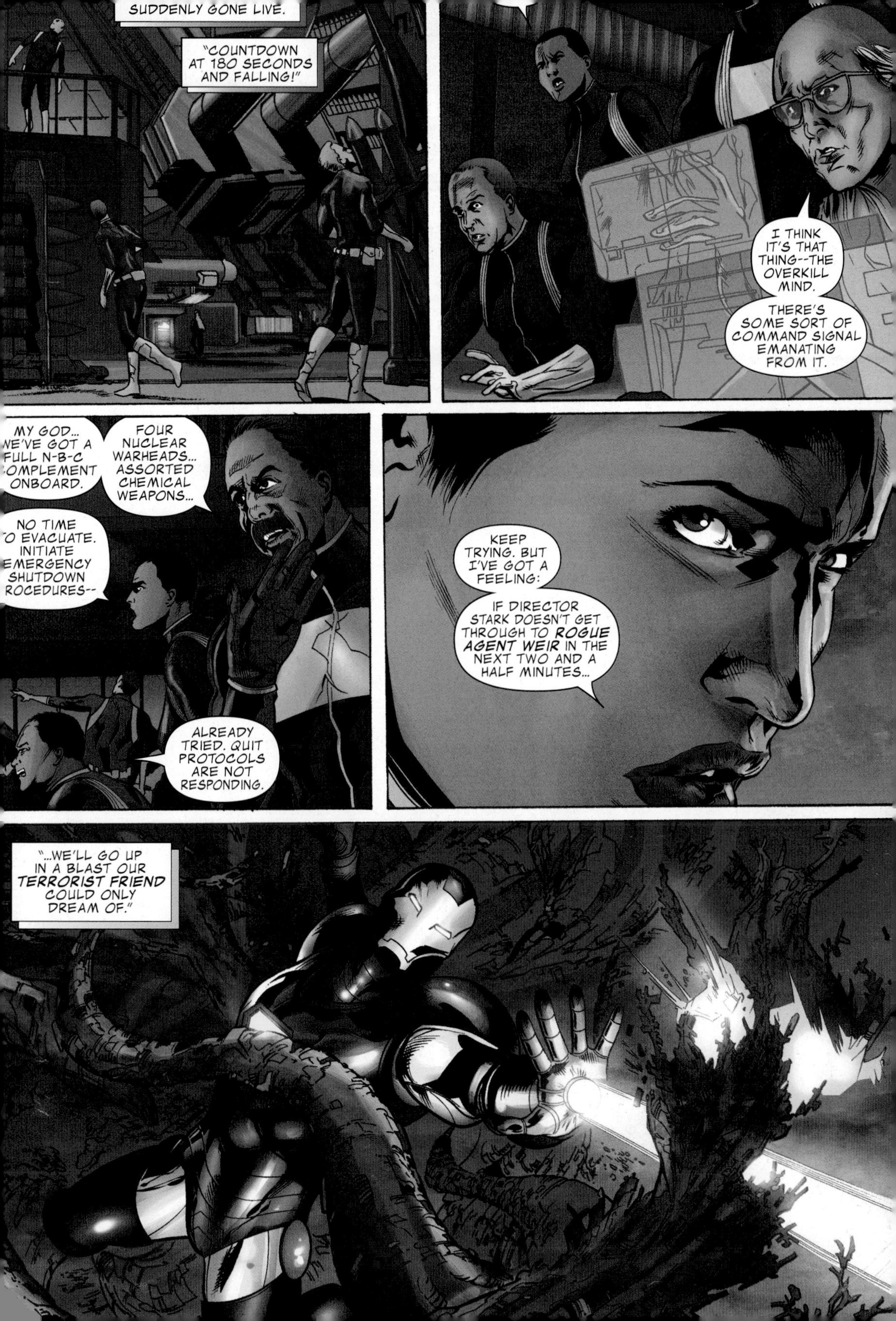
SUDDENLY GONE LIVE.
"COUNTDOWN AT 180 SECONDS AND FALLING!"
I THINK IT'S THAT THING--THE OVERKILL MIND.
THERE'S SOME SORT OF COMMAND SIGNAL EMANATING FROM IT.
MY GOD... WE'VE GOT A FULL N-B-C COMPLEMENT ONBOARD.
FOUR NUCLEAR WARHEADS... ASSORTED CHEMICAL WEAPONS...
NO TIME TO EVACUATE. INITIATE EMERGENCY SHUTDOWN PROCEDURES--
ALREADY TRIED. QUIT PROTOCOLS ARE NOT RESPONDING.
KEEP TRYING. BUT I'VE GOT A FEELING:
IF DIRECTOR STARK DOESN'T GET THROUGH TO ROGUE AGENT WEIR IN THE NEXT TWO AND A HALF MINUTES...
"...WE'LL GO UP IN A BLAST OUR TERRORIST FRIEND COULD ONLY DREAM OF."

#32

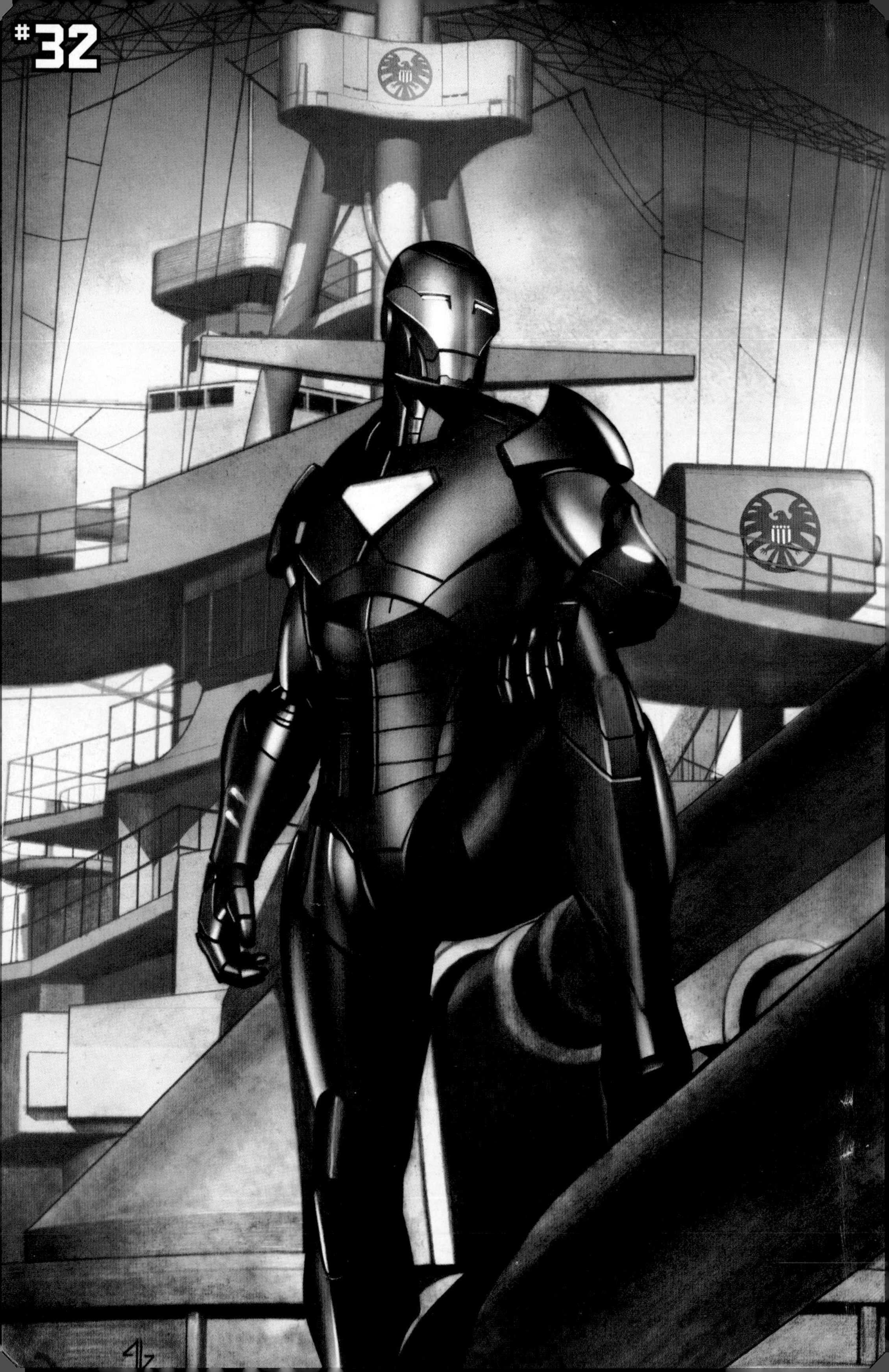

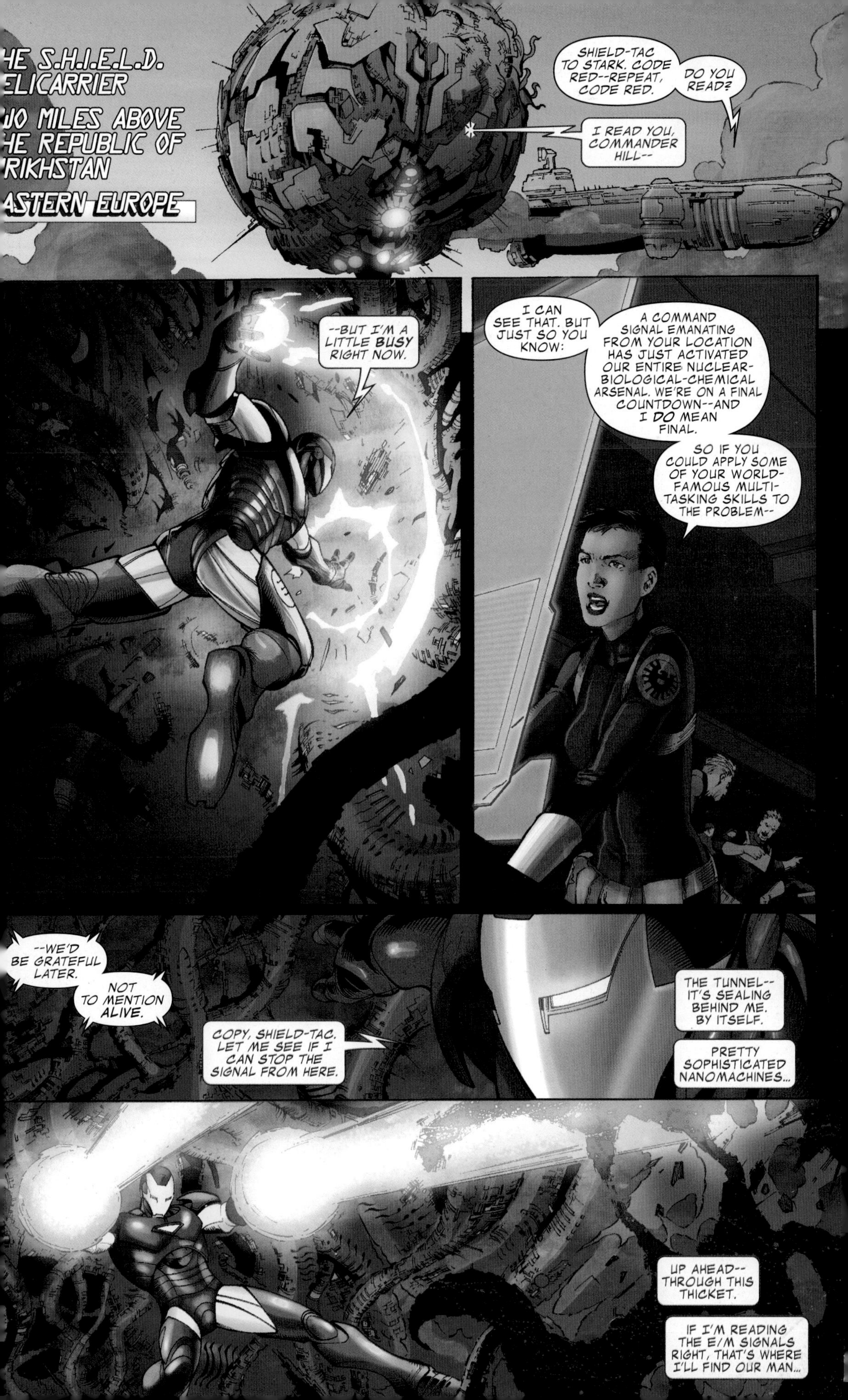
HE S.H.I.E.L.D.
ELICARRIER
JO MILES ABOVE
HE REPUBLIC OF
RIKHSTAN
ASTERN EUROPE
SHIELD-TAC TO STARK. CODE RED--REPEAT, CODE RED.
DO YOU READ?
I READ YOU, COMMANDER HILL--
--BUT I'M A LITTLE BUSY RIGHT NOW.
I CAN SEE THAT. BUT JUST SO YOU KNOW:
A COMMAND SIGNAL EMANATING FROM YOUR LOCATION HAS JUST ACTIVATED OUR ENTIRE NUCLEAR-BIOLOGICAL-CHEMICAL ARSENAL. WE'RE ON A FINAL COUNTDOWN--AND I DO MEAN FINAL.
SO IF YOU COULD APPLY SOME OF YOUR WORLD-FAMOUS MULTI-TASKING SKILLS TO THE PROBLEM--
--WE'D BE GRATEFUL LATER.
NOT TO MENTION ALIVE.
COPY, SHIELD-TAC. LET ME SEE IF I CAN STOP THE SIGNAL FROM HERE.
THE TUNNEL-- IT'S SEALING BEHIND ME. BY ITSELF.
PRETTY SOPHISTICATED NANOMACHINES...
UP AHEAD-- THROUGH THIS THICKET.
IF I'M READING THE E/M SIGNALS RIGHT, THAT'S WHERE I'LL FIND OUR MAN...

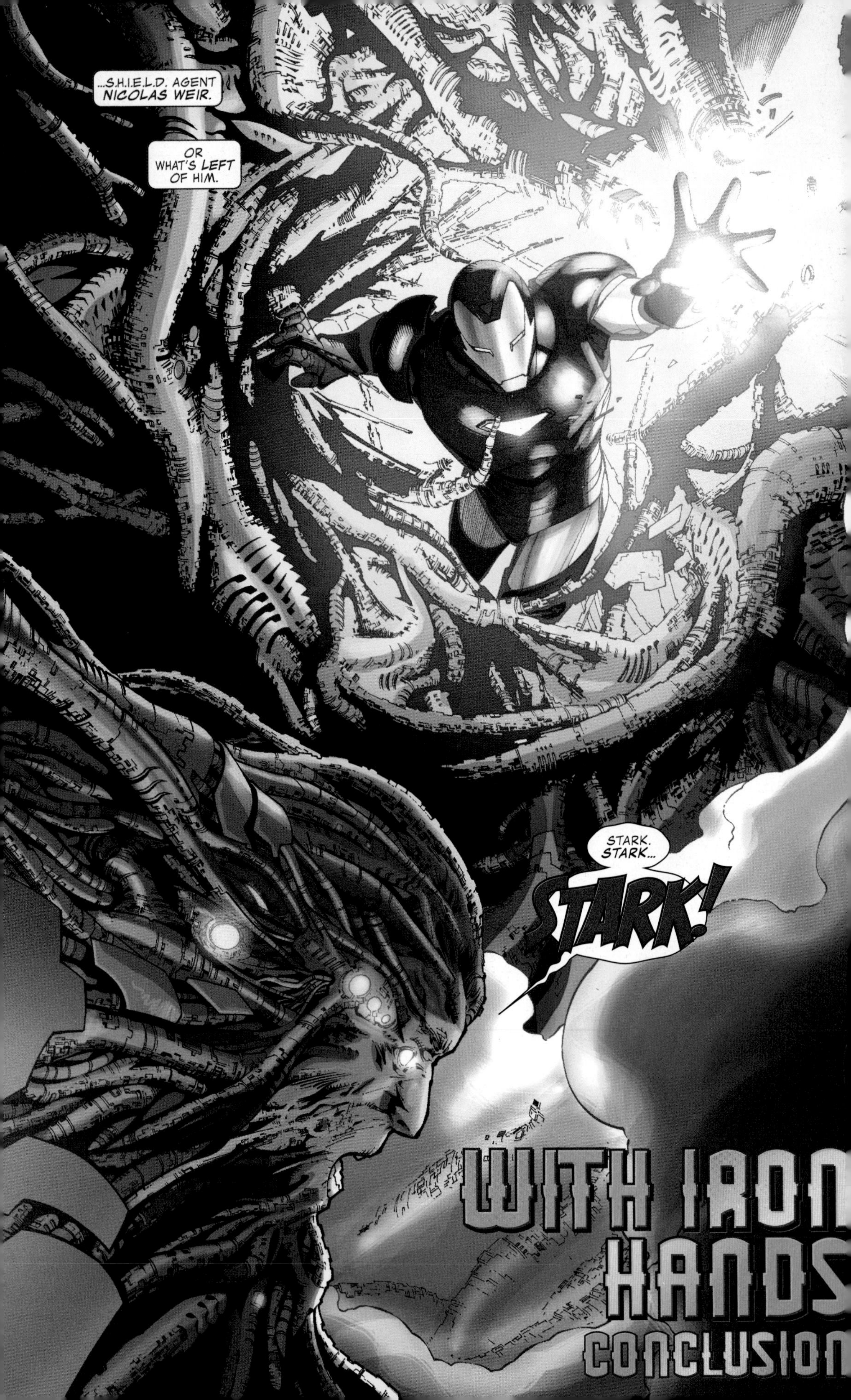

...S.H.I.E.L.D. AGENT NICOLAS WEIR.
OR WHAT'S LEFT OF HIM.
STARK. STARK...
STARK!
WITH IRON HANDS
CONCLUSION

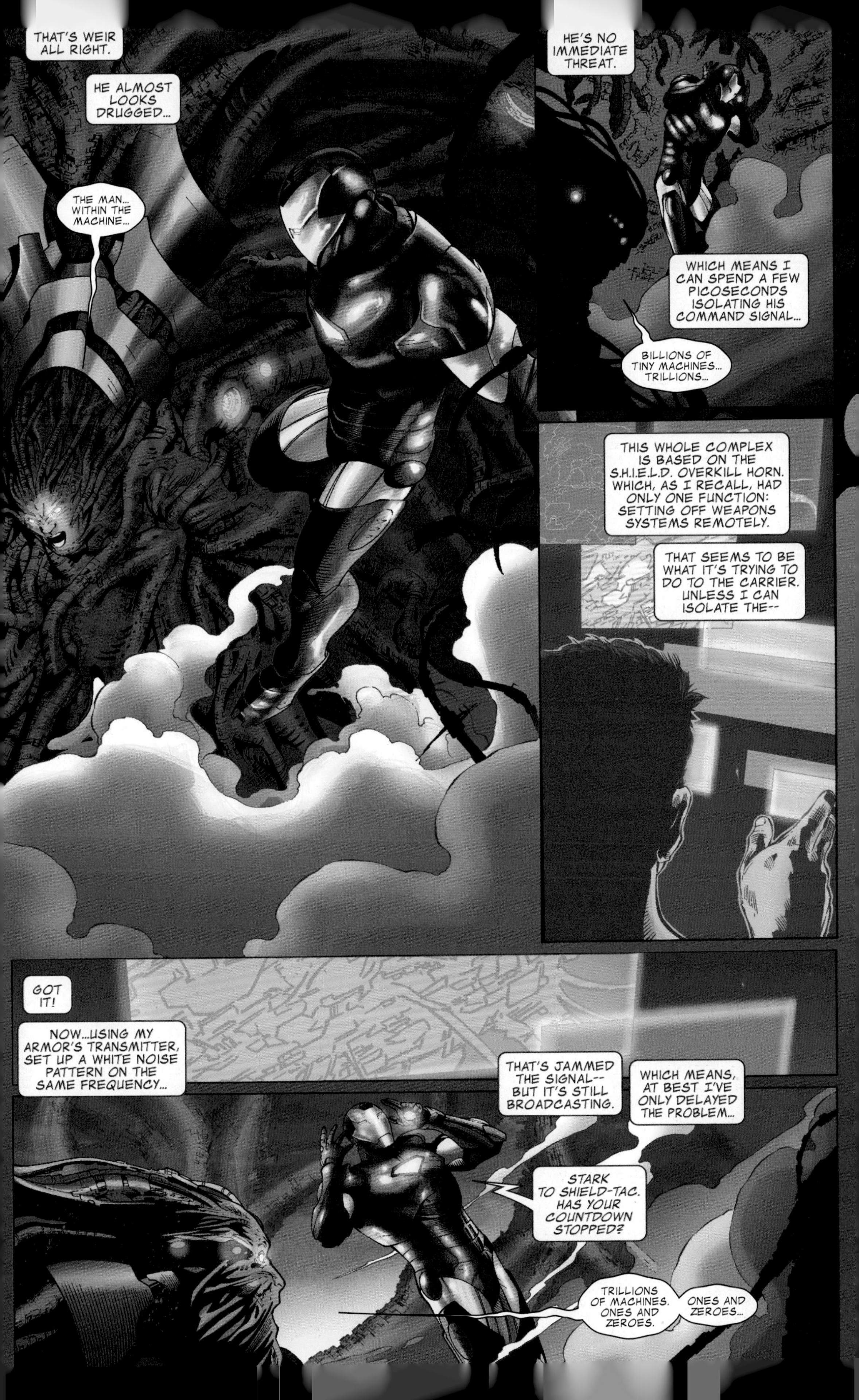
THAT'S WEIR ALL RIGHT.
HE ALMOST LOOKS DRUGGED...
THE MAN... WITHIN THE MACHINE...
HE'S NO IMMEDIATE THREAT.
WHICH MEANS I CAN SPEND A FEW PICOSECONDS ISOLATING HIS COMMAND SIGNAL...
BILLIONS OF TINY MACHINES... TRILLIONS...
THIS WHOLE COMPLEX IS BASED ON THE S.H.I.E.L.D. OVERKILL HORN. WHICH, AS I RECALL, HAD ONLY ONE FUNCTION: SETTING OFF WEAPONS SYSTEMS REMOTELY.
THAT SEEMS TO BE WHAT IT'S TRYING TO DO TO THE CARRIER. UNLESS I CAN ISOLATE THE--
GOT IT!
NOW...USING MY ARMOR'S TRANSMITTER, SET UP A WHITE NOISE PATTERN ON THE SAME FREQUENCY...
THAT'S JAMMED THE SIGNAL-- BUT IT'S STILL BROADCASTING.
WHICH MEANS, AT BEST I'VE ONLY DELAYED THE PROBLEM...
STARK TO SHIELD-TAC. HAS YOUR COUNTDOWN STOPPED?
TRILLIONS OF MACHINES. ONES AND ZEROES.
ONES AND ZEROES...

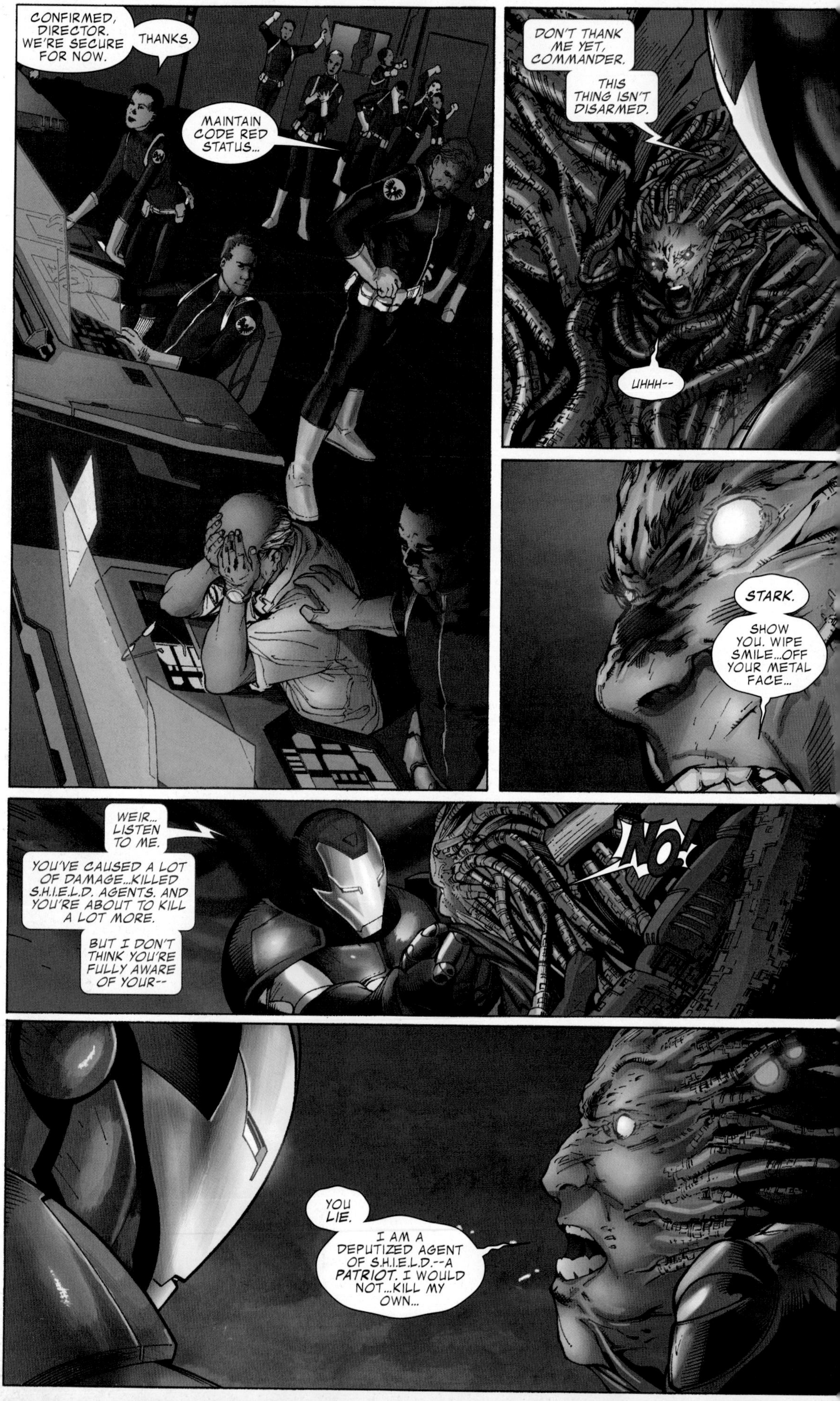
CONFIRMED, DIRECTOR. WE'RE SECURE FOR NOW.
THANKS.
MAINTAIN CODE RED STATUS...
DON'T THANK ME YET, COMMANDER.
THIS THING ISN'T DISARMED.
UHHH--
STARK.
SHOW YOU. WIPE SMILE...OFF YOUR METAL FACE...
WEIR... LISTEN TO ME.
YOU'VE CAUSED A LOT OF DAMAGE...KILLED S.H.I.E.L.D. AGENTS. AND YOU'RE ABOUT TO KILL A LOT MORE.
BUT I DON'T THINK YOU'RE FULLY AWARE OF YOUR--
NO!
YOU LIE.
I AM A DEPUTIZED AGENT OF S.H.I.E.L.D.--A PATRIOT. I WOULD NOT...KILL MY OWN...

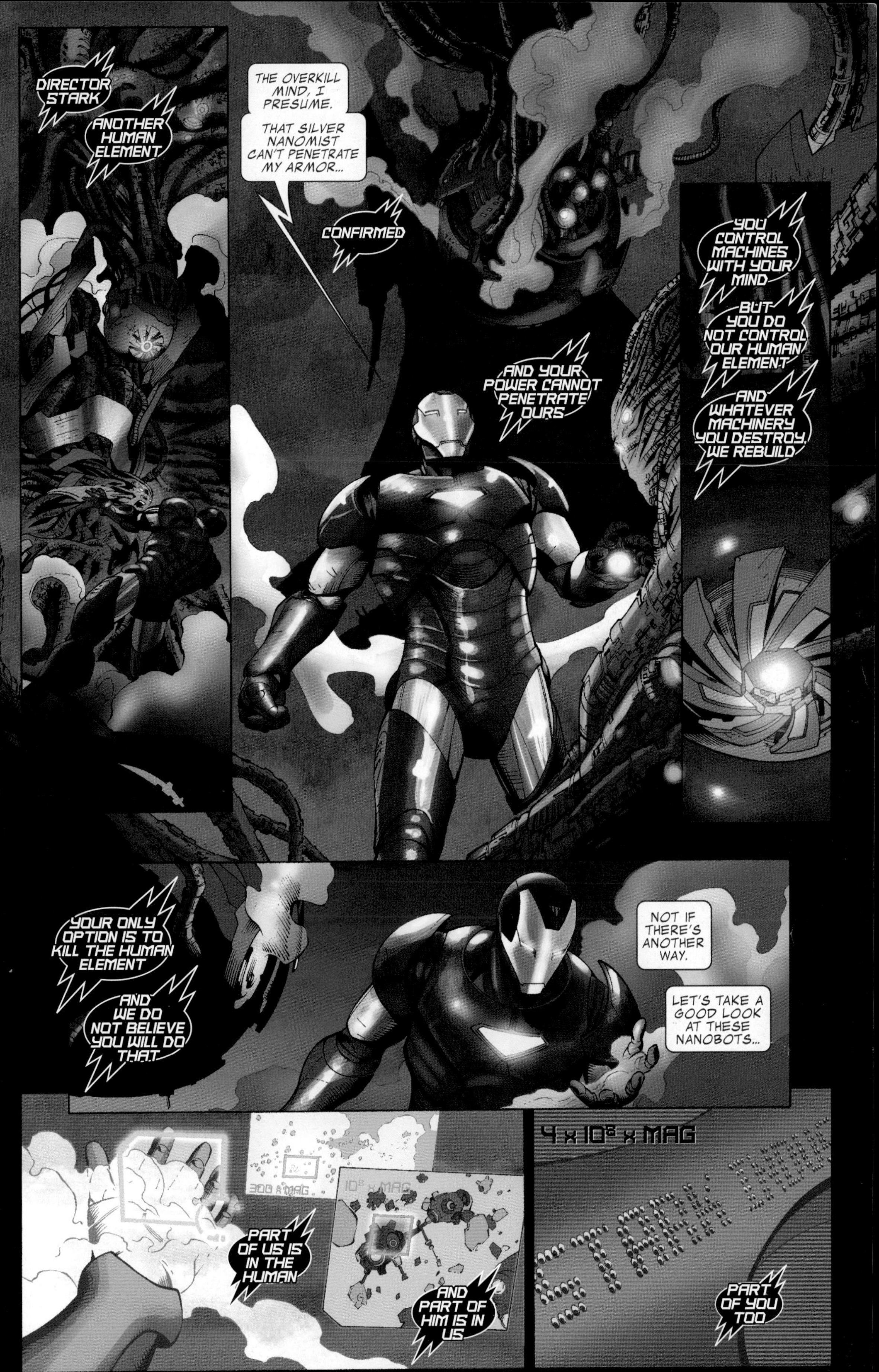
DIRECTOR STARK
ANOTHER HUMAN ELEMENT
THE OVERKILL MIND, I PRESUME.
THAT SILVER NANOMIST CAN'T PENETRATE MY ARMOR...
CONFIRMED
YOU CONTROL MACHINES WITH YOUR MIND
BUT YOU DO NOT CONTROL OUR HUMAN ELEMENT
AND YOUR POWER CANNOT PENETRATE OURS
AND WHATEVER MACHINERY YOU DESTROY, WE REBUILD
YOUR ONLY OPTION IS TO KILL THE HUMAN ELEMENT
AND WE DO NOT BELIEVE YOU WILL DO THAT
NOT IF THERE'S ANOTHER WAY.
LET'S TAKE A GOOD LOOK AT THESE NANOBOTS...
300 x MAG
10⁸ x MAG
PART OF US IS IN THE HUMAN
AND PART OF HIM IS IN US
4 x 10⁸ x MAG
PART OF YOU TOO

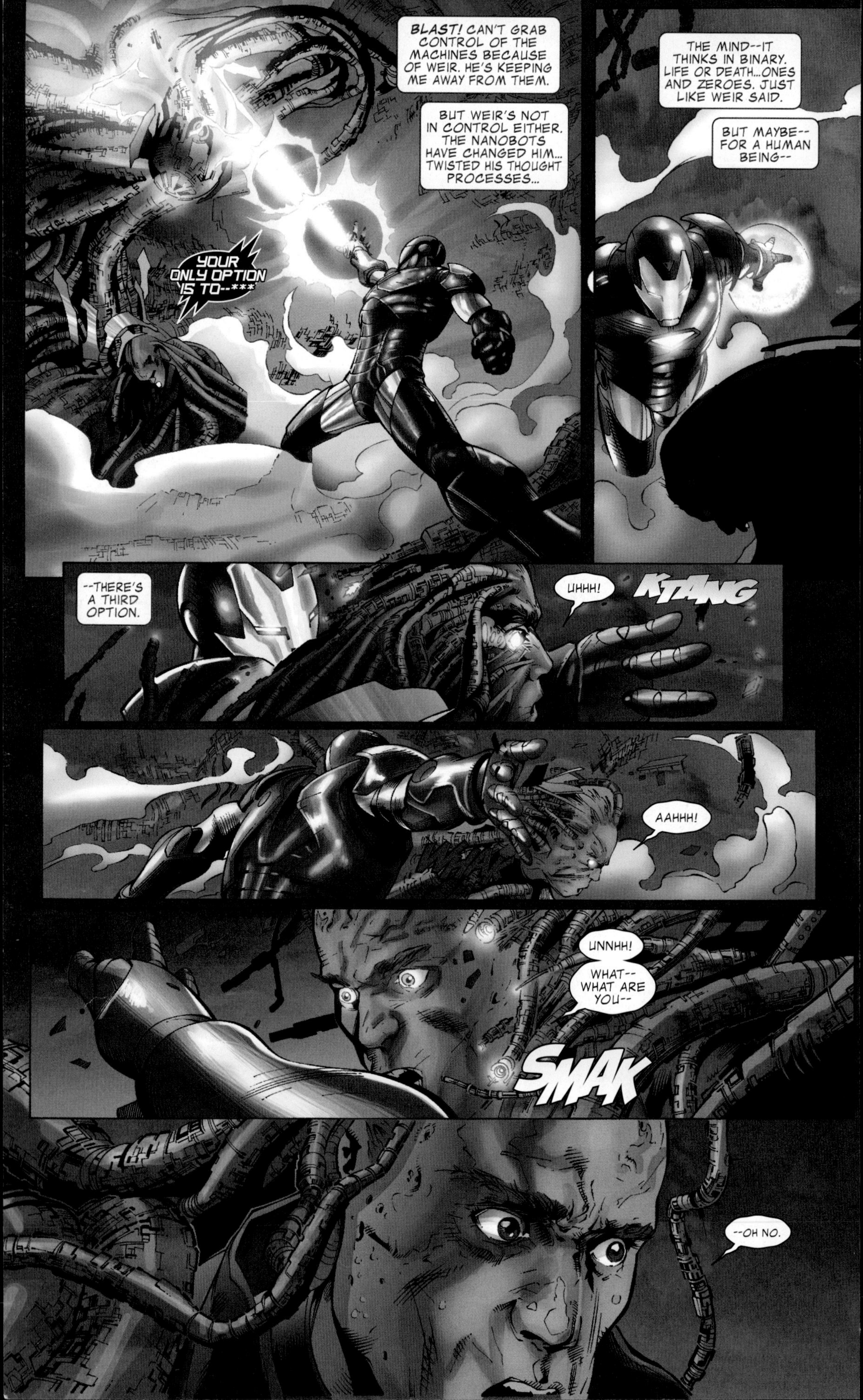
BLAST! CAN'T GRAB CONTROL OF THE MACHINES BECAUSE OF WEIR. HE'S KEEPING ME AWAY FROM THEM.
BUT WEIR'S NOT IN CONTROL EITHER. THE NANOBOTS HAVE CHANGED HIM... TWISTED HIS THOUGHT PROCESSES...
YOUR ONLY OPTION IS TO--***
THE MIND--IT THINKS IN BINARY. LIFE OR DEATH...ONES AND ZEROES. JUST LIKE WEIR SAID.
BUT MAYBE-- FOR A HUMAN BEING--
--THERE'S A THIRD OPTION.
UHHH!
KTANG
AAHHH!
UNNHH!
WHAT-- WHAT ARE YOU--
SMAK
--OH NO.

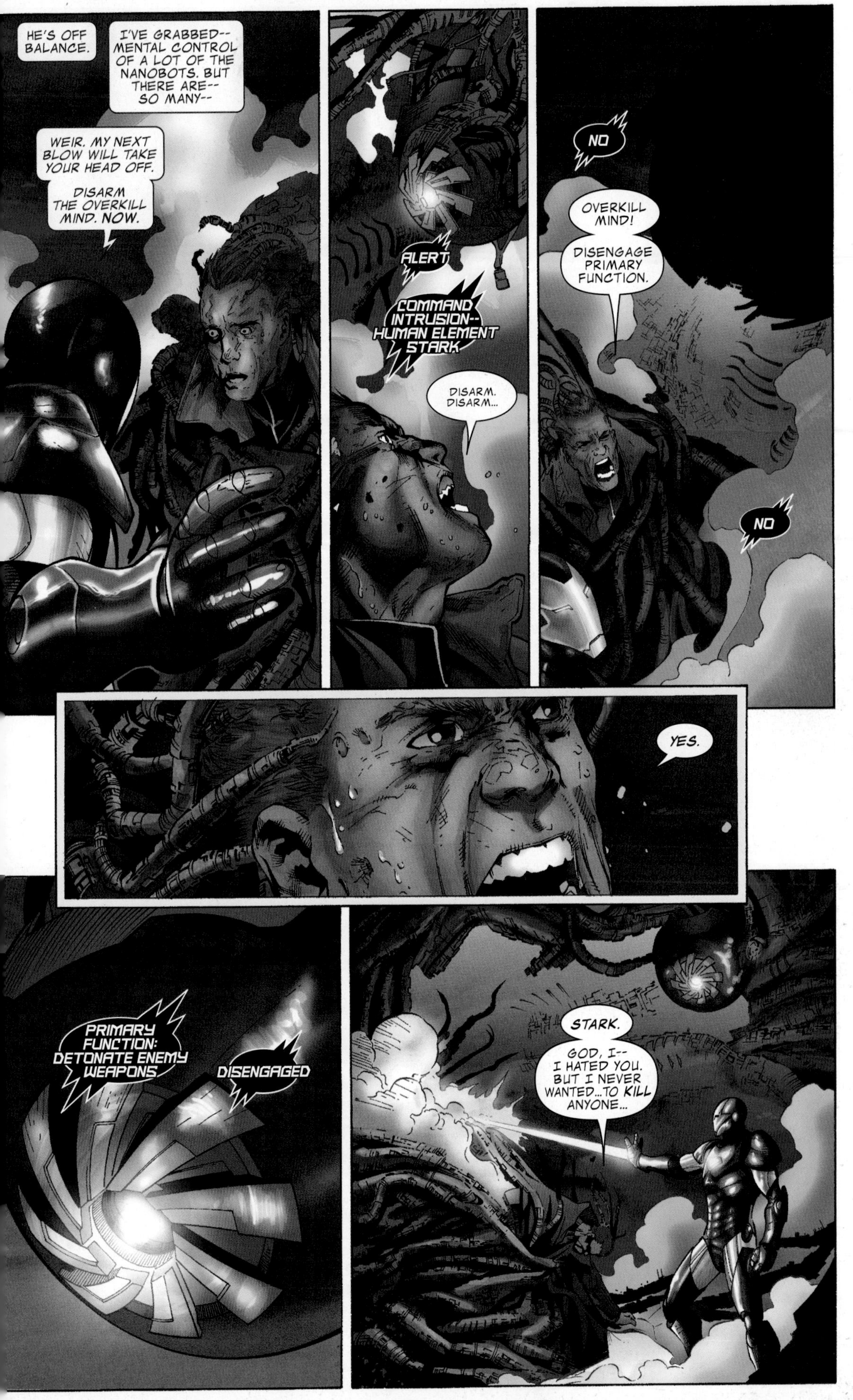
HE'S OFF BALANCE.
I'VE GRABBED-- MENTAL CONTROL OF A LOT OF THE NANOBOTS. BUT THERE ARE-- SO MANY--
WEIR. MY NEXT BLOW WILL TAKE YOUR HEAD OFF.
DISARM THE OVERKILL MIND. NOW.
ALERT
COMMAND INTRUSION-- HUMAN ELEMENT STARK
DISARM. DISARM...
NO
OVERKILL MIND!
DISENGAGE PRIMARY FUNCTION.
NO
YES.
PRIMARY FUNCTION: DETONATE ENEMY WEAPONS
DISENGAGED
STARK.
GOD, I-- I HATED YOU. BUT I NEVER WANTED...TO KILL ANYONE...

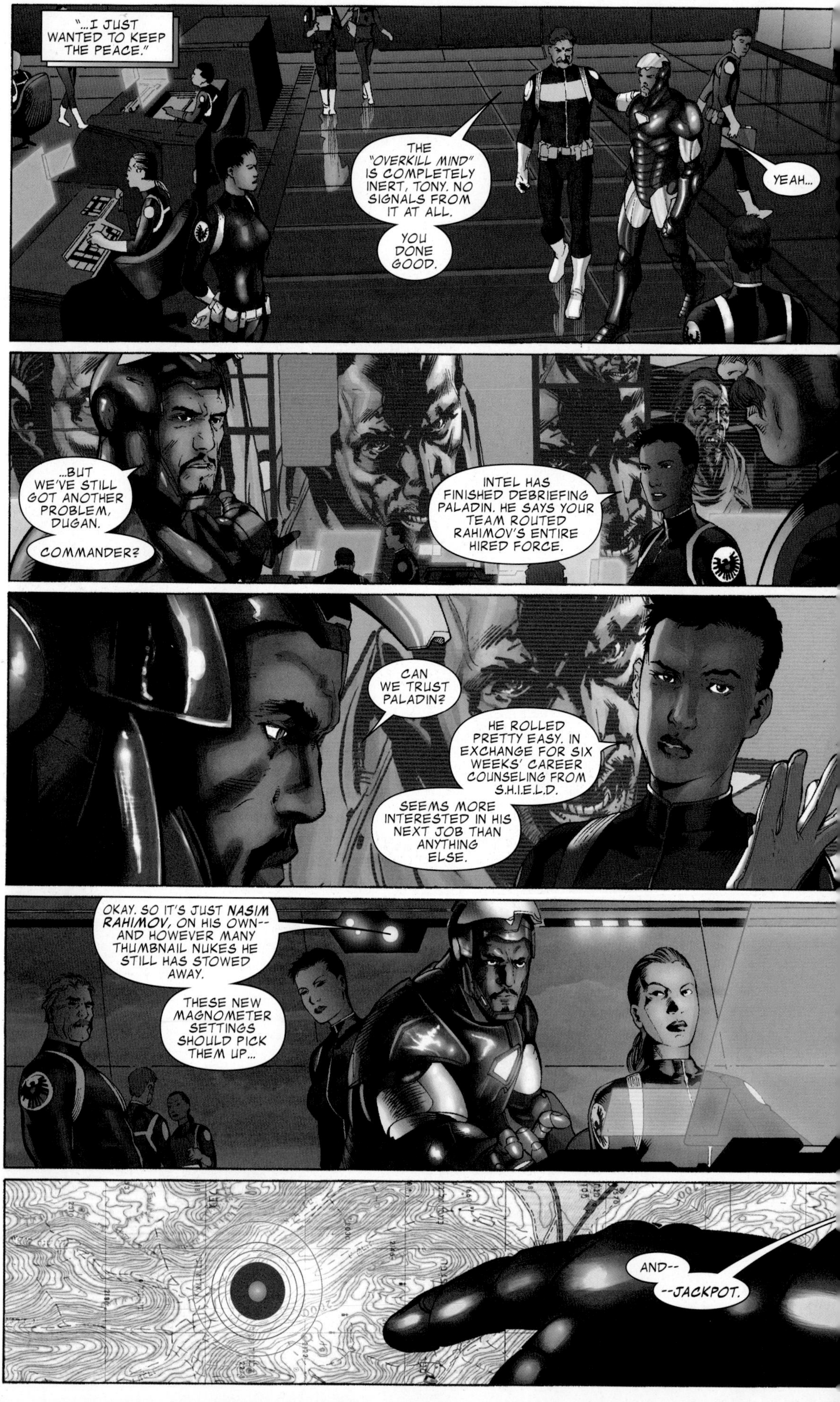
"...I JUST WANTED TO KEEP THE PEACE."
THE "OVERKILL MIND" IS COMPLETELY INERT, TONY. NO SIGNALS FROM IT AT ALL.
YOU DONE GOOD.
YEAH...
...BUT WE'VE STILL GOT ANOTHER PROBLEM, DUGAN.
COMMANDER?
INTEL HAS FINISHED DEBRIEFING PALADIN. HE SAYS YOUR TEAM ROUTED RAHIMOV'S ENTIRE HIRED FORCE.
CAN WE TRUST PALADIN?
HE ROLLED PRETTY EASY. IN EXCHANGE FOR SIX WEEKS' CAREER COUNSELING FROM S.H.I.E.L.D.
SEEMS MORE INTERESTED IN HIS NEXT JOB THAN ANYTHING ELSE.
OKAY. SO IT'S JUST NASIM RAHIMOV, ON HIS OWN-- AND HOWEVER MANY THUMBNAIL NUKES HE STILL HAS STOWED AWAY.
THESE NEW MAGNOMETER SETTINGS SHOULD PICK THEM UP...
AND--
--JACKPOT.

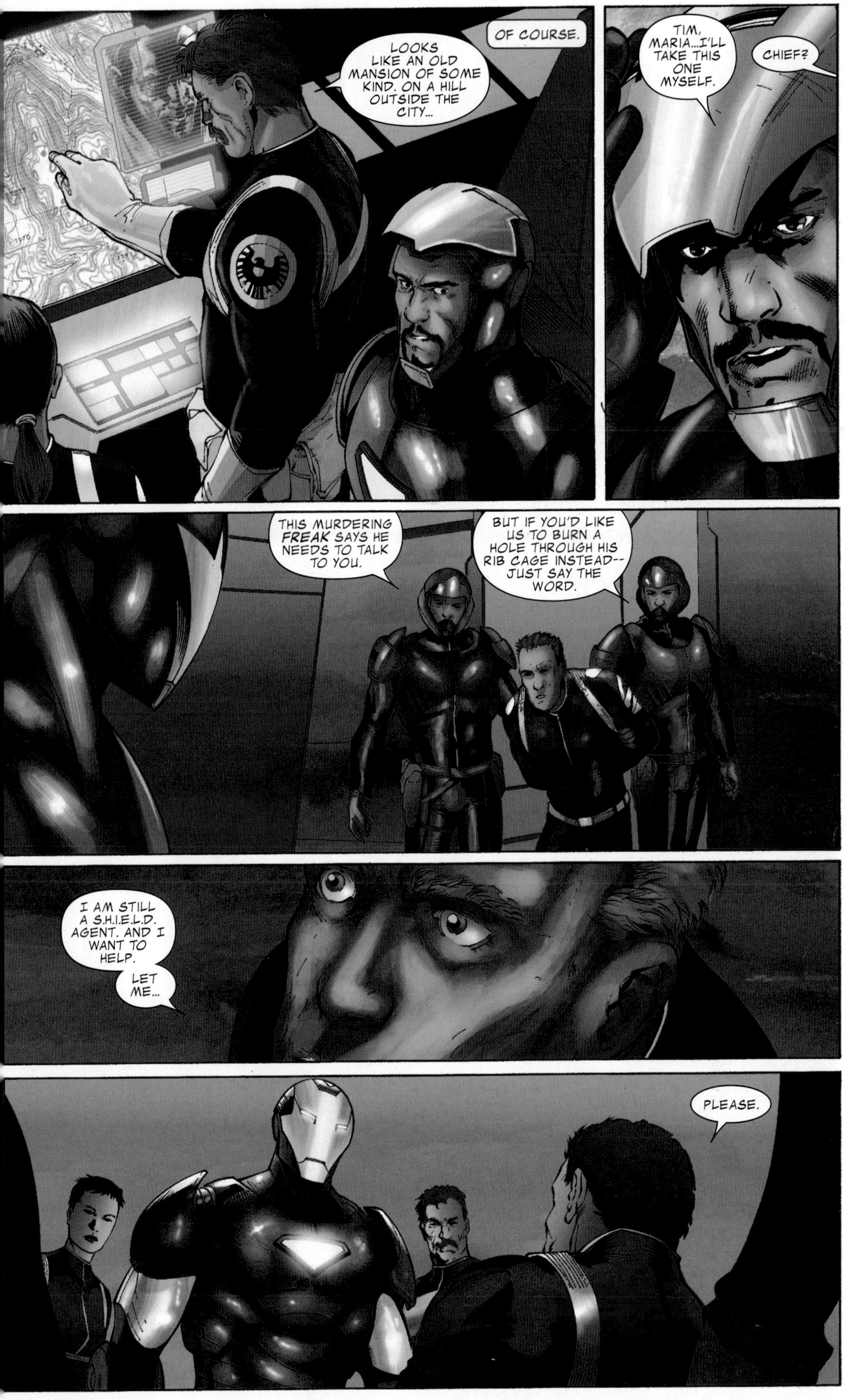
LOOKS LIKE AN OLD MANSION OF SOME KIND. ON A HILL OUTSIDE THE CITY...
OF COURSE.
TIM, MARIA...I'LL TAKE THIS ONE MYSELF.
CHIEF?
THIS MURDERING FREAK SAYS HE NEEDS TO TALK TO YOU.
BUT IF YOU'D LIKE US TO BURN A HOLE THROUGH HIS RIB CAGE INSTEAD-- JUST SAY THE WORD.
I AM STILL A S.H.I.E.L.D. AGENT. AND I WANT TO HELP.
LET ME...
PLEASE.

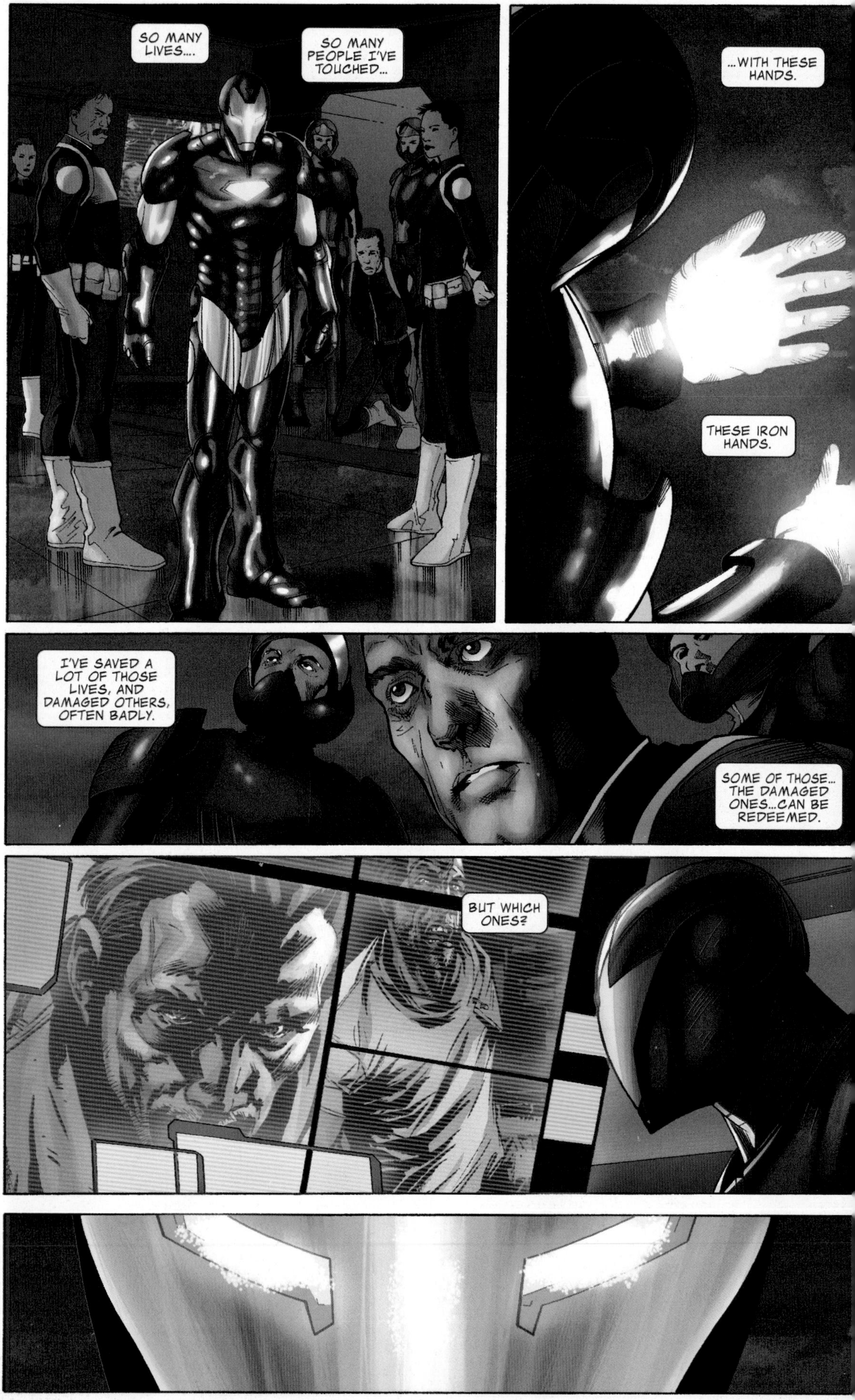
SO MANY LIVES....
SO MANY PEOPLE I'VE TOUCHED...
...WITH THESE HANDS.
THESE IRON HANDS.
I'VE SAVED A LOT OF THOSE LIVES, AND DAMAGED OTHERS, OFTEN BADLY.
SOME OF THOSE... THE DAMAGED ONES...CAN BE REDEEMED.
BUT WHICH ONES?

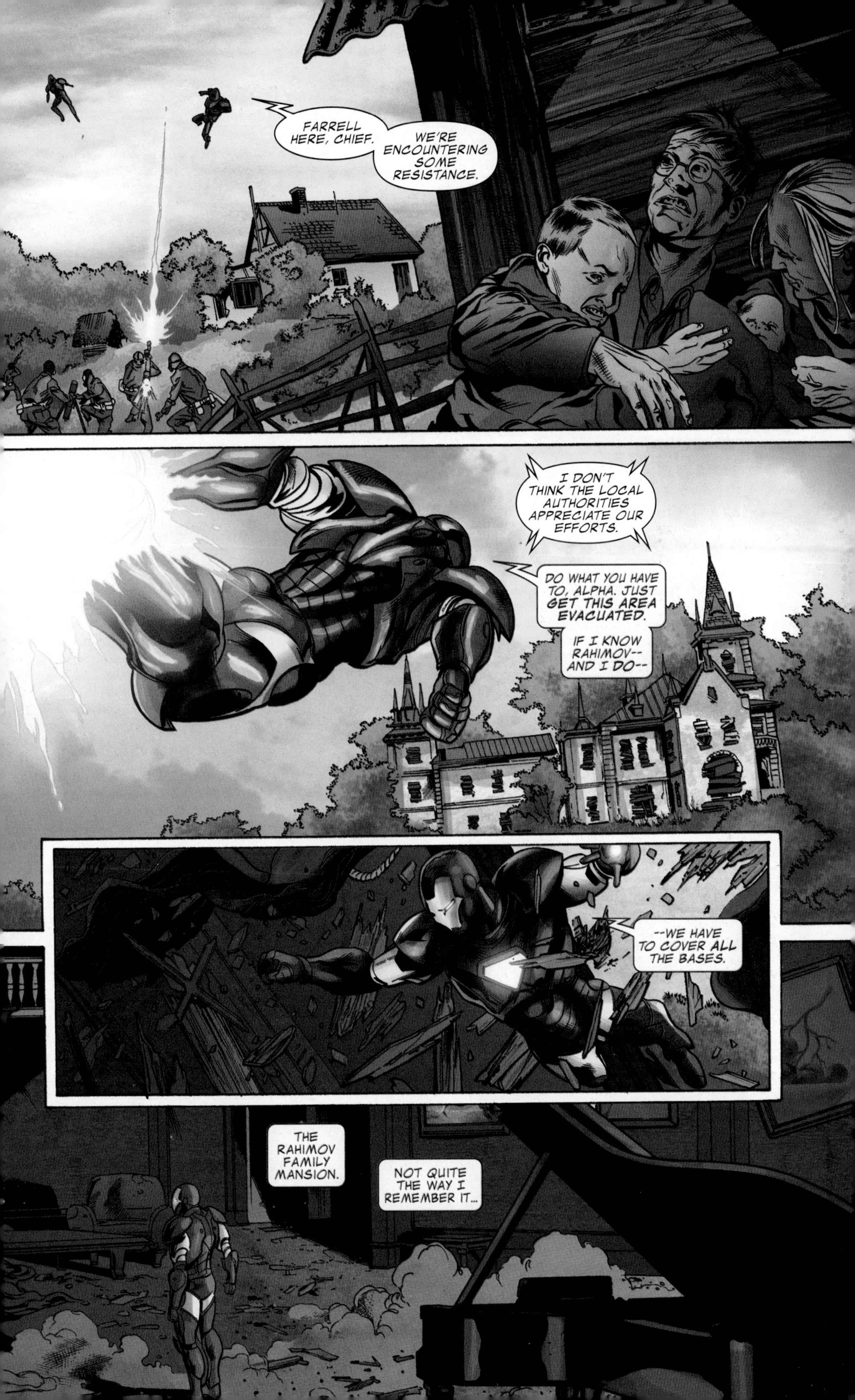
FARRELL HERE, CHIEF.
WE'RE ENCOUNTERING SOME RESISTANCE.
I DON'T THINK THE LOCAL AUTHORITIES APPRECIATE OUR EFFORTS.
DO WHAT YOU HAVE TO, ALPHA. JUST GET THIS AREA EVACUATED.
IF I KNOW RAHIMOV-- AND I DO--
--WE HAVE TO COVER ALL THE BASES.
THE RAHIMOV FAMILY MANSION.
NOT QUITE THE WAY I REMEMBER IT...

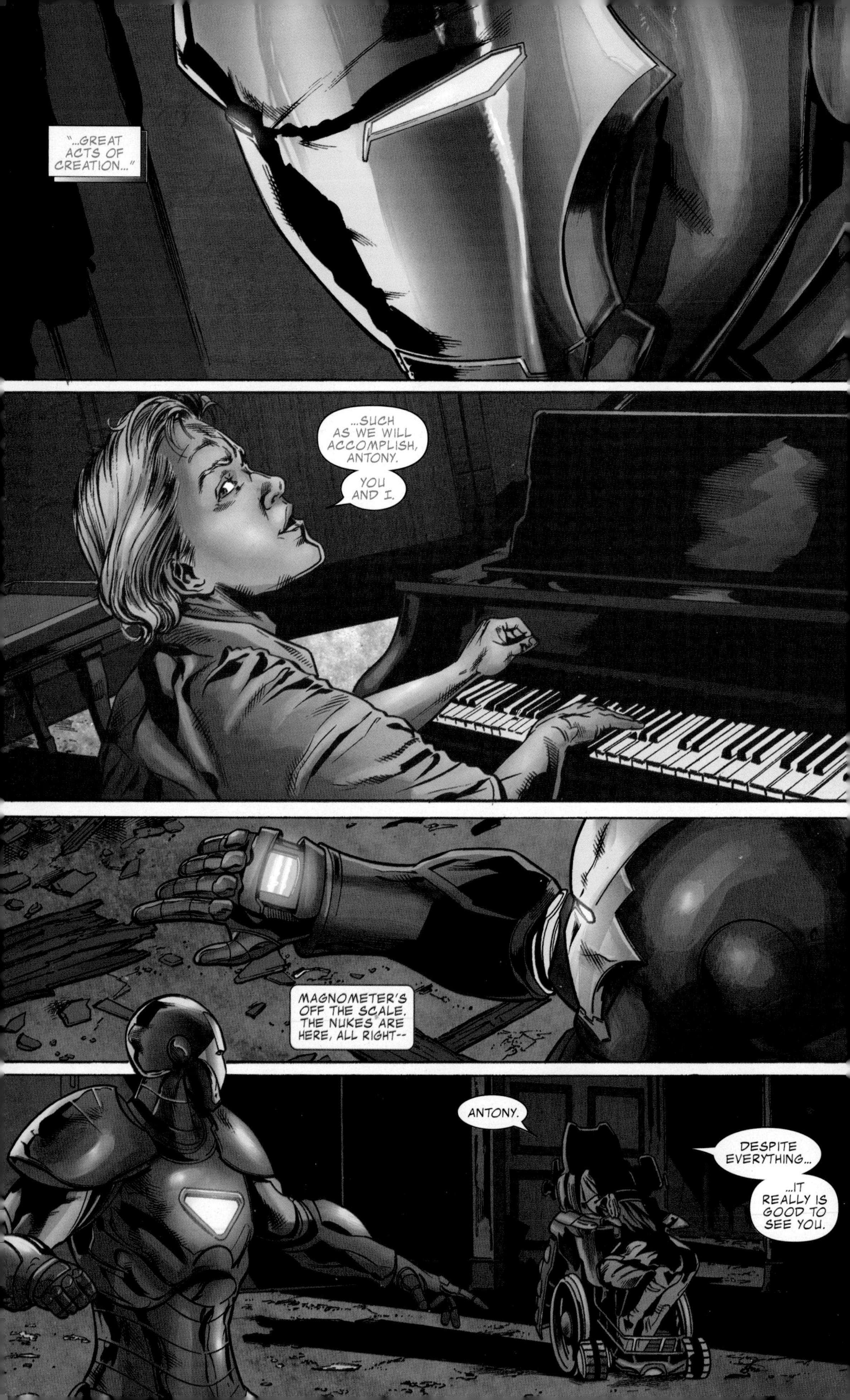
"...GREAT ACTS OF CREATION..."
...SUCH AS WE WILL ACCOMPLISH, ANTONY.
YOU AND I.
MAGNOMETER'S OFF THE SCALE. THE NUKES ARE HERE, ALL RIGHT--
ANTONY.
DESPITE EVERYTHING...
...IT REALLY IS GOOD TO SEE YOU.

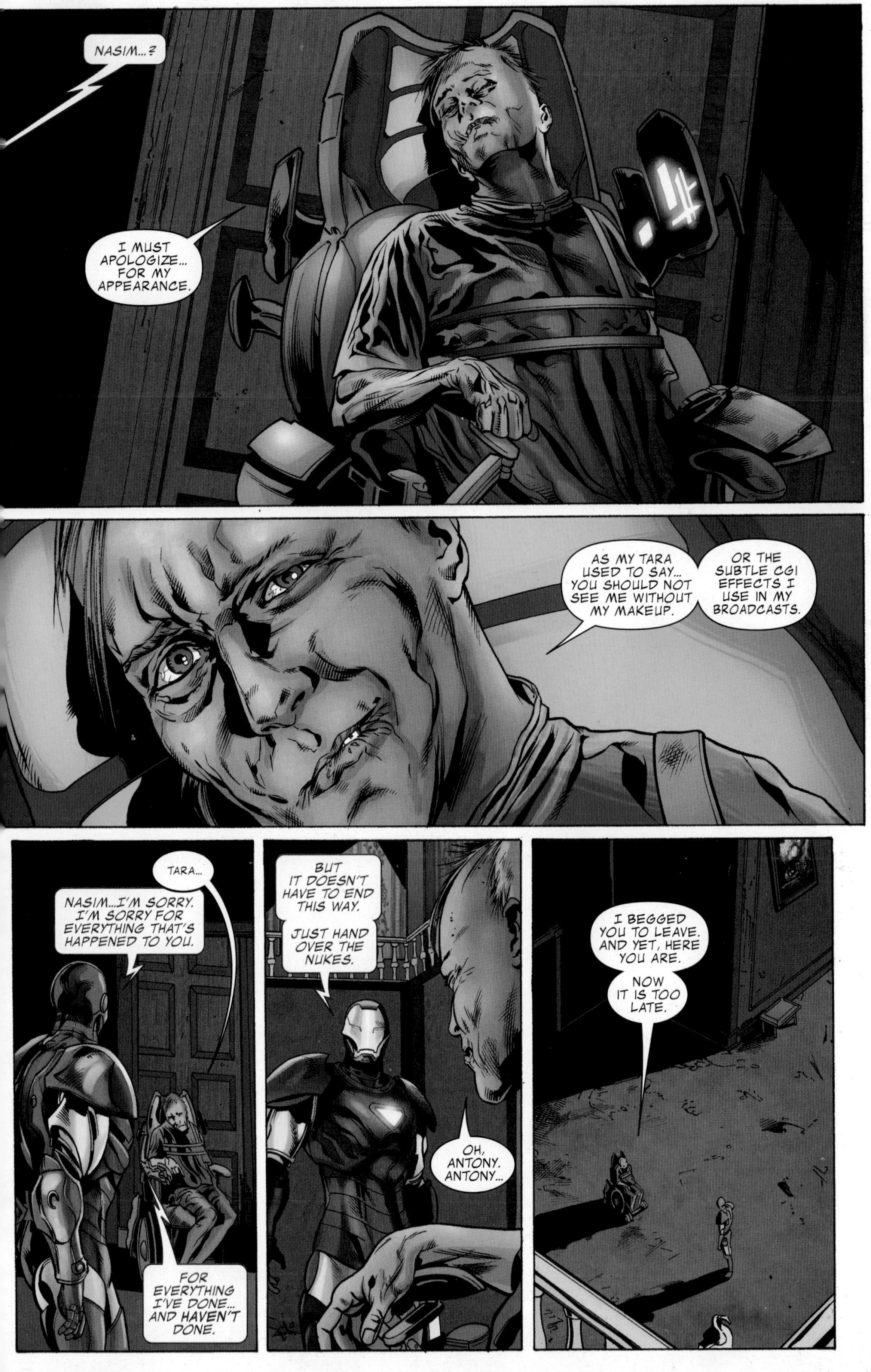
NASIM...?
I MUST APOLOGIZE... FOR MY APPEARANCE.
AS MY TARA USED TO SAY... YOU SHOULD NOT SEE ME WITHOUT MY MAKEUP.
OR THE SUBTLE CGI EFFECTS I USE IN MY BROADCASTS.
TARA...
NASIM...I'M SORRY. I'M SORRY FOR EVERYTHING THAT'S HAPPENED TO YOU.
FOR EVERYTHING I'VE DONE... AND HAVEN'T DONE.
BUT IT DOESN'T HAVE TO END THIS WAY.
JUST HAND OVER THE NUKES.
OH, ANTONY. ANTONY...
I BEGGED YOU TO LEAVE. AND YET, HERE YOU ARE.
NOW IT IS TOO LATE.

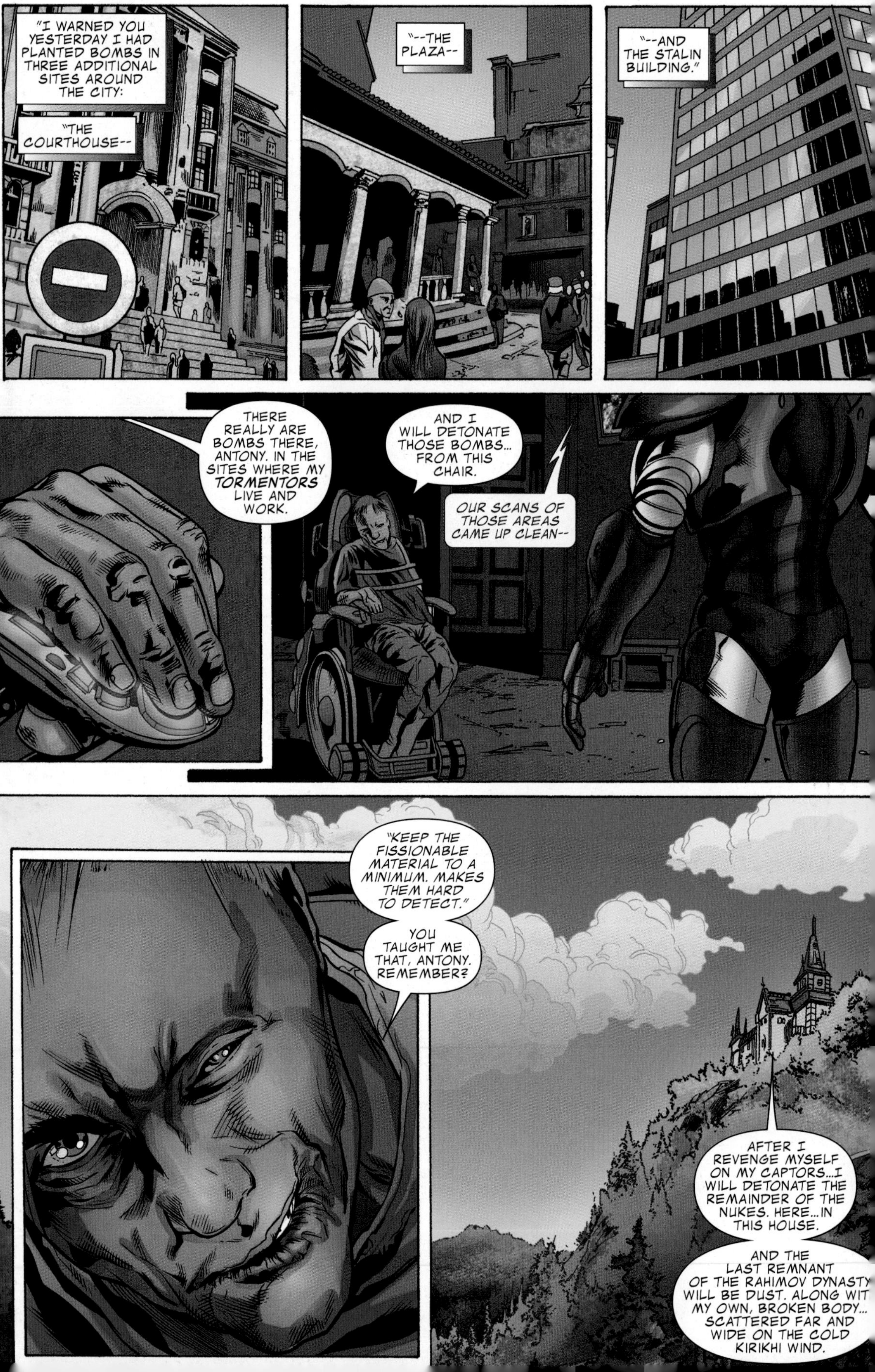
"I WARNED YOU YESTERDAY I HAD PLANTED BOMBS IN THREE ADDITIONAL SITES AROUND THE CITY:
"THE COURTHOUSE--
"--THE PLAZA--
"--AND THE STALIN BUILDING."
THERE REALLY ARE BOMBS THERE, ANTONY. IN THE SITES WHERE MY *TORMENTORS* LIVE AND WORK.
AND I WILL DETONATE THOSE BOMBS... FROM THIS CHAIR.
OUR SCANS OF THOSE AREAS CAME UP CLEAN--
"KEEP THE FISSIONABLE MATERIAL TO A MINIMUM. MAKES THEM HARD TO DETECT."
YOU TAUGHT ME THAT, ANTONY. REMEMBER?
AFTER I REVENGE MYSELF ON MY CAPTORS...I WILL DETONATE THE REMAINDER OF THE NUKES. HERE...IN THIS HOUSE.
AND THE LAST REMNANT OF THE RAHIMOV DYNASTY WILL BE DUST. ALONG WIT MY OWN, BROKEN BODY... SCATTERED FAR AND WIDE ON THE COLD KIRIKHI WIND.

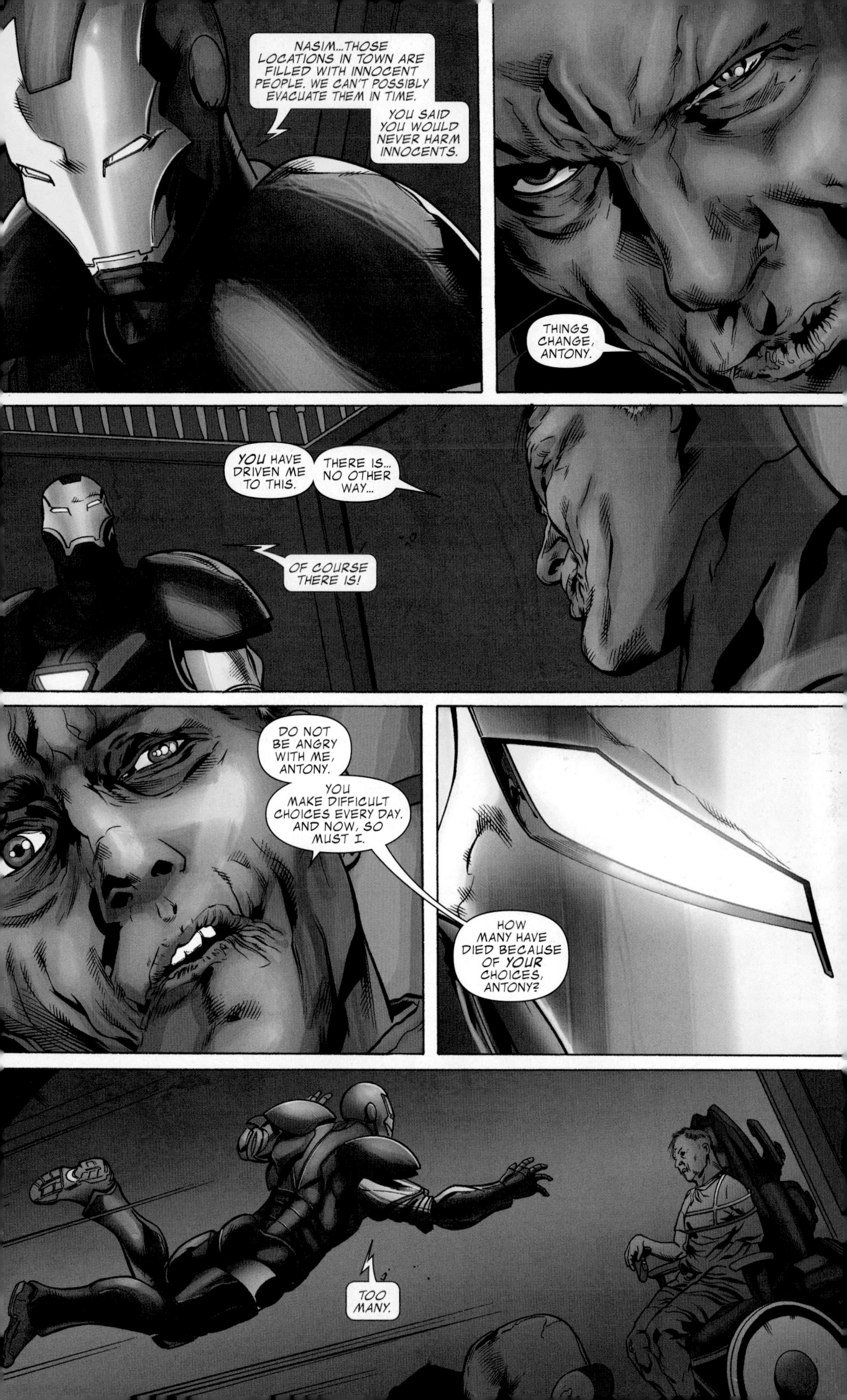
NASIM...THOSE LOCATIONS IN TOWN ARE FILLED WITH INNOCENT PEOPLE. WE CAN'T POSSIBLY EVACUATE THEM IN TIME.
YOU SAID YOU WOULD NEVER HARM INNOCENTS.
THINGS CHANGE, ANTONY.
YOU HAVE DRIVEN ME TO THIS.
THERE IS... NO OTHER WAY...
OF COURSE THERE IS!
DO NOT BE ANGRY WITH ME, ANTONY.
YOU MAKE DIFFICULT CHOICES EVERY DAY. AND NOW, SO MUST I.
HOW MANY HAVE DIED BECAUSE OF YOUR CHOICES, ANTONY?
TOO MANY.

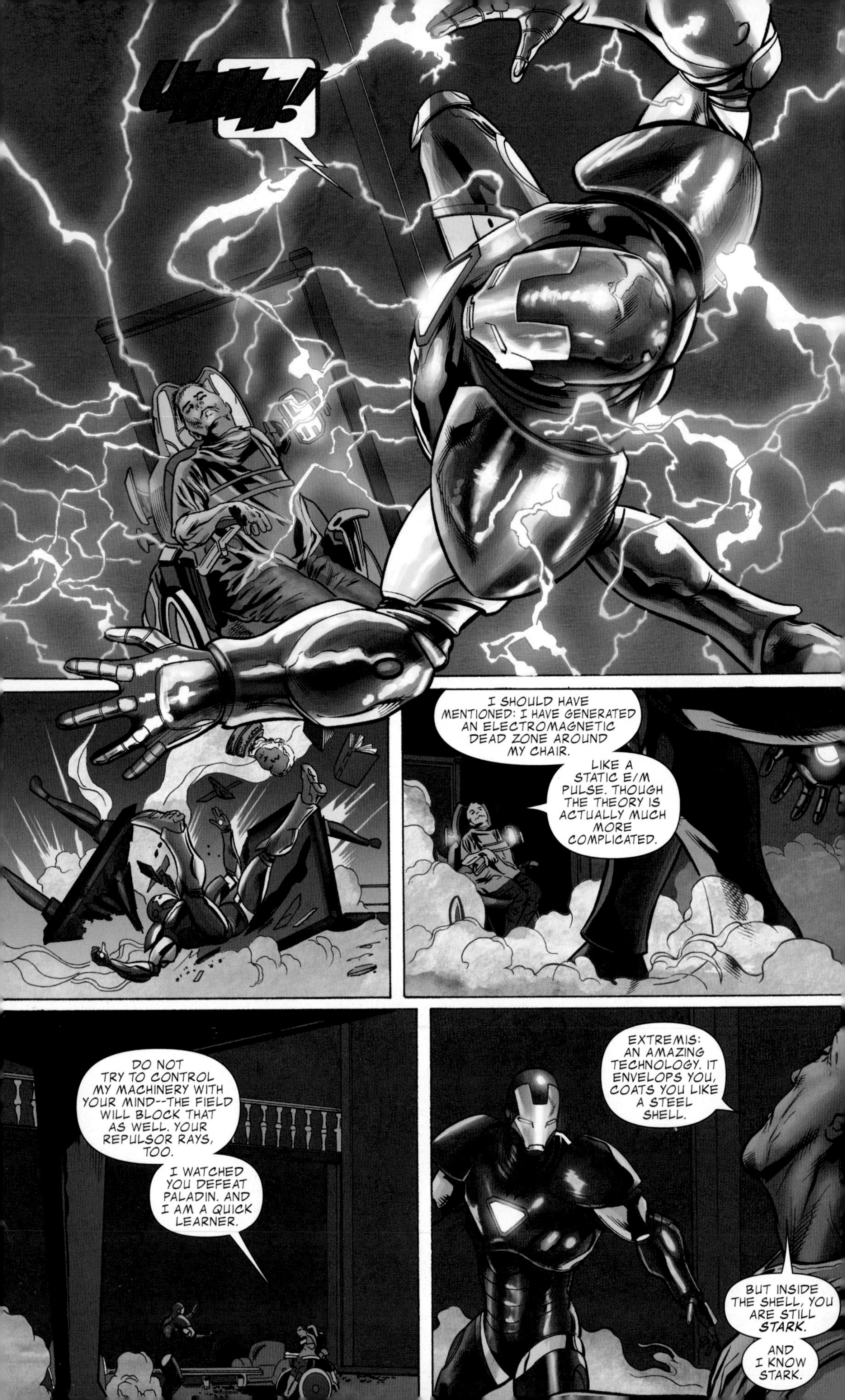
UNNH!
I SHOULD HAVE MENTIONED: I HAVE GENERATED AN ELECTROMAGNETIC DEAD ZONE AROUND MY CHAIR.
LIKE A STATIC E/M PULSE. THOUGH THE THEORY IS ACTUALLY MUCH MORE COMPLICATED.
DO NOT TRY TO CONTROL MY MACHINERY WITH YOUR MIND--THE FIELD WILL BLOCK THAT AS WELL. YOUR REPULSOR RAYS, TOO.
I WATCHED YOU DEFEAT PALADIN. AND I AM A QUICK LEARNER.
EXTREMIS: AN AMAZING TECHNOLOGY. IT ENVELOPS YOU, COATS YOU LIKE A STEEL SHELL.
BUT INSIDE THE SHELL, YOU ARE STILL *STARK.*
AND I KNOW STARK.

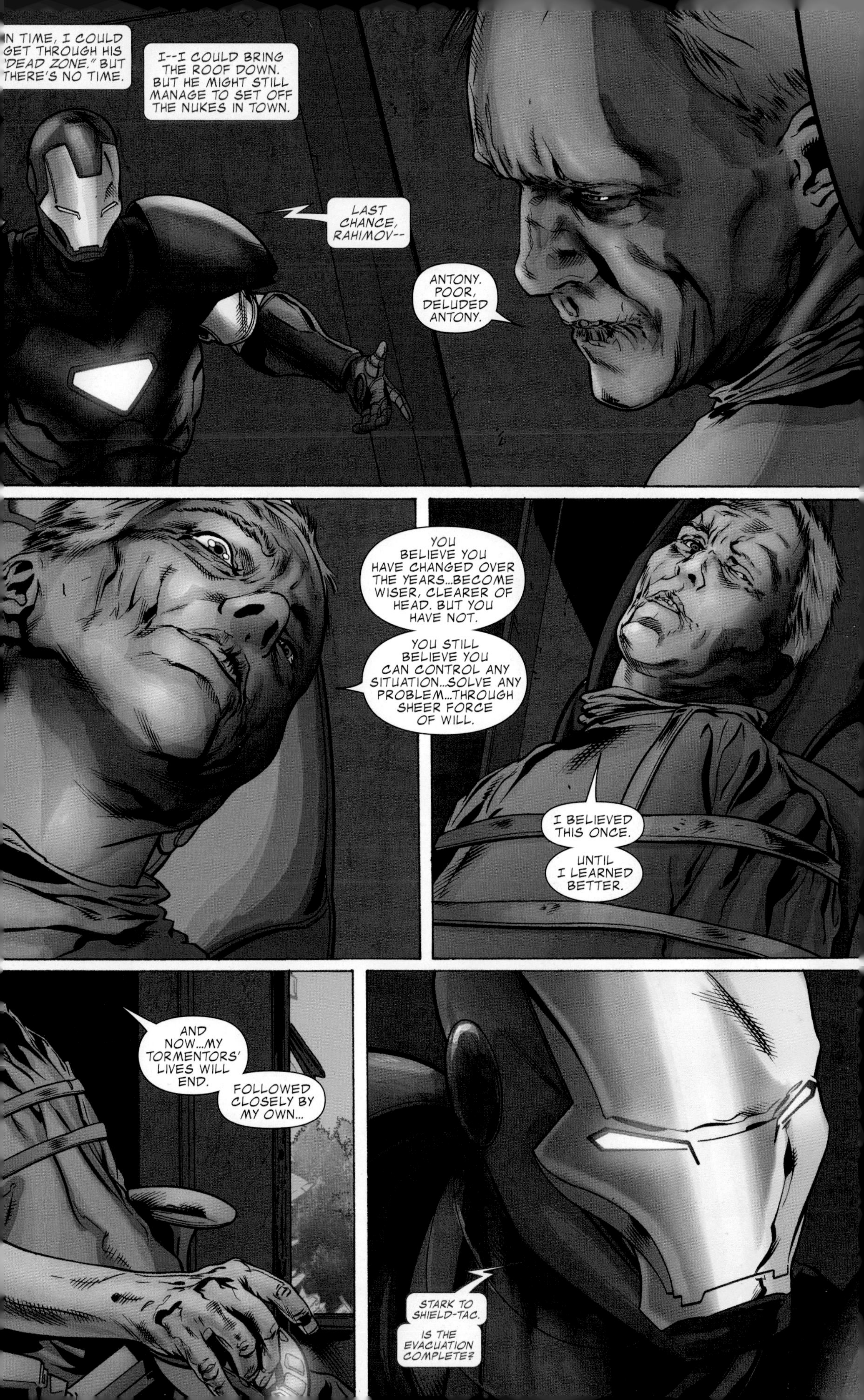
IN TIME, I COULD GET THROUGH HIS "DEAD ZONE." BUT THERE'S NO TIME.
I--I COULD BRING THE ROOF DOWN. BUT HE MIGHT STILL MANAGE TO SET OFF THE NUKES IN TOWN.
LAST CHANCE, RAHIMOV--
ANTONY. POOR, DELUDED ANTONY.
YOU BELIEVE YOU HAVE CHANGED OVER THE YEARS...BECOME WISER, CLEARER OF HEAD. BUT YOU HAVE NOT.
YOU STILL BELIEVE YOU CAN CONTROL ANY SITUATION...SOLVE ANY PROBLEM...THROUGH SHEER FORCE OF WILL.
I BELIEVED THIS ONCE.
UNTIL I LEARNED BETTER.
AND NOW...MY TORMENTORS' LIVES WILL END.
FOLLOWED CLOSELY BY MY OWN...
STARK TO SHIELD-TAC.
IS THE EVACUATION COMPLETE?

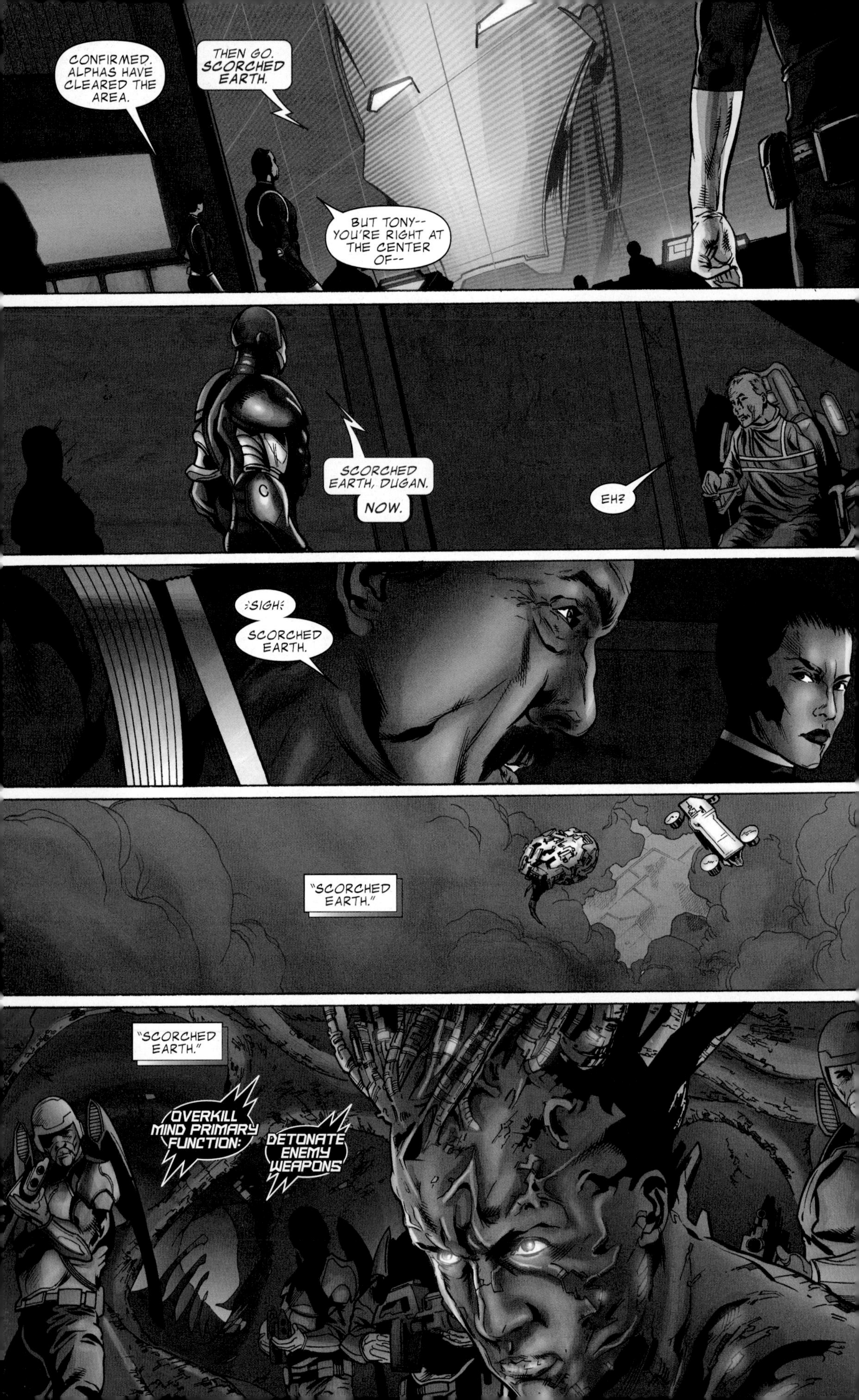
CONFIRMED. ALPHAS HAVE CLEARED THE AREA.
THEN GO. SCORCHED EARTH.
BUT TONY-- YOU'RE RIGHT AT THE CENTER OF--
SCORCHED EARTH, DUGAN.
NOW.
EH?
SIGH
SCORCHED EARTH.
"SCORCHED EARTH."
"SCORCHED EARTH."
OVERKILL MIND PRIMARY FUNCTION:
DETONATE ENEMY WEAPONS

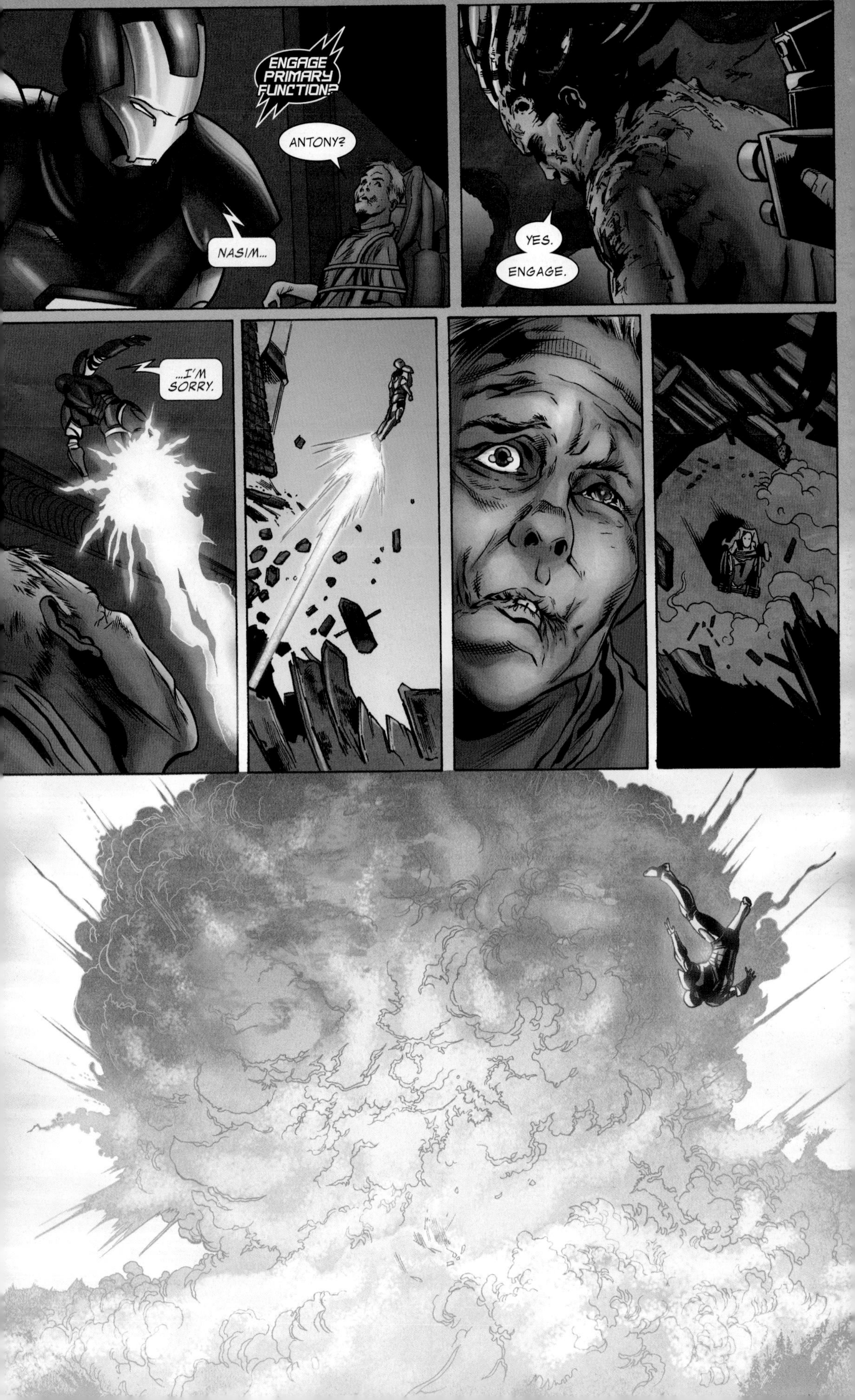
ENGAGE PRIMARY FUNCTION?
ANTONY?
NASIM...
YES. ENGAGE.
...I'M SORRY.

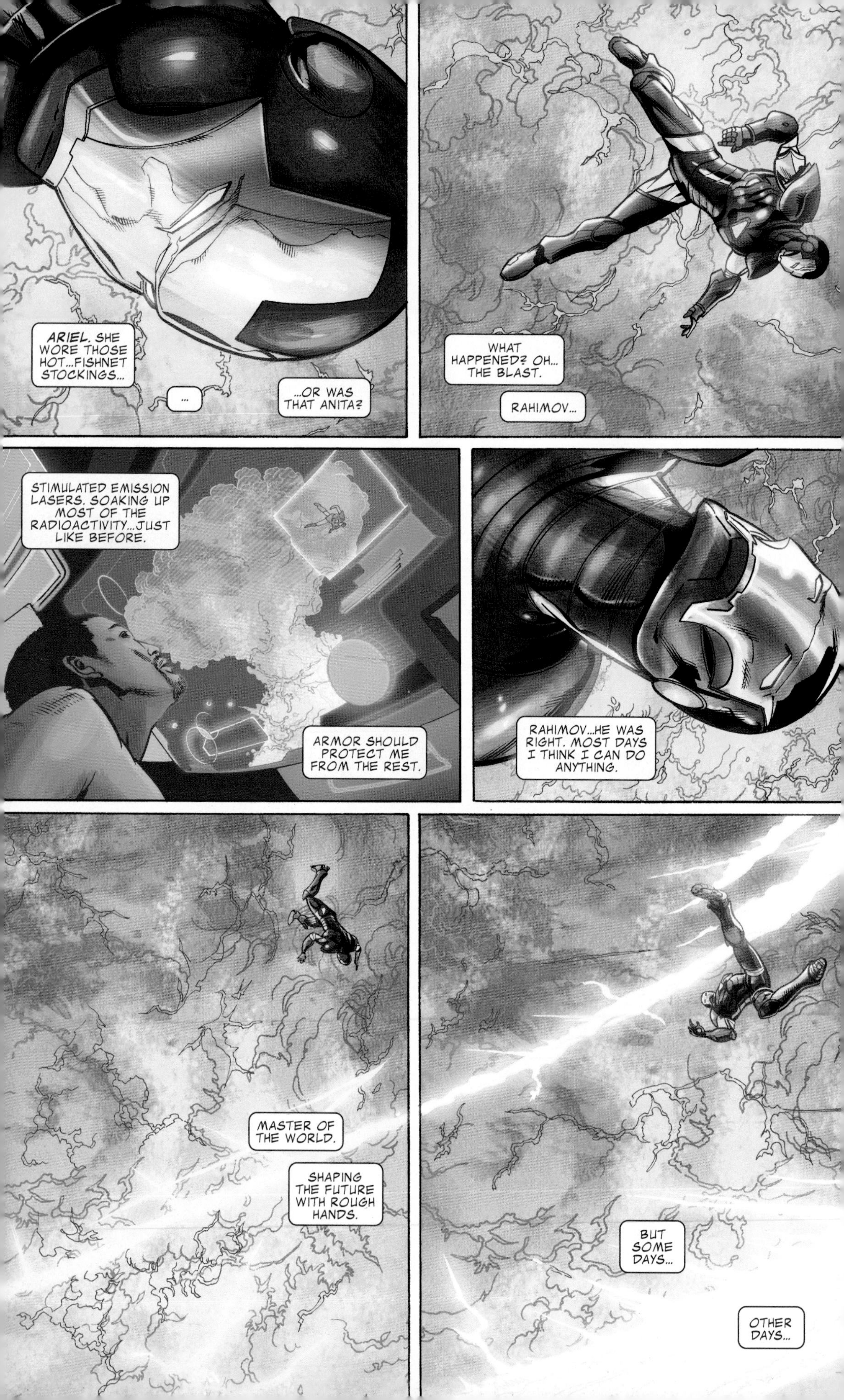
ARIEL. SHE WORE THOSE HOT...FISHNET STOCKINGS...
...
...OR WAS THAT ANITA?
WHAT HAPPENED? OH... THE BLAST.
RAHIMOV...
STIMULATED EMISSION LASERS. SOAKING UP MOST OF THE RADIOACTIVITY...JUST LIKE BEFORE.
ARMOR SHOULD PROTECT ME FROM THE REST.
RAHIMOV...HE WAS RIGHT. MOST DAYS I THINK I CAN DO ANYTHING.
MASTER OF THE WORLD.
SHAPING THE FUTURE WITH ROUGH HANDS.
BUT SOME DAYS...
OTHER DAYS...

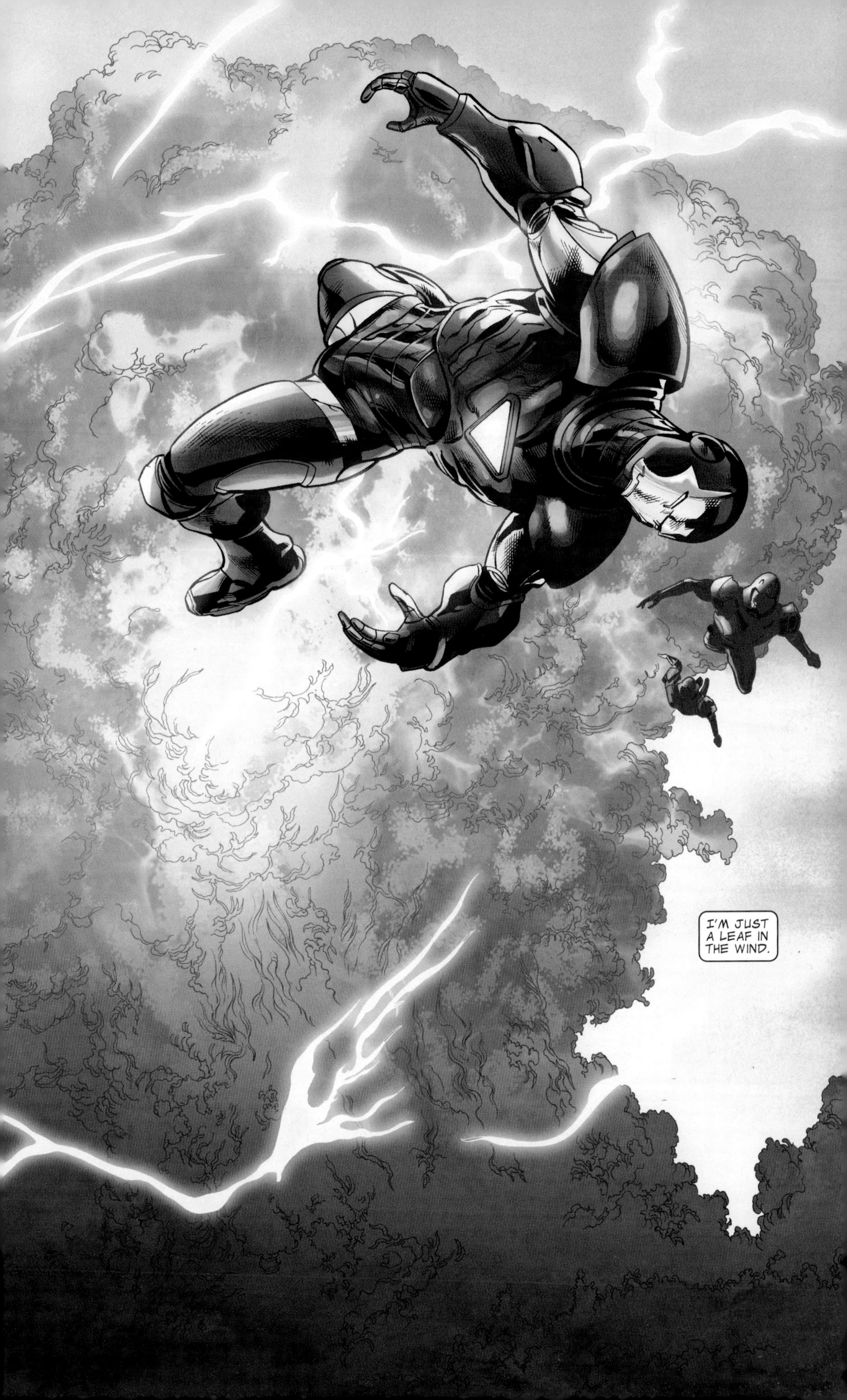
I'M JUST A LEAF IN THE WIND.

RAHIMOV WAS RIGHT.

BUT I WAS RIGHT, TOO.

"HOW MANY HAVE DIED?" HE ASKED.

"TOO MANY," I SAID.

BUT I DIDN'T TELL HIM THE REST. WHAT HAPPENS WHEN YOU...MAKE THOSE DECISIONS.

ALL THOSE PEOPLE I'VE TOUCHED...

...I REMEMBER THEM.

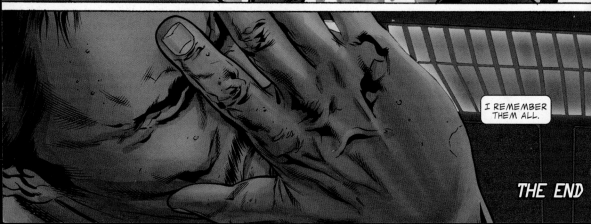

I REMEMBER THEM ALL.

THE END

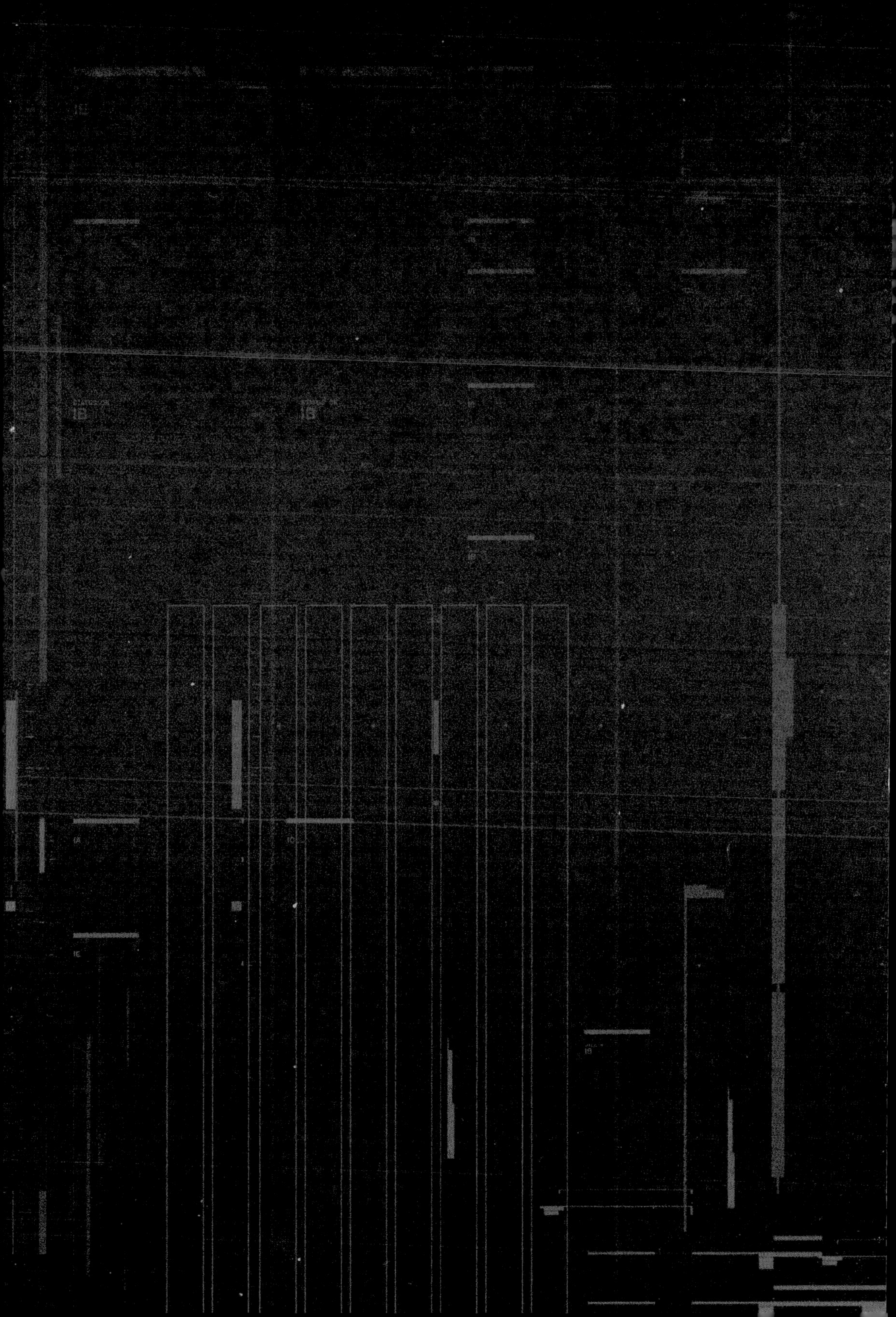

Iron Man (1998) #36

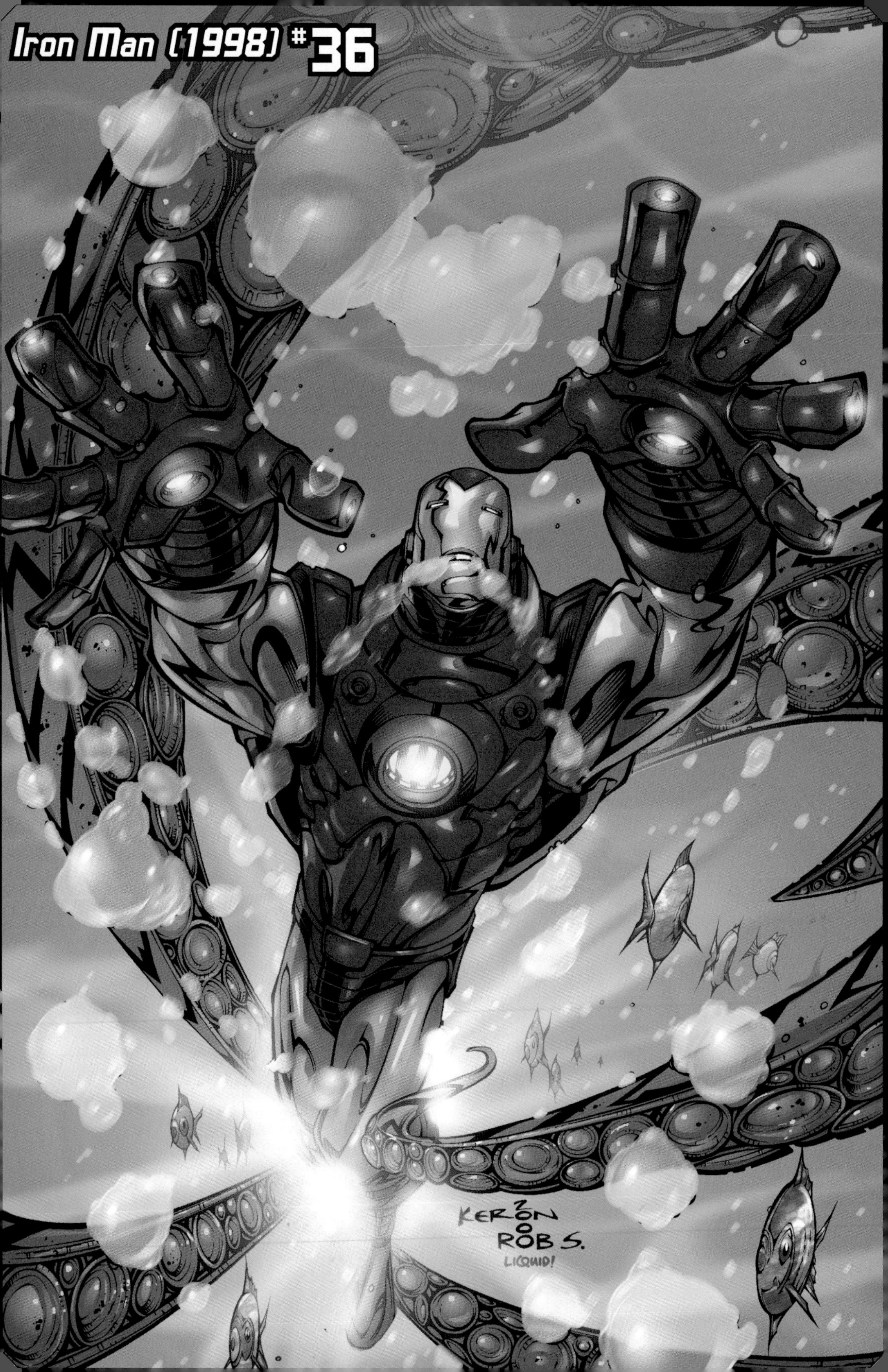
KERON
ROB S.
LIQUID!

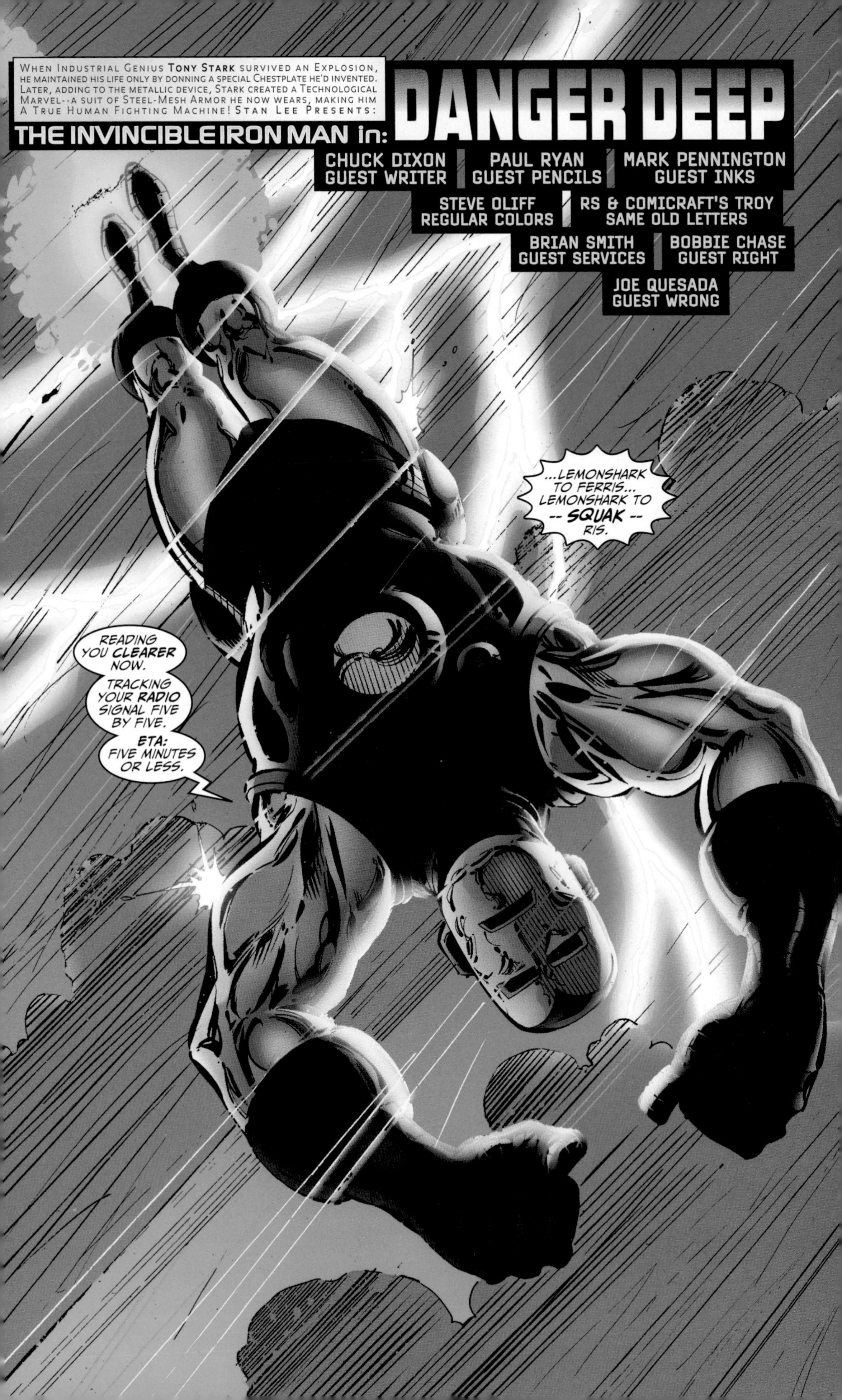

When Industrial Genius Tony Stark survived an Explosion, he maintained his life only by donning a special Chestplate he'd invented. Later, adding to the metallic device, Stark created a Technological Marvel--a suit of Steel-Mesh Armor he now wears, making him A True Human Fighting Machine! Stan Lee Presents:
THE INVINCIBLE IRON MAN in: DANGER DEEP
CHUCK DIXON GUEST WRITER
PAUL RYAN GUEST PENCILS
MARK PENNINGTON GUEST INKS
STEVE OLIFF REGULAR COLORS
RS & COMICRAFT'S TROY SAME OLD LETTERS
BRIAN SMITH GUEST SERVICES
BOBBIE CHASE GUEST RIGHT
JOE QUESADA GUEST WRONG
...LEMONSHARK TO FERRIS... LEMONSHARK TO -- SQUAK -- RIS.
READING YOU CLEARER NOW. TRACKING YOUR RADIO SIGNAL FIVE BY FIVE. ETA: FIVE MINUTES OR LESS.

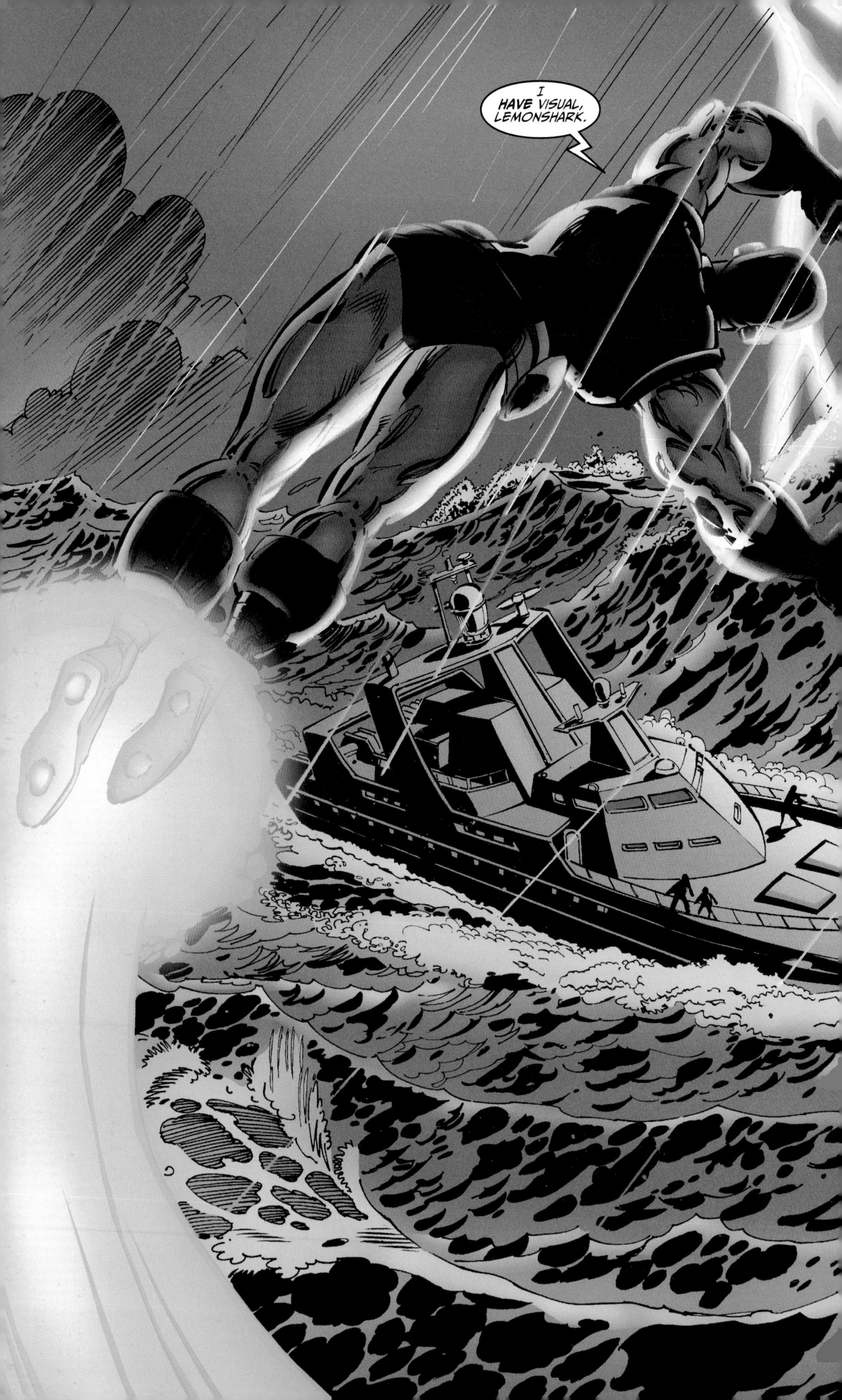
I HAVE VISUAL, LEMONSHARK.

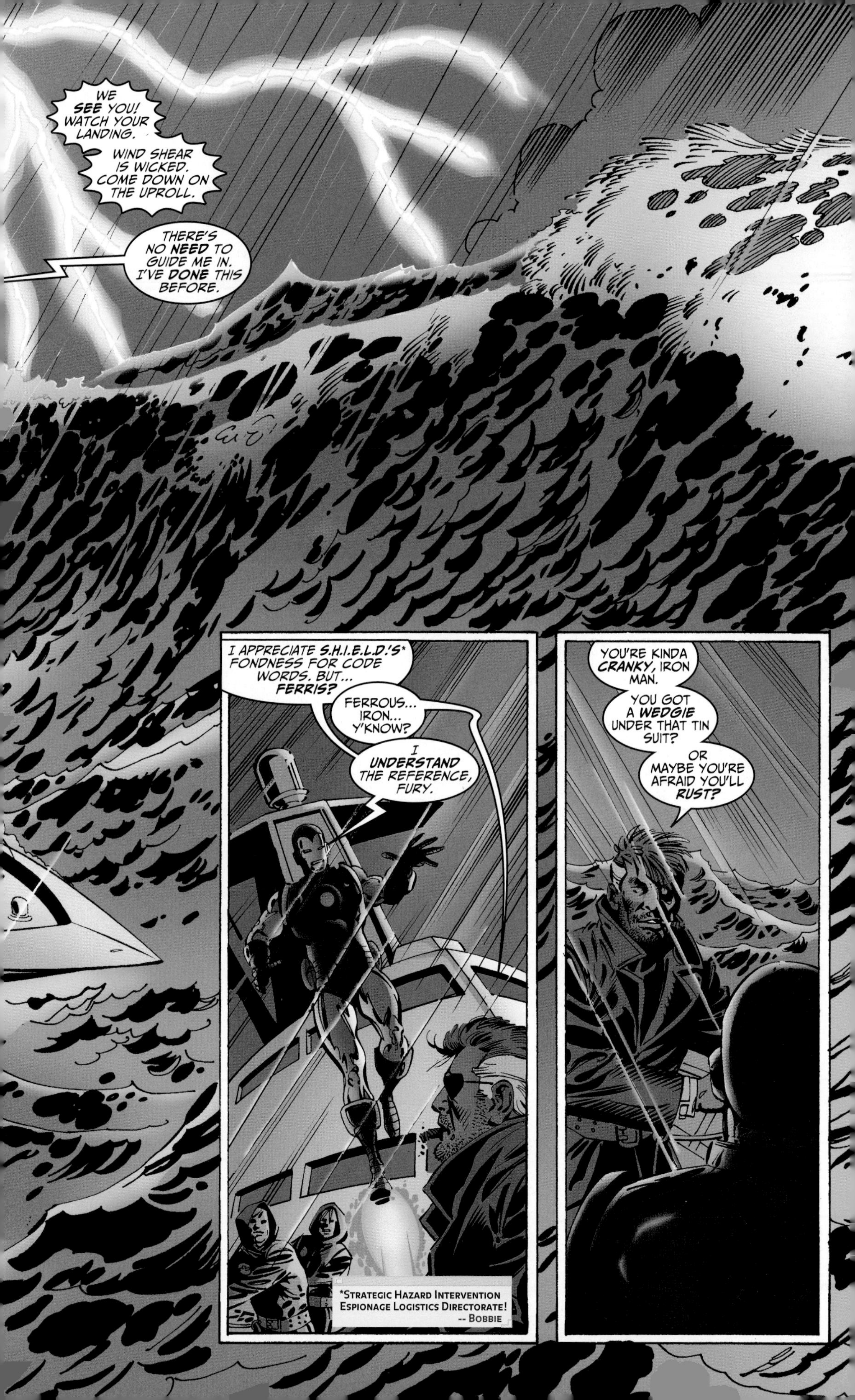
WE SEE YOU! WATCH YOUR LANDING.
WIND SHEAR IS WICKED. COME DOWN ON THE UPROLL.
THERE'S NO NEED TO GUIDE ME IN. I'VE DONE THIS BEFORE.
I APPRECIATE S.H.I.E.L.D.'S* FONDNESS FOR CODE WORDS. BUT... FERRIS?
FERROUS... IRON... Y'KNOW?
I UNDERSTAND THE REFERENCE, FURY.
*STRATEGIC HAZARD INTERVENTION ESPIONAGE LOGISTICS DIRECTORATE! -- BOBBIE
YOU'RE KINDA CRANKY, IRON MAN.
YOU GOT A WEDGIE UNDER THAT TIN SUIT?
OR MAYBE YOU'RE AFRAID YOU'LL RUST?

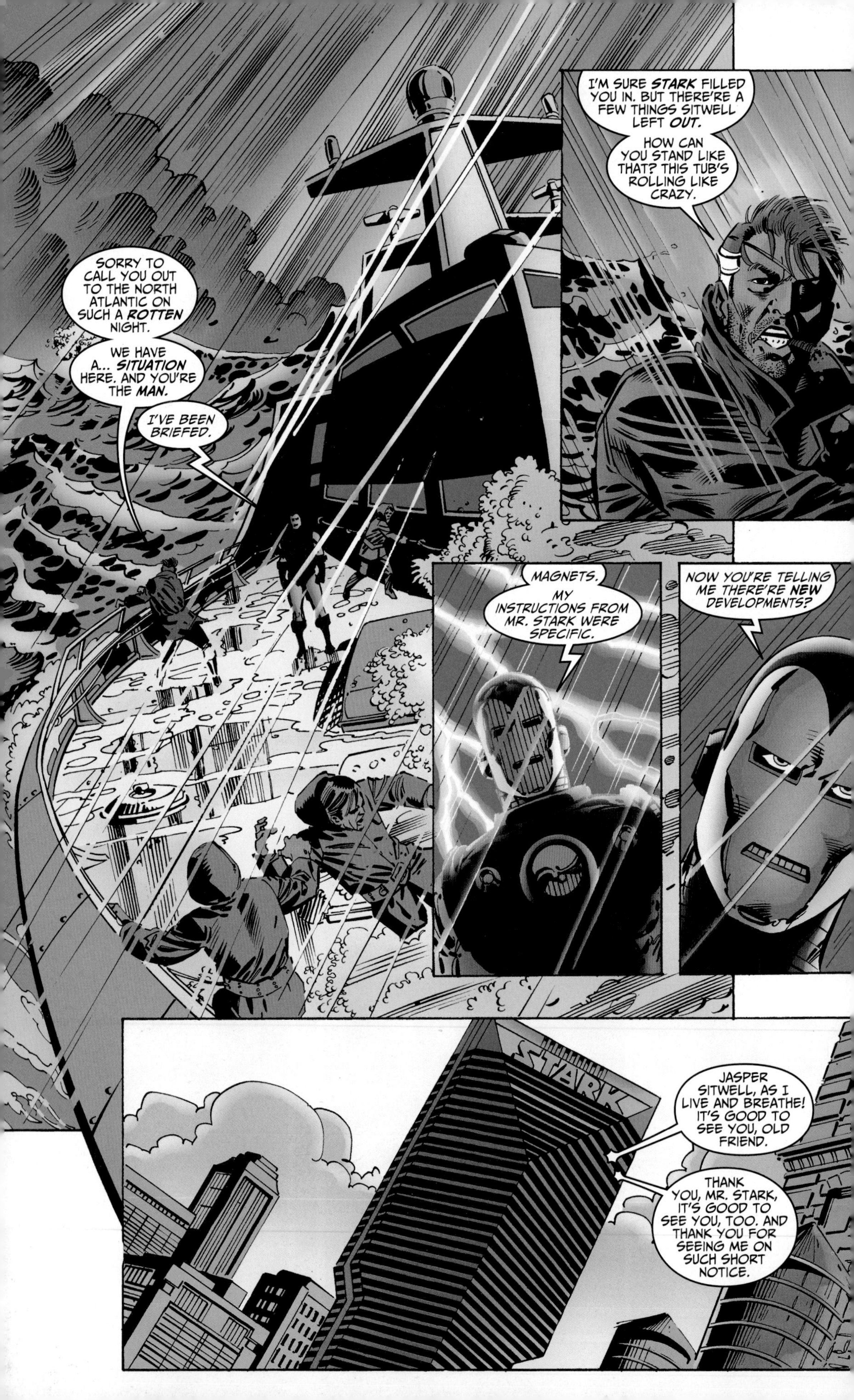
SORRY TO CALL YOU OUT TO THE NORTH ATLANTIC ON SUCH A ROTTEN NIGHT.
WE HAVE A... SITUATION HERE. AND YOU'RE THE MAN.
I'VE BEEN BRIEFED.
I'M SURE STARK FILLED YOU IN. BUT THERE'RE A FEW THINGS SITWELL LEFT OUT.
HOW CAN YOU STAND LIKE THAT? THIS TUB'S ROLLING LIKE CRAZY.
MAGNETS. MY INSTRUCTIONS FROM MR. STARK WERE SPECIFIC.
NOW YOU'RE TELLING ME THERE'RE NEW DEVELOPMENTS?
STARK
JASPER SITWELL, AS I LIVE AND BREATHE! IT'S GOOD TO SEE YOU, OLD FRIEND.
THANK YOU, MR. STARK, IT'S GOOD TO SEE YOU, TOO. AND THANK YOU FOR SEEING ME ON SUCH SHORT NOTICE.

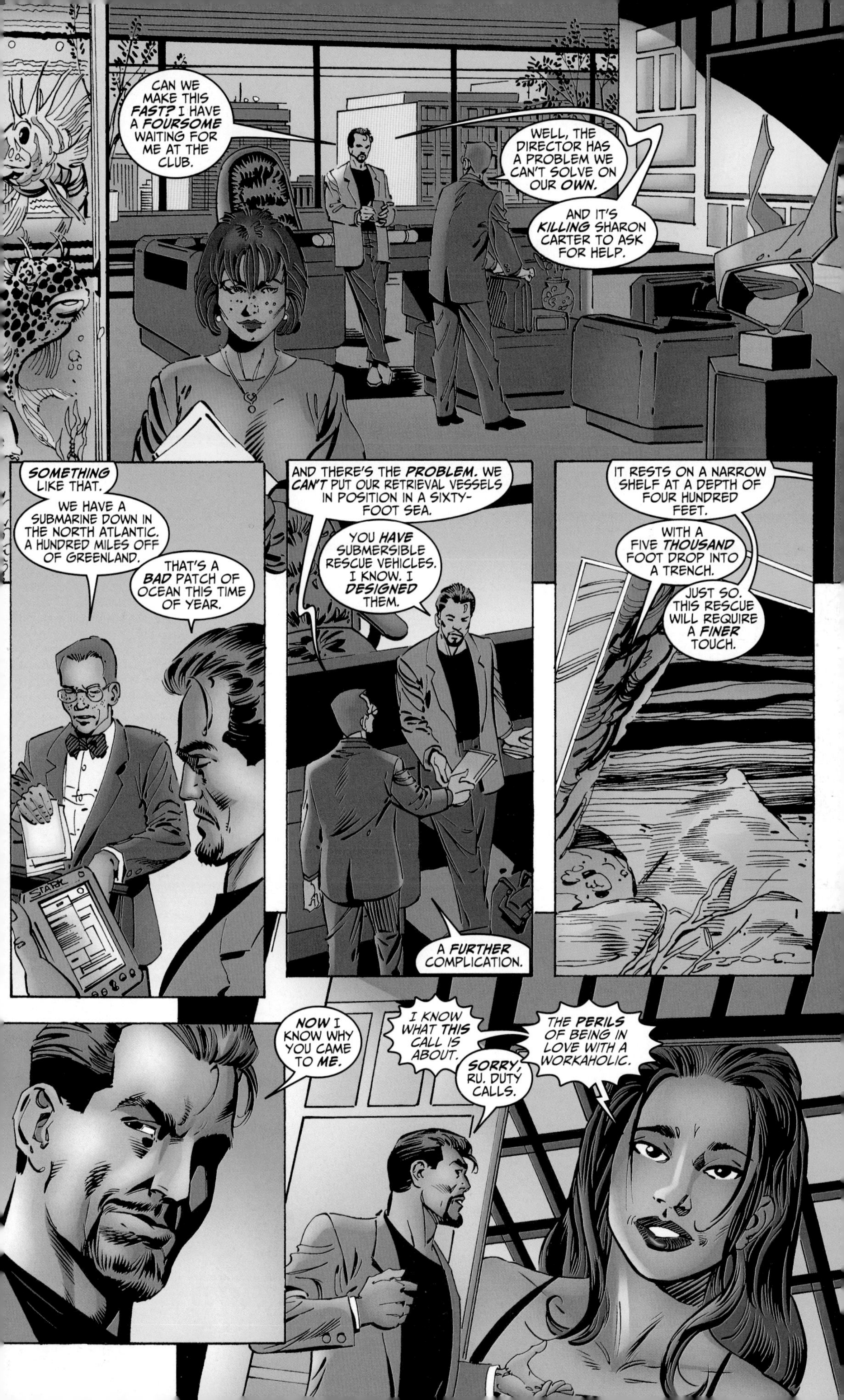
CAN WE MAKE THIS FAST? I HAVE A FOURSOME WAITING FOR ME AT THE CLUB.
WELL, THE DIRECTOR HAS A PROBLEM WE CAN'T SOLVE ON OUR OWN.
AND IT'S KILLING SHARON CARTER TO ASK FOR HELP.
SOMETHING LIKE THAT.
WE HAVE A SUBMARINE DOWN IN THE NORTH ATLANTIC. A HUNDRED MILES OFF OF GREENLAND.
THAT'S A BAD PATCH OF OCEAN THIS TIME OF YEAR.
STARK
AND THERE'S THE PROBLEM. WE CAN'T PUT OUR RETRIEVAL VESSELS IN POSITION IN A SIXTY-FOOT SEA.
YOU HAVE SUBMERSIBLE RESCUE VEHICLES. I KNOW. I DESIGNED THEM.
A FURTHER COMPLICATION.
IT RESTS ON A NARROW SHELF AT A DEPTH OF FOUR HUNDRED FEET.
WITH A FIVE THOUSAND FOOT DROP INTO A TRENCH.
JUST SO. THIS RESCUE WILL REQUIRE A FINER TOUCH.
NOW I KNOW WHY YOU CAME TO ME.
I KNOW WHAT THIS CALL IS ABOUT.
THE PERILS OF BEING IN LOVE WITH A WORKAHOLIC.
SORRY, RU. DUTY CALLS.

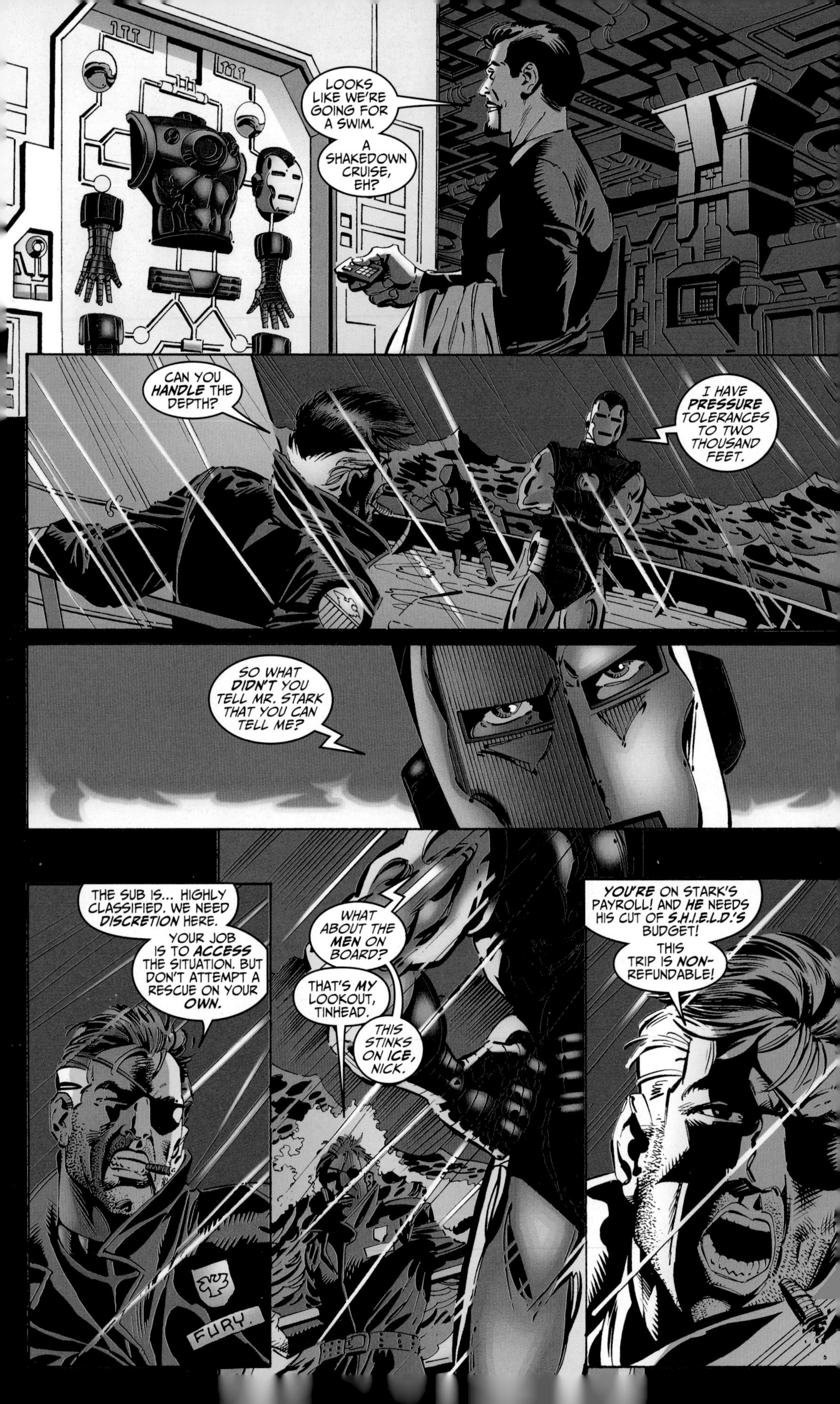
LOOKS LIKE WE'RE GOING FOR A SWIM.
A SHAKEDOWN CRUISE, EH?
CAN YOU HANDLE THE DEPTH?
I HAVE PRESSURE TOLERANCES TO TWO THOUSAND FEET.
SO WHAT DIDN'T YOU TELL MR. STARK THAT YOU CAN TELL ME?
THE SUB IS... HIGHLY CLASSIFIED. WE NEED DISCRETION HERE.
YOUR JOB IS TO ACCESS THE SITUATION. BUT DON'T ATTEMPT A RESCUE ON YOUR OWN.
WHAT ABOUT THE MEN ON BOARD?
THAT'S MY LOOKOUT, TINHEAD.
THIS STINKS ON ICE, NICK.
YOU'RE ON STARK'S PAYROLL! AND HE NEEDS HIS CUT OF S.H.I.E.L.D.'S BUDGET!
THIS TRIP IS NON-REFUNDABLE!
FURY

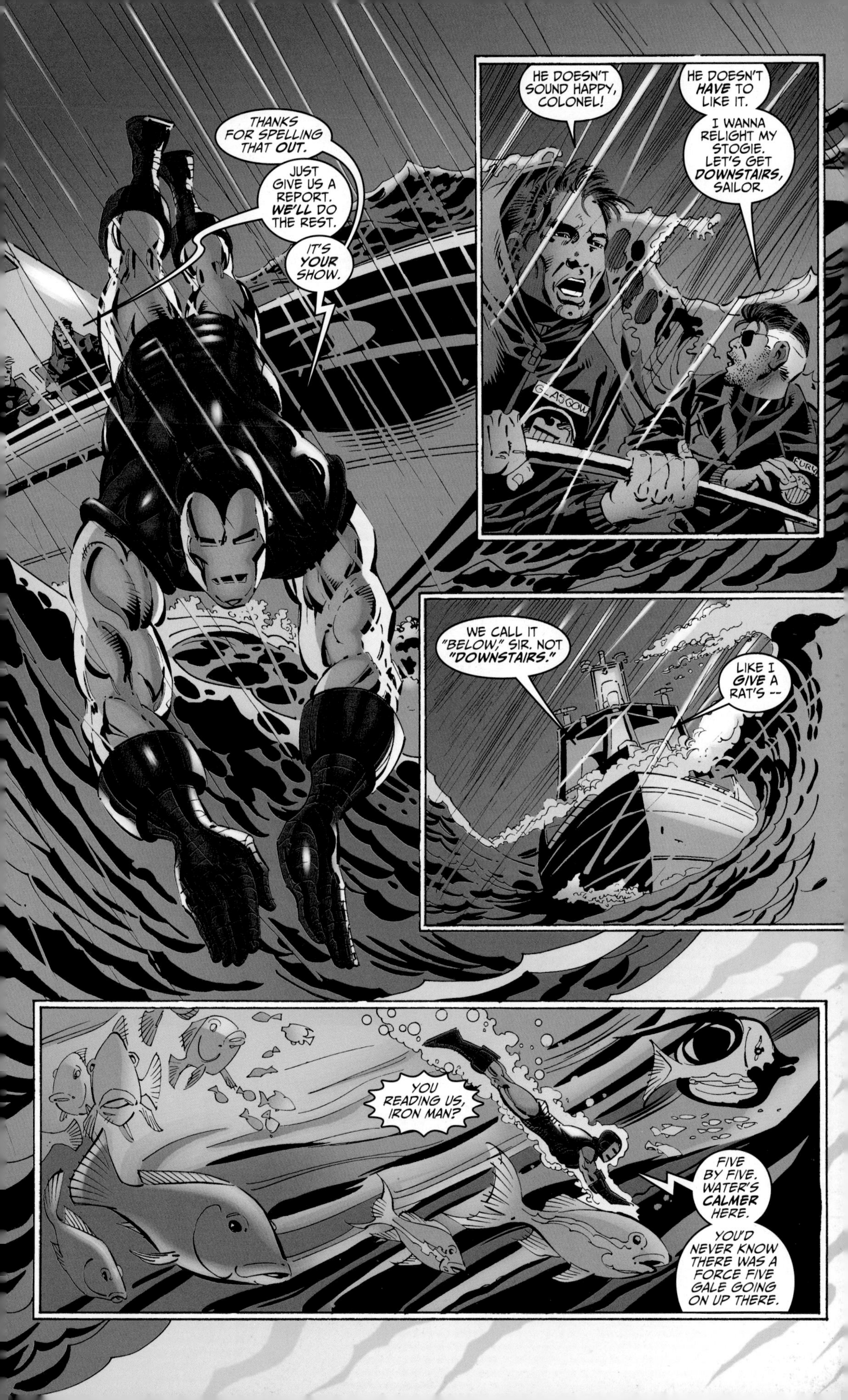

THANKS FOR SPELLING THAT OUT.
JUST GIVE US A REPORT. WE'LL DO THE REST.
IT'S YOUR SHOW.
HE DOESN'T SOUND HAPPY, COLONEL!
HE DOESN'T HAVE TO LIKE IT.
I WANNA RELIGHT MY STOGIE. LET'S GET DOWNSTAIRS, SAILOR.
GLASGOW
FURY
WE CALL IT "BELOW," SIR. NOT "DOWNSTAIRS."
LIKE I GIVE A RAT'S --
YOU READING US, IRON MAN?
FIVE BY FIVE. WATER'S CALMER HERE.
YOU'D NEVER KNOW THERE WAS A FORCE FIVE GALE GOING ON UP THERE.

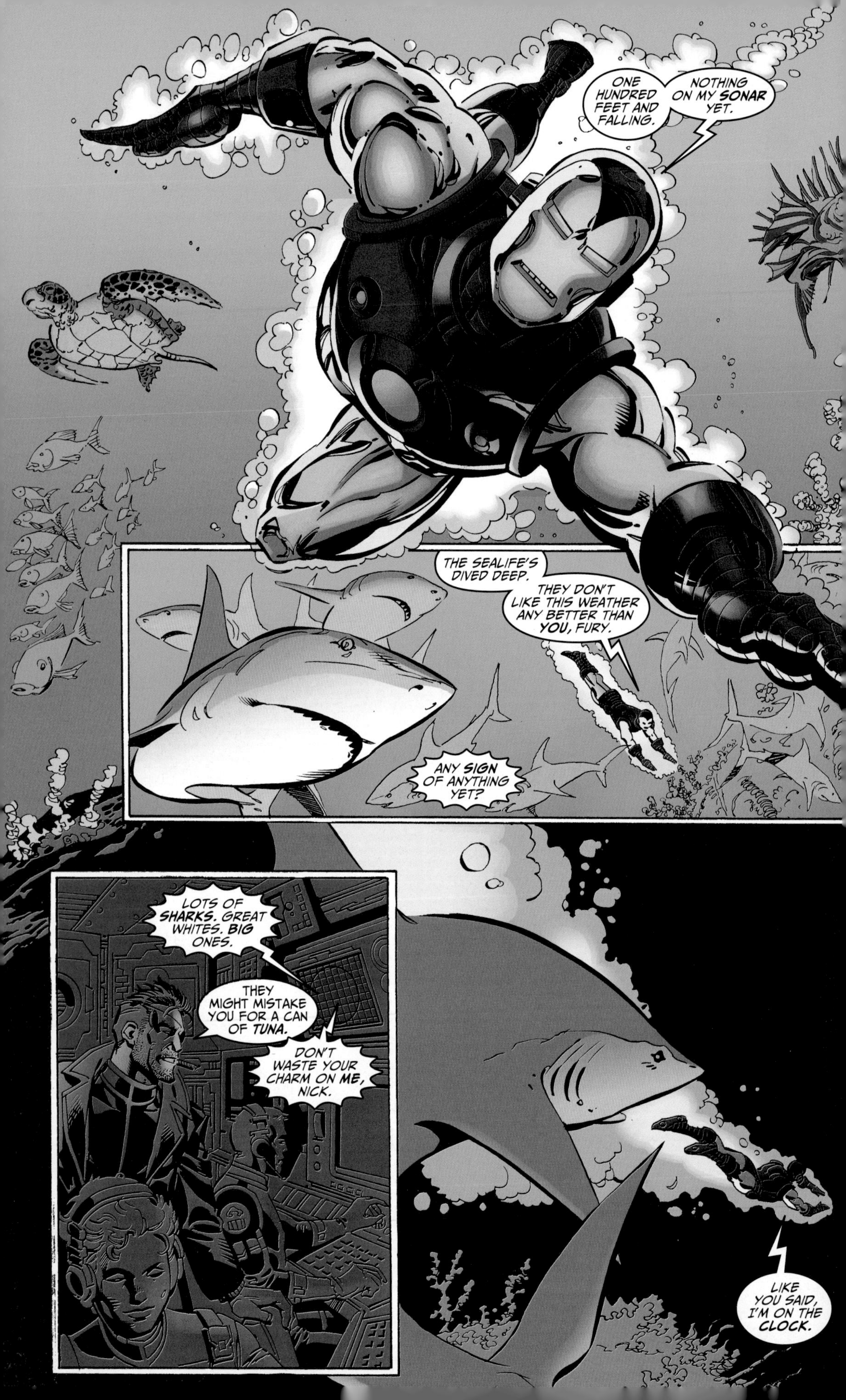
ONE HUNDRED FEET AND FALLING.
NOTHING ON MY SONAR YET.
THE SEALIFE'S DIVED DEEP.
THEY DON'T LIKE THIS WEATHER ANY BETTER THAN YOU, FURY.
ANY SIGN OF ANYTHING YET?
LOTS OF SHARKS. GREAT WHITES. BIG ONES.
THEY MIGHT MISTAKE YOU FOR A CAN OF TUNA.
DON'T WASTE YOUR CHARM ON ME, NICK.
LIKE YOU SAID, I'M ON THE CLOCK.

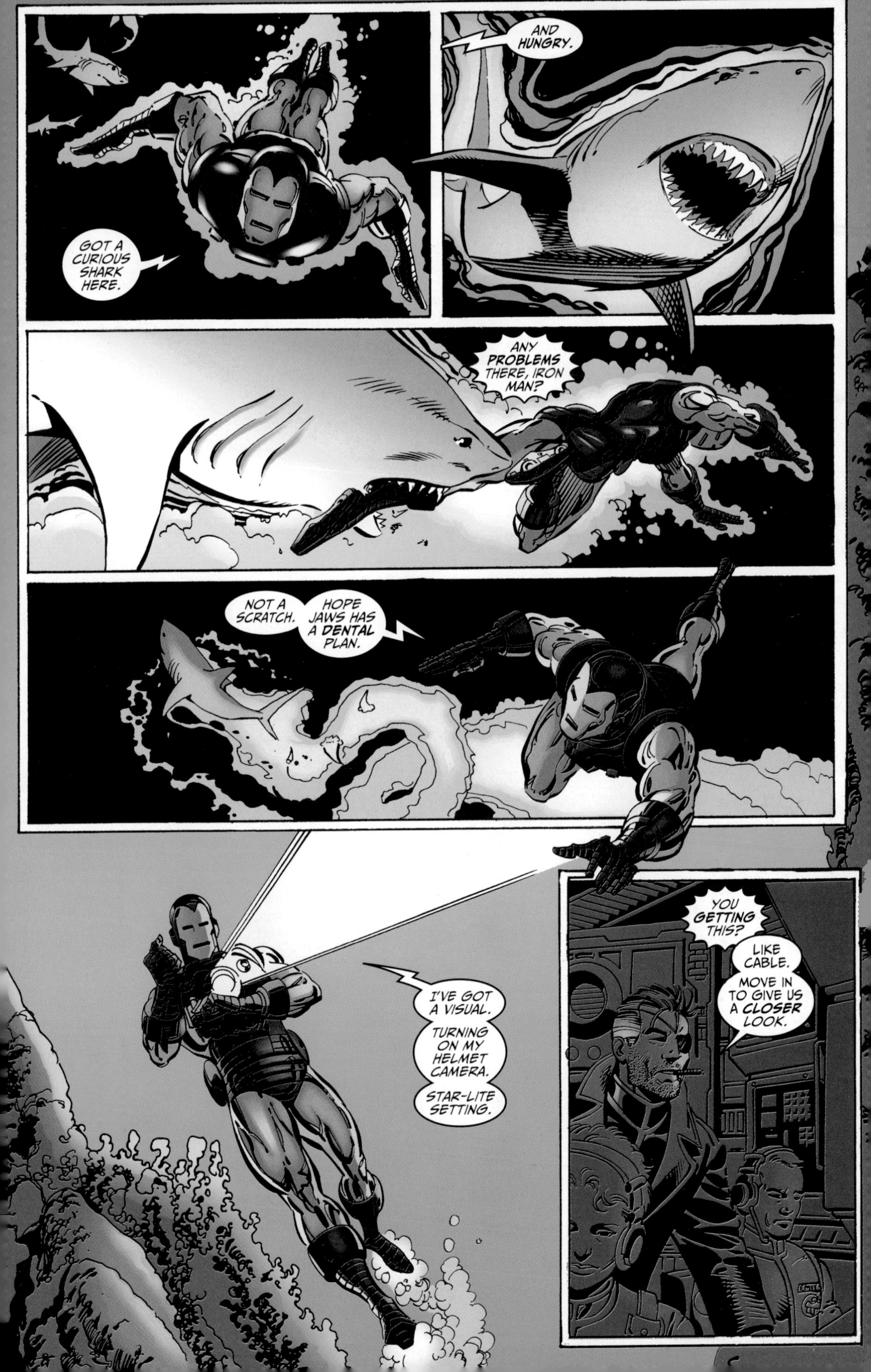
GOT A CURIOUS SHARK HERE.
AND HUNGRY.
ANY PROBLEMS THERE, IRON MAN?
NOT A SCRATCH.
HOPE JAWS HAS A DENTAL PLAN.
I'VE GOT A VISUAL.
TURNING ON MY HELMET CAMERA.
STAR-LITE SETTING.
YOU GETTING THIS?
LIKE CABLE.
MOVE IN TO GIVE US A CLOSER LOOK.

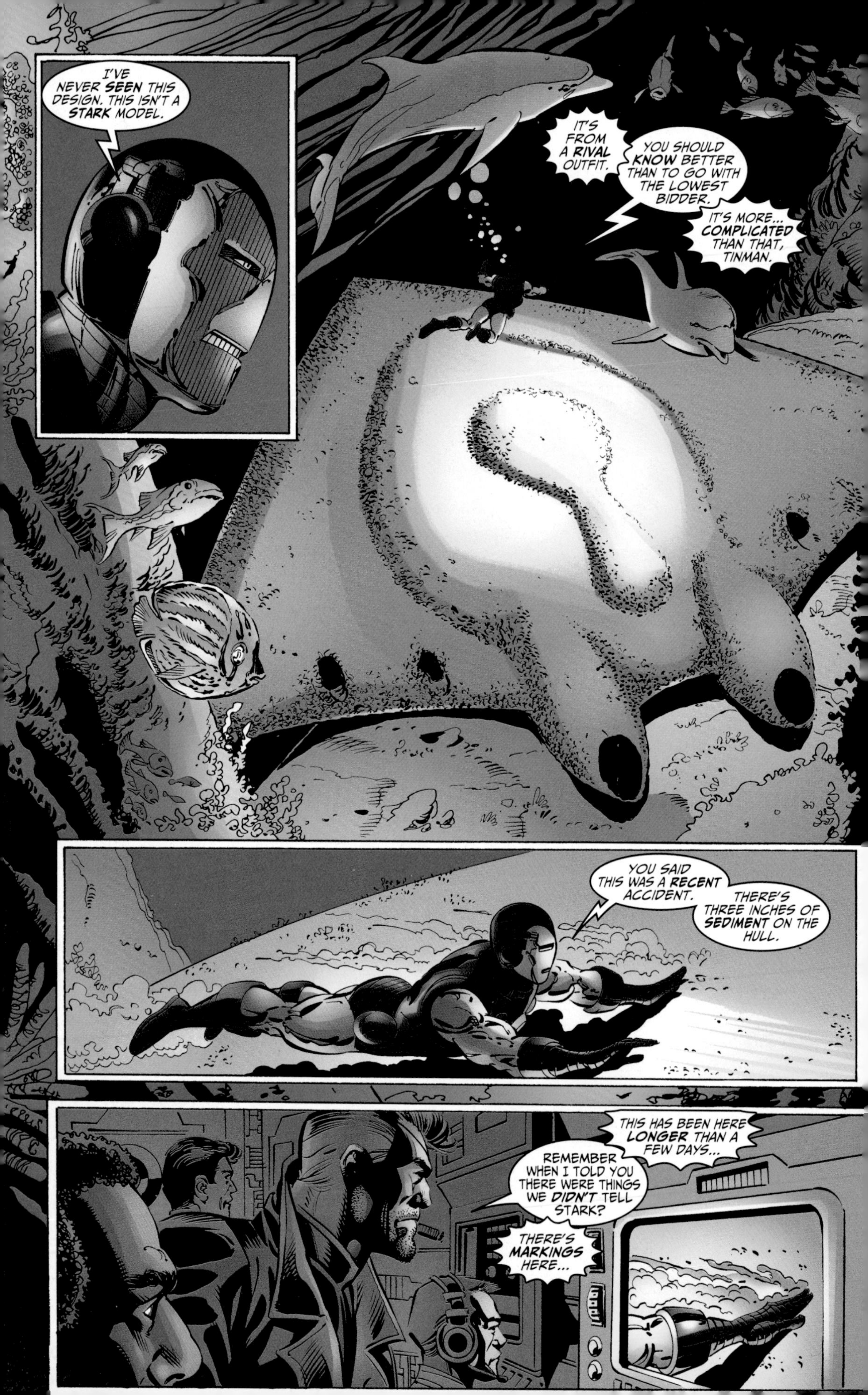
I'VE NEVER SEEN THIS DESIGN. THIS ISN'T A STARK MODEL.
IT'S FROM A RIVAL OUTFIT.
YOU SHOULD KNOW BETTER THAN TO GO WITH THE LOWEST BIDDER.
IT'S MORE... COMPLICATED THAN THAT, TINMAN.
YOU SAID THIS WAS A RECENT ACCIDENT.
THERE'S THREE INCHES OF SEDIMENT ON THE HULL.
THIS HAS BEEN HERE LONGER THAN A FEW DAYS...
REMEMBER WHEN I TOLD YOU THERE WERE THINGS WE DIDN'T TELL STARK?
THERE'S MARKINGS HERE...

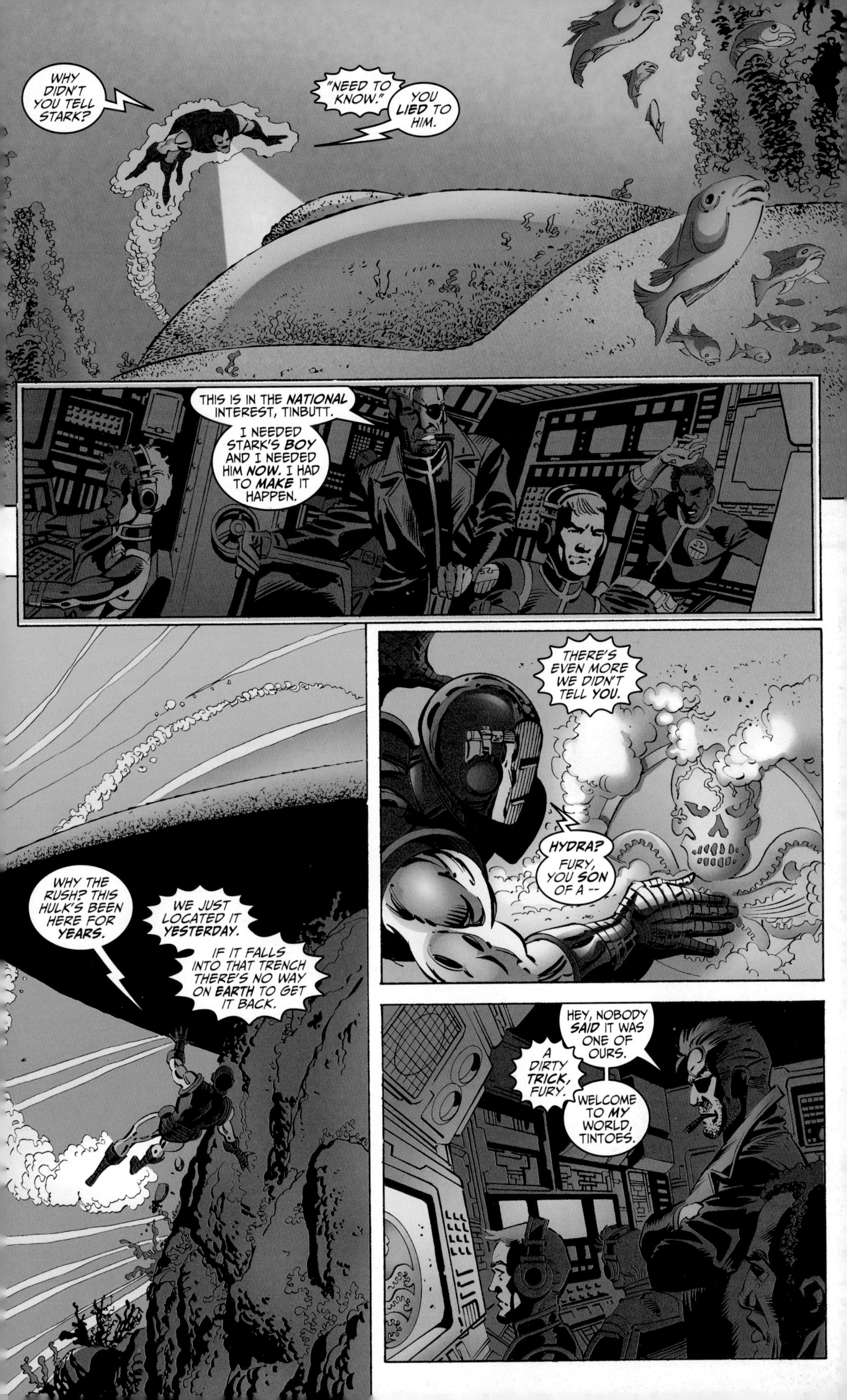
WHY DIDN'T YOU TELL STARK?
"NEED TO KNOW."
YOU LIED TO HIM.
THIS IS IN THE NATIONAL INTEREST, TINBUTT.
I NEEDED STARK'S BOY AND I NEEDED HIM NOW. I HAD TO MAKE IT HAPPEN.
WHY THE RUSH? THIS HULK'S BEEN HERE FOR YEARS.
WE JUST LOCATED IT YESTERDAY.
IF IT FALLS INTO THAT TRENCH THERE'S NO WAY ON EARTH TO GET IT BACK.
THERE'S EVEN MORE WE DIDN'T TELL YOU.
HYDRA? FURY, YOU SON OF A --
A DIRTY TRICK, FURY.
HEY, NOBODY SAID IT WAS ONE OF OURS.
WELCOME TO MY WORLD, TINTOES.

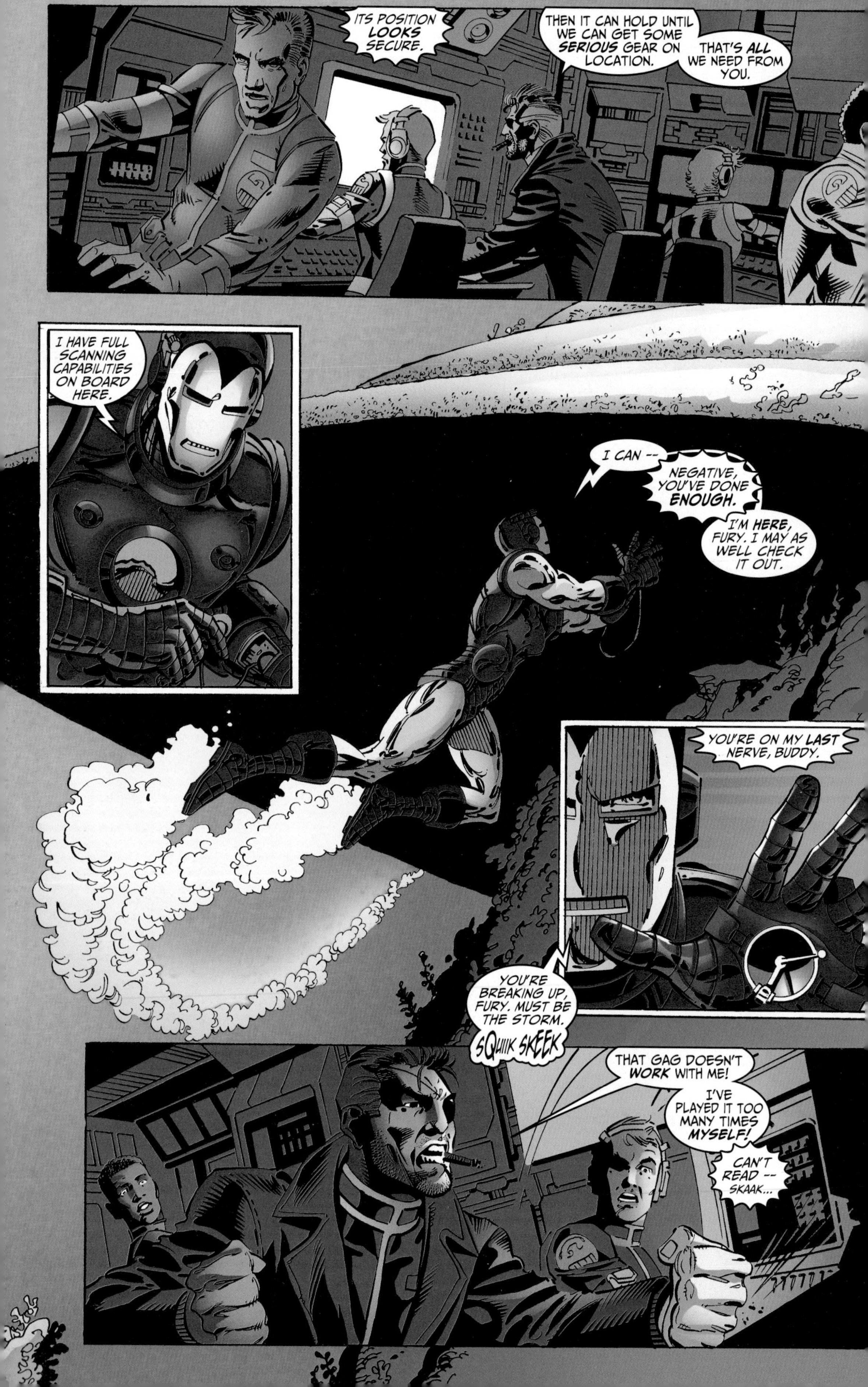

ITS POSITION LOOKS SECURE.
THEN IT CAN HOLD UNTIL WE CAN GET SOME SERIOUS GEAR ON LOCATION.
THAT'S ALL WE NEED FROM YOU.
I HAVE FULL SCANNING CAPABILITIES ON BOARD HERE.
I CAN --
NEGATIVE, YOU'VE DONE ENOUGH.
I'M HERE, FURY. I MAY AS WELL CHECK IT OUT.
YOU'RE ON MY LAST NERVE, BUDDY.
YOU'RE BREAKING UP, FURY. MUST BE THE STORM.
SQUIIK SKEEK
THAT GAG DOESN'T WORK WITH ME!
I'VE PLAYED IT TOO MANY TIMES MYSELF!
CAN'T READ -- SKAAK...

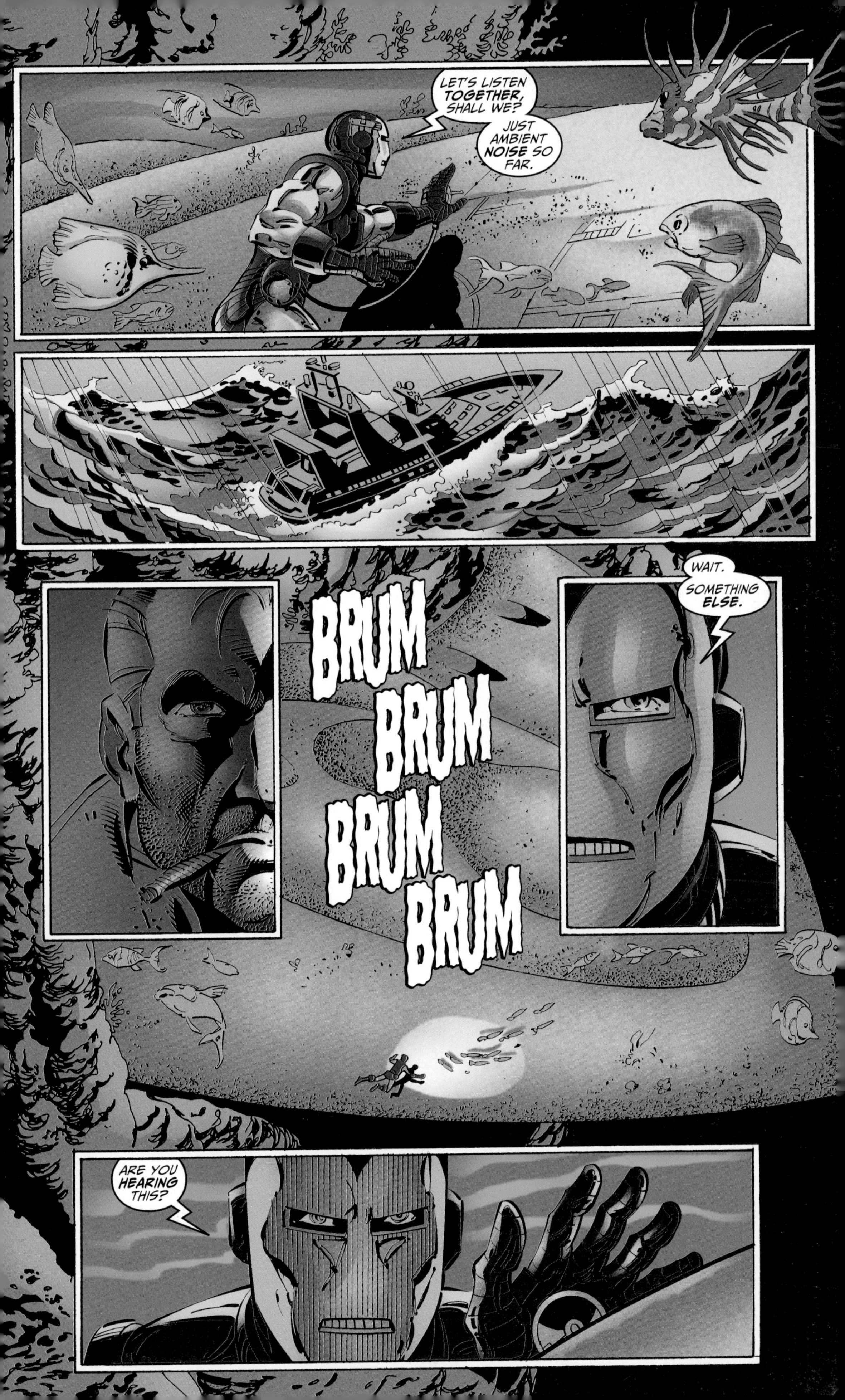
LET'S LISTEN TOGETHER, SHALL WE?
JUST AMBIENT NOISE SO FAR.
BRUM BRUM BRUM BRUM
WAIT. SOMETHING ELSE.
ARE YOU HEARING THIS?

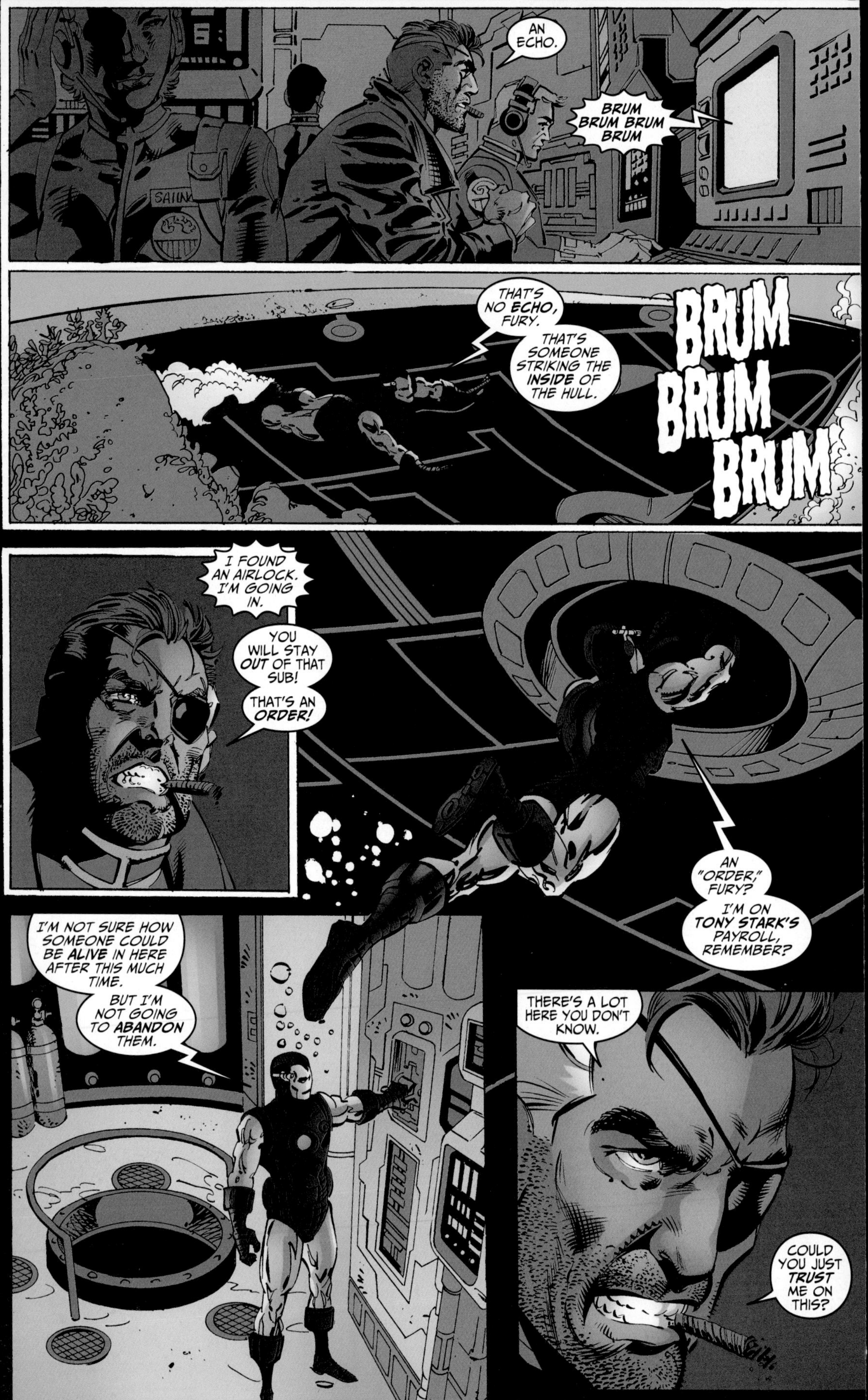
AN ECHO.
BRUM BRUM BRUM BRUM
THAT'S NO ECHO, FURY.
THAT'S SOMEONE STRIKING THE INSIDE OF THE HULL.
BRUM BRUM BRUM
I FOUND AN AIRLOCK. I'M GOING IN.
YOU WILL STAY OUT OF THAT SUB!
THAT'S AN ORDER!
AN "ORDER," FURY?
I'M ON TONY STARK'S PAYROLL, REMEMBER?
I'M NOT SURE HOW SOMEONE COULD BE ALIVE IN HERE AFTER THIS MUCH TIME.
BUT I'M NOT GOING TO ABANDON THEM.
THERE'S A LOT HERE YOU DON'T KNOW.
COULD YOU JUST TRUST ME ON THIS?

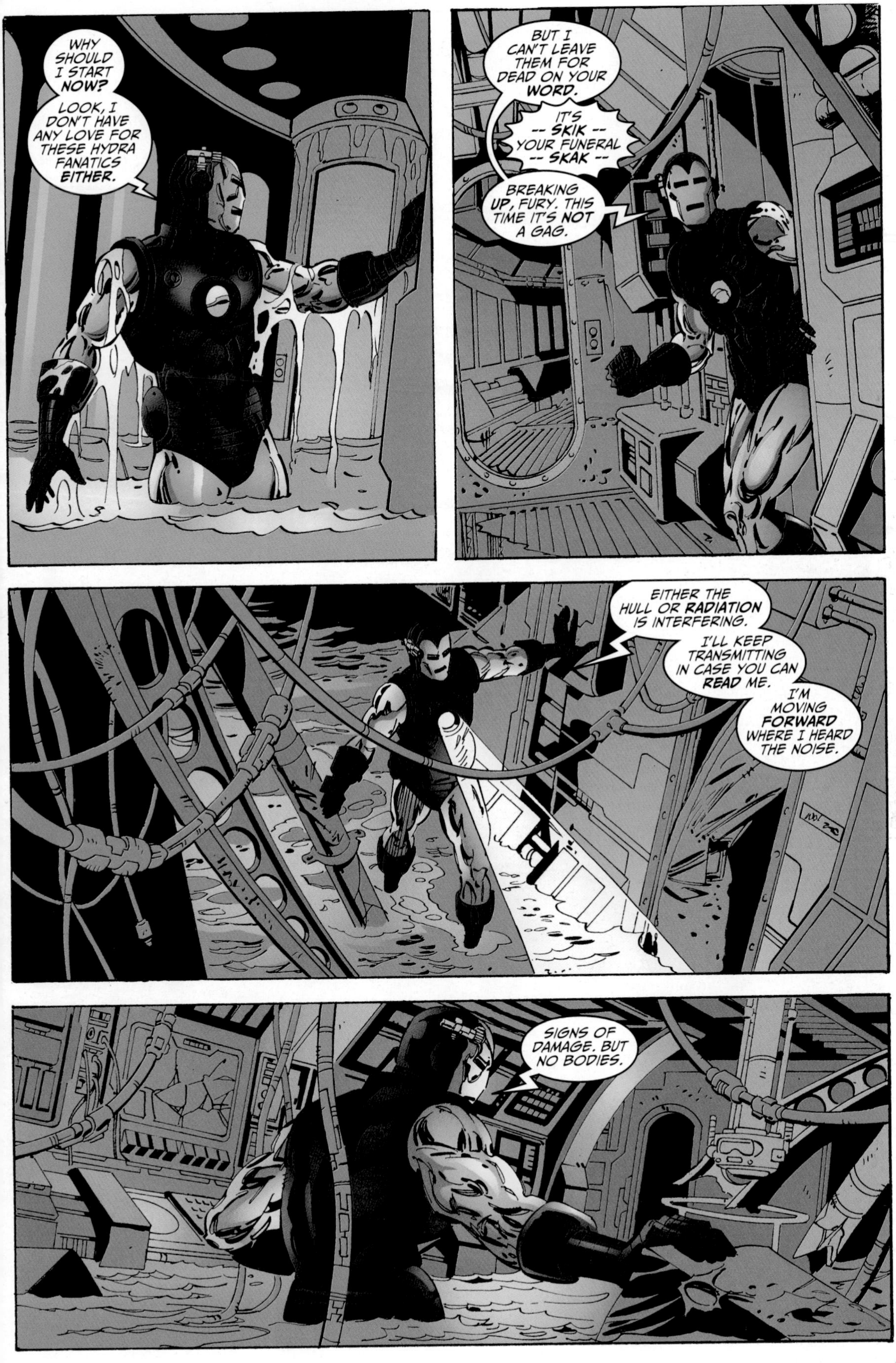
WHY SHOULD I START NOW?
LOOK, I DON'T HAVE ANY LOVE FOR THESE HYDRA FANATICS EITHER.
BUT I CAN'T LEAVE THEM FOR DEAD ON YOUR WORD.
IT'S -- SKIK -- YOUR FUNERAL -- SKAK --
BREAKING UP, FURY. THIS TIME IT'S NOT A GAG.
EITHER THE HULL OR RADIATION IS INTERFERING.
I'LL KEEP TRANSMITTING IN CASE YOU CAN READ ME.
I'M MOVING FORWARD WHERE I HEARD THE NOISE.
SIGNS OF DAMAGE. BUT NO BODIES.

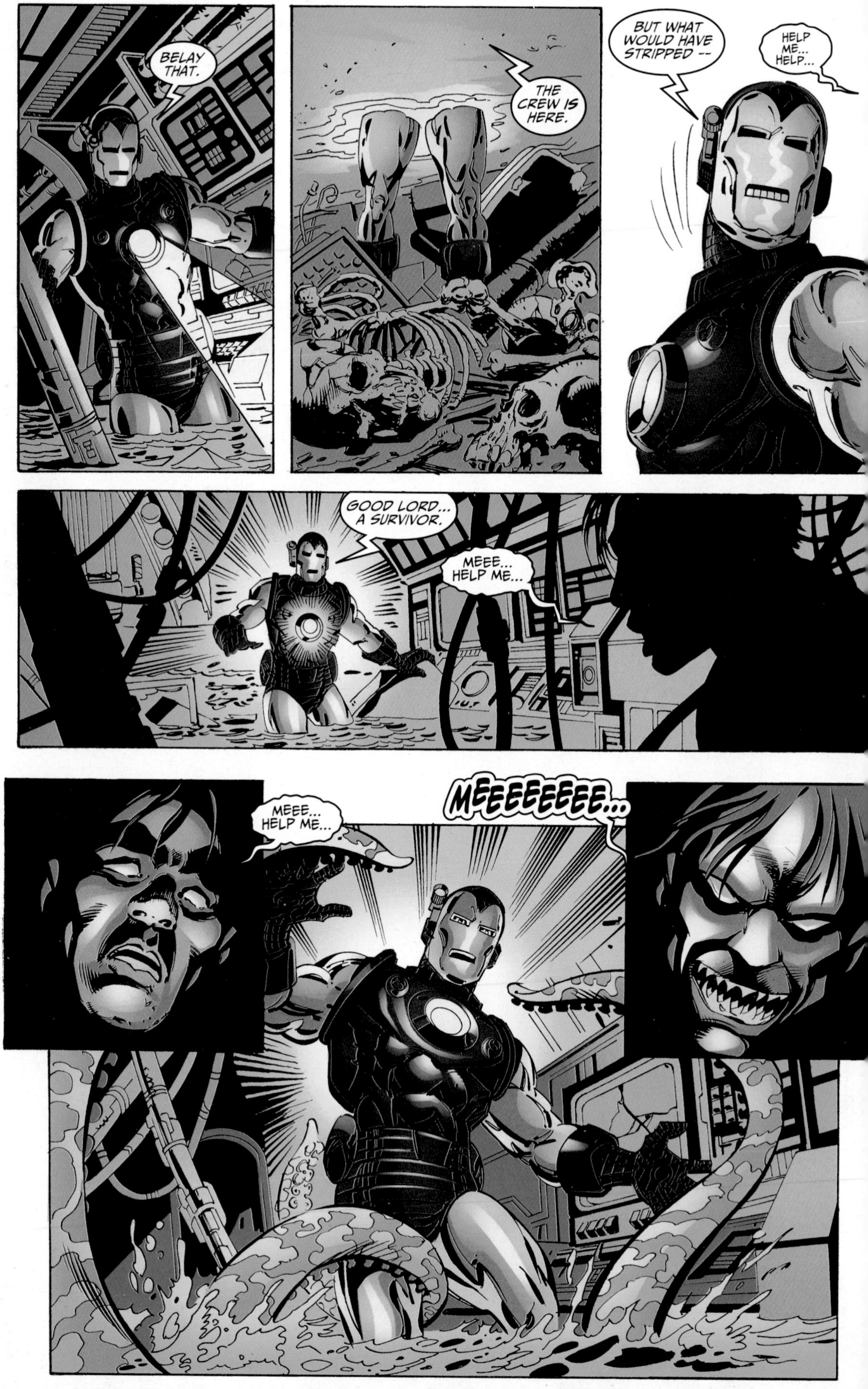
BELAY THAT.
THE CREW IS HERE.
BUT WHAT WOULD HAVE STRIPPED --
HELP ME... HELP...
GOOD LORD... A SURVIVOR.
MEEE... HELP ME...
MEEE... HELP ME...
MEEEEEEEEE...

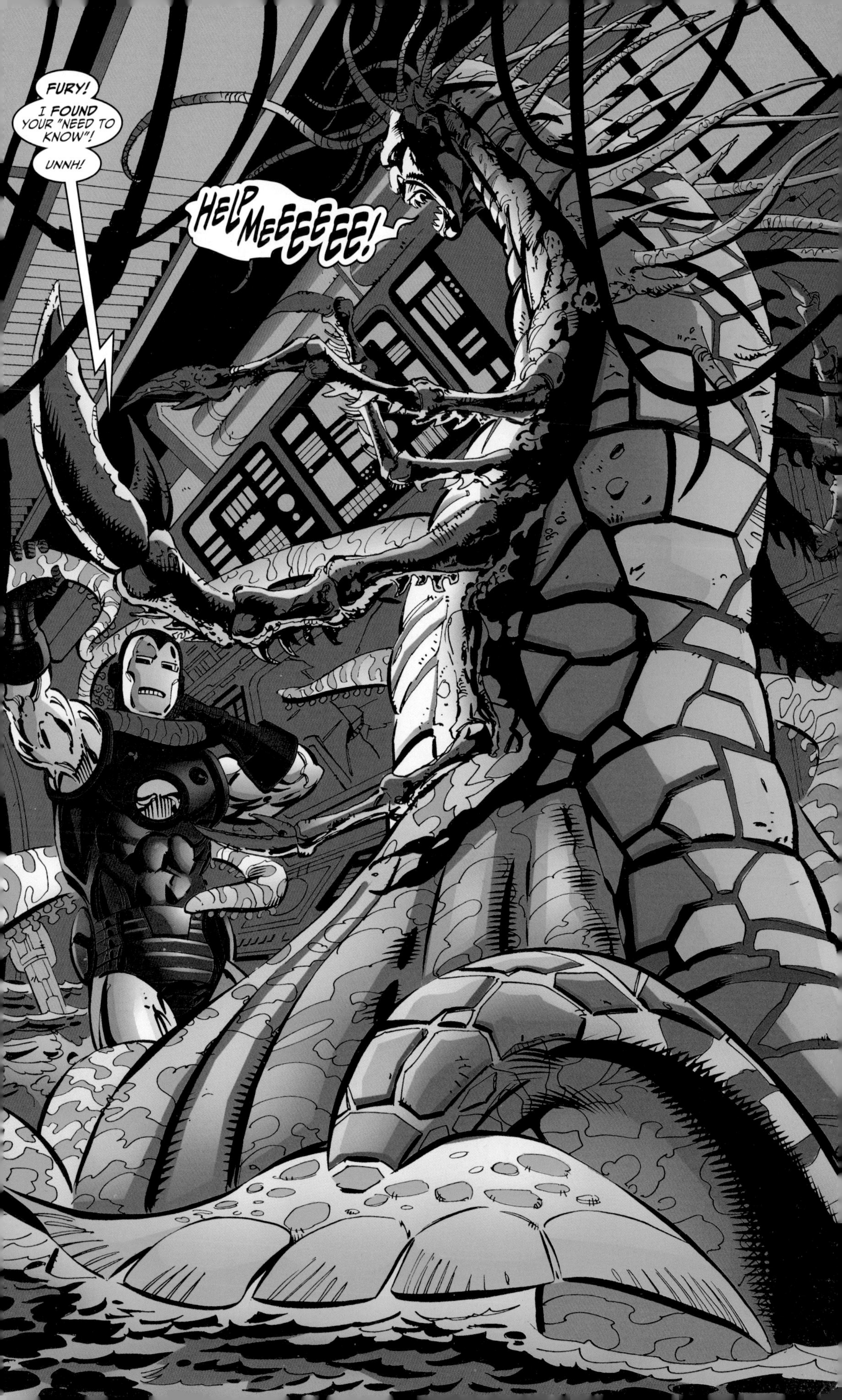
FURY!
I FOUND YOUR "NEED TO KNOW"!
UNNH!
HELP MEEEEEEE!

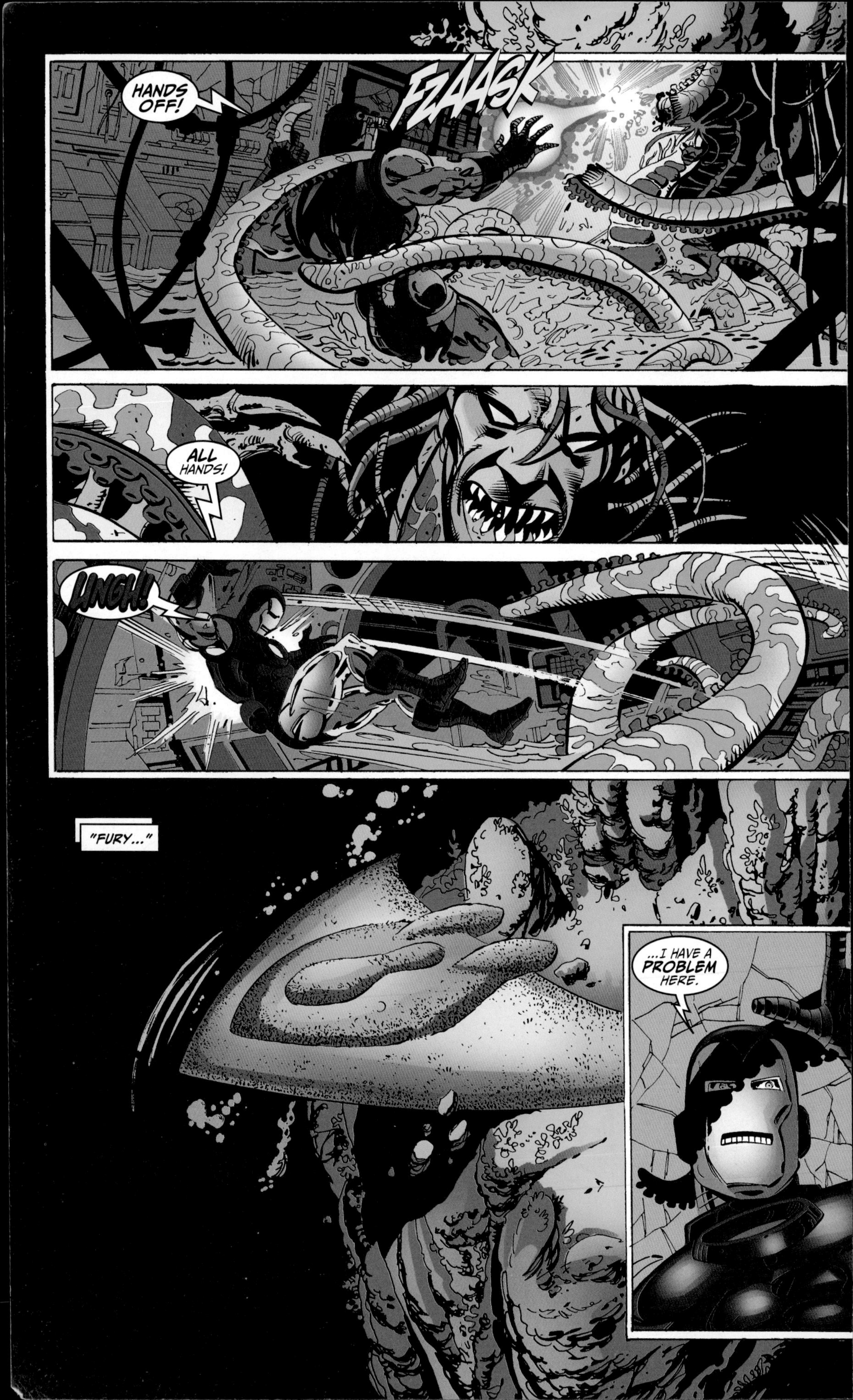
HANDS OFF!
FZAASK
ALL HANDS!
UNGH!
"FURY..."
...I HAVE A PROBLEM HERE.

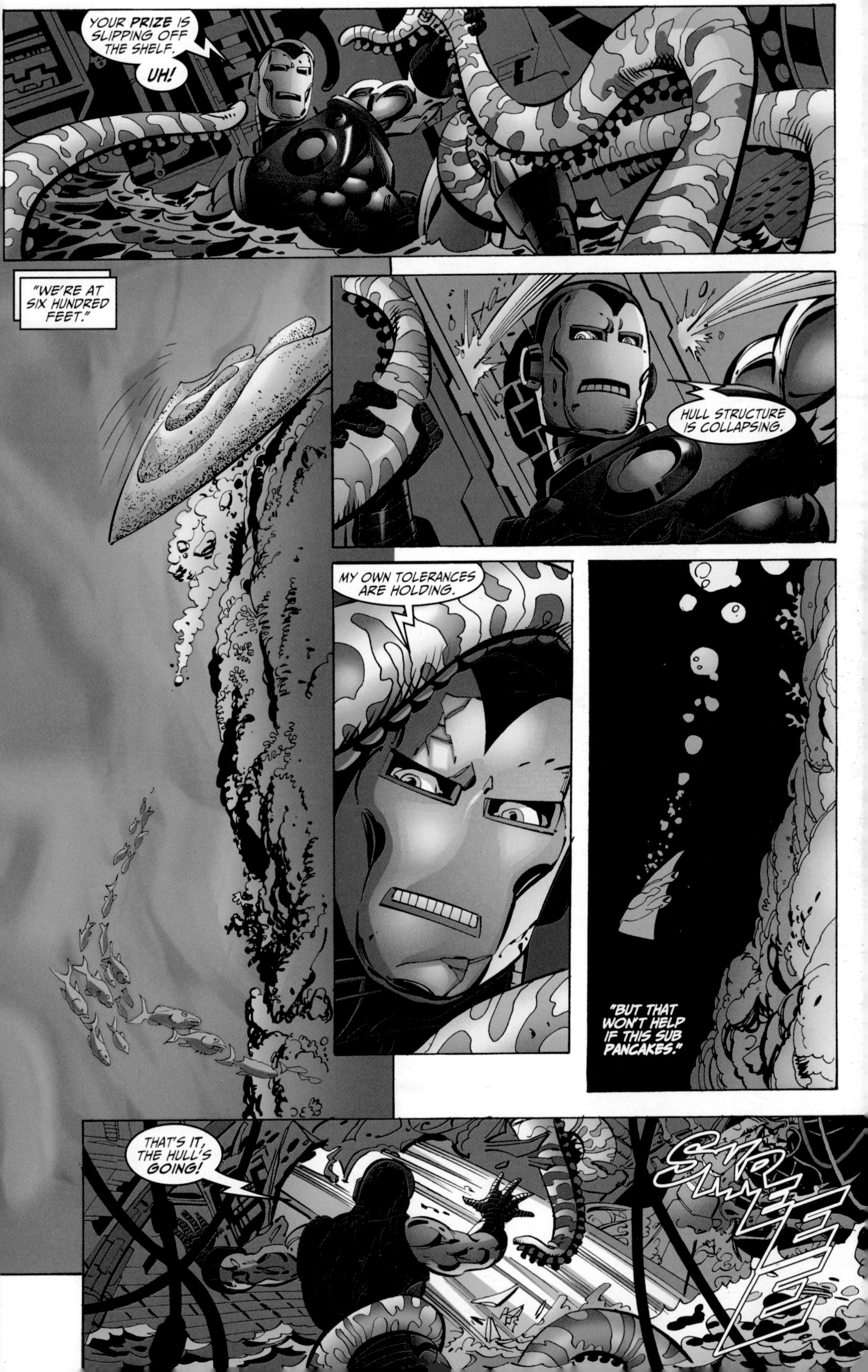
YOUR PRIZE IS SLIPPING OFF THE SHELF.
UH!
"WE'RE AT SIX HUNDRED FEET."
HULL STRUCTURE IS COLLAPSING.
MY OWN TOLERANCES ARE HOLDING.
"BUT THAT WON'T HELP IF THIS SUB PANCAKES."
THAT'S IT, THE HULL'S GOING!

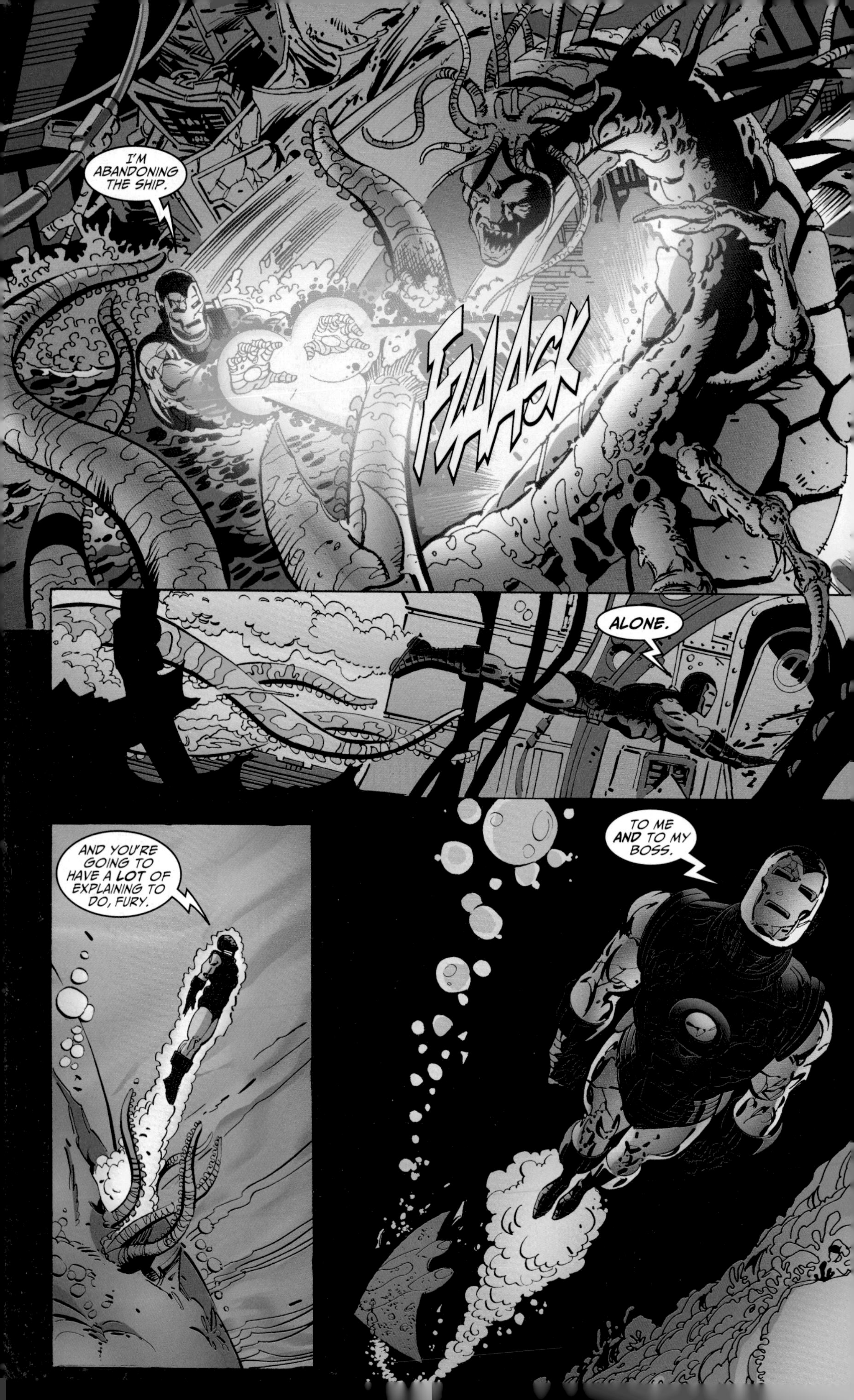
I'M ABANDONING THE SHIP.
FZAASK
ALONE.
AND YOU'RE GOING TO HAVE A LOT OF EXPLAINING TO DO, FURY.
TO ME AND TO MY BOSS.

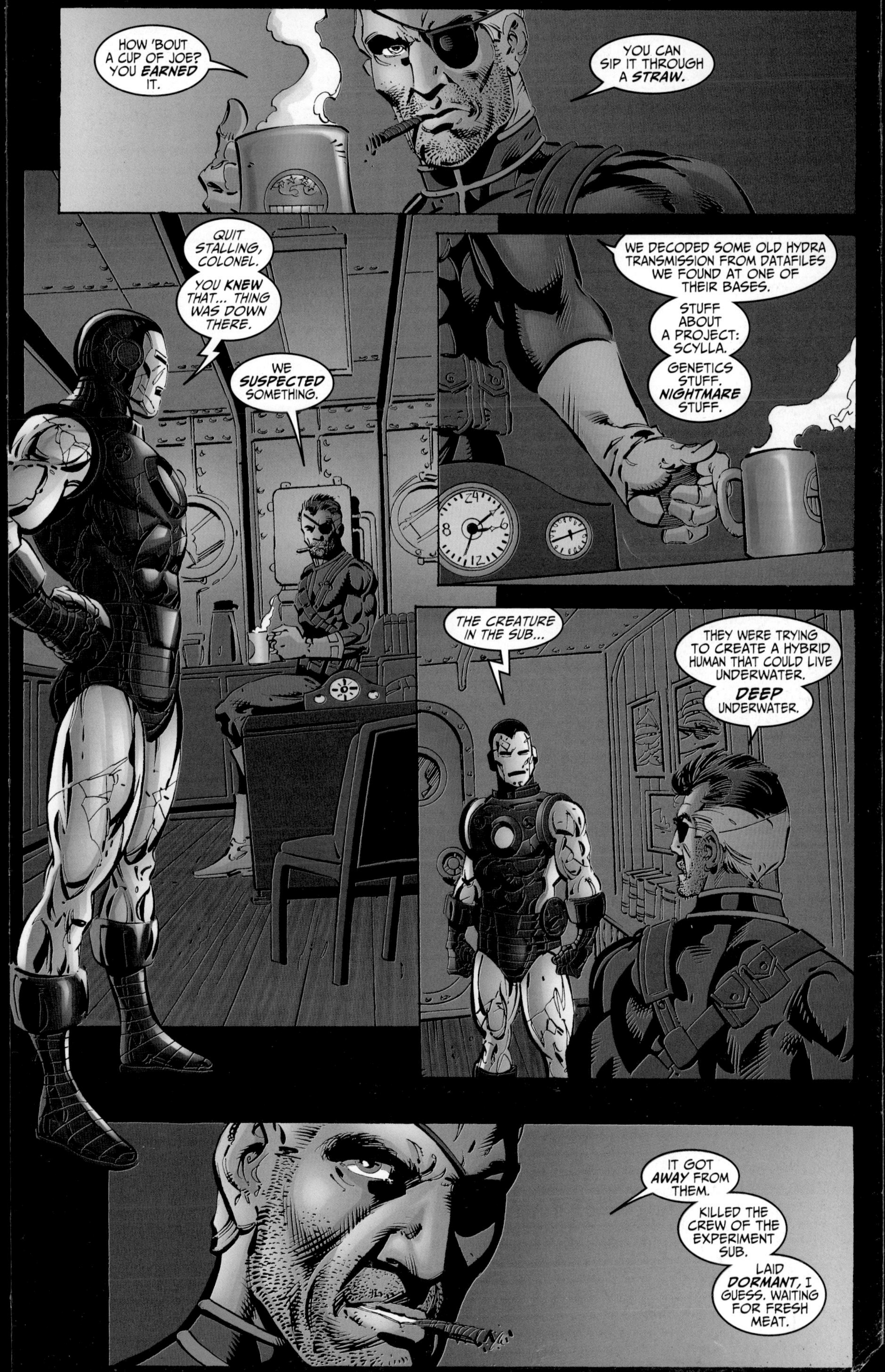
HOW 'BOUT A CUP OF JOE? YOU EARNED IT.
YOU CAN SIP IT THROUGH A STRAW.
QUIT STALLING, COLONEL.
YOU KNEW THAT... THING WAS DOWN THERE.
WE SUSPECTED SOMETHING.
WE DECODED SOME OLD HYDRA TRANSMISSION FROM DATAFILES WE FOUND AT ONE OF THEIR BASES.
STUFF ABOUT A PROJECT: SCYLLA.
GENETICS STUFF. NIGHTMARE STUFF.
THE CREATURE IN THE SUB...
THEY WERE TRYING TO CREATE A HYBRID HUMAN THAT COULD LIVE UNDERWATER.
DEEP UNDERWATER.
IT GOT AWAY FROM THEM.
KILLED THE CREW OF THE EXPERIMENT SUB.
LAID DORMANT, I GUESS. WAITING FOR FRESH MEAT.

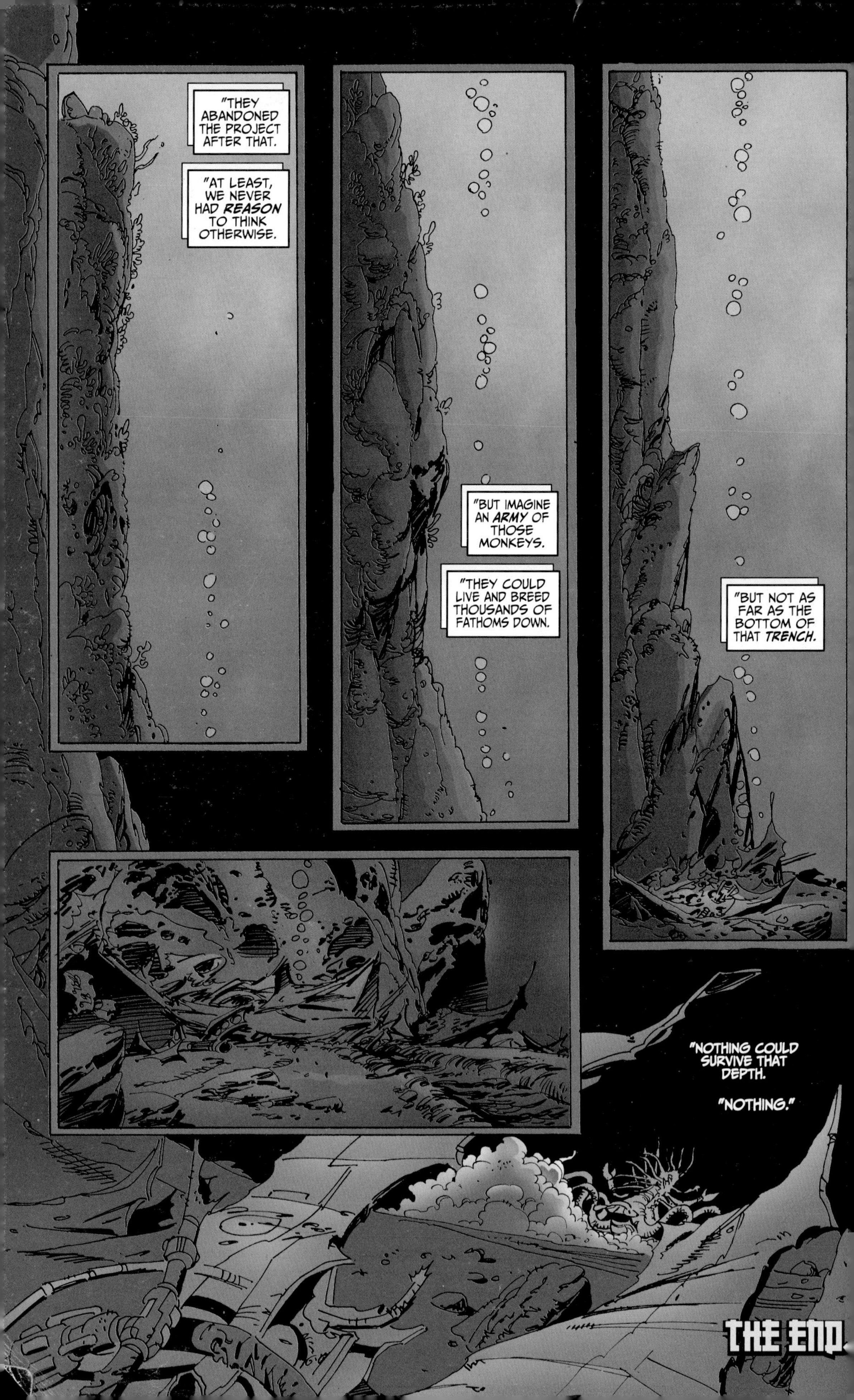
"THEY ABANDONED THE PROJECT AFTER THAT.
"AT LEAST, WE NEVER HAD REASON TO THINK OTHERWISE.
"BUT IMAGINE AN ARMY OF THOSE MONKEYS.
"THEY COULD LIVE AND BREED THOUSANDS OF FATHOMS DOWN.
"BUT NOT AS FAR AS THE BOTTOM OF THAT TRENCH.
"NOTHING COULD SURVIVE THAT DEPTH.
"NOTHING."
THE END